"Introduced by Vaia Tsolas and Christine Anzieu-Premmereur, and with chapters by prestigious authors such as Julia Kristeva, Laurence Kahn, Jacqueline Schaeffer, Rosemary Balsam and others, this original and compelling book addresses the shifting forms of pleasure from their Freudian roots to the world of technology, artificial intelligence, online meetings, and sessions. In these times where the body seems absent, should we rethink notions as desire, love, and thought? Major metapsychological concepts such as drive, hallucinatory satisfaction, après-coup, object, and dis-objectivation are questioned and bring to light a new conception of pleasure."

Marilia Aisenstein, *past president (Paris Society) and past president (Paris Institute of Psychosomatics), the author of* An Analytic Journey: From the Art of Archery to the Art of Psychoanalysis *(Karnac Books 2017) and* Désir, douleur, pensée *(Ithaque 2020)*

"Beginning with the assumption that 'pleasure, in its metapsychological meaning, not merely as a sensation or experience' 'has been undertheorized in psychoanalytic literature despite its position as one of Freud's main fascinations in his inquiries into the human psyche,' this extraordinary interdisciplinary collection of essays addresses 'the malaise of the contemporary individual "and some would say contemporary psychoanalysis!" desperately trying to survive and to secure some satisfaction in combating the overwhelming, overpowering climate of ethical and political impotence.' Central to its argument is the demonstration of the theoretical necessity and clinical relevance of Freudian drive theory and the restoration of the economic point of view to its 'rightful place as the motivating force of human existence.'"

Howard B. Levine, *editor-in-chief of the Routledge W.R. Bion Studies Series, author of* Affect, Representation and Language: Between the Silence and the Cry *(Routledge 2022)*

"This fascinating series of essays is particularly timely in exploring the destiny of humanity and our inner experiences after the pandemic. Contemporary psychoanalytic exploration reveals that the search for pleasure shows new and unexpected implications compared with classical analytic knowledge. The very distinguished and multi-disciplinary contributors that participated in this book explore the different implications of the catastrophic changes in a time of crisis, facing the rise of different forms of private and public violence, together with several original manifestations of people's desperate attempts to find pleasure, sometimes in new and original ways. This book is a must-read for a wider understanding of the new social horizons and man's deep psychology that characterize our contemporary world."

Riccardo Lombardi, *author of* Body-Mind Dissociation in Psychoanalysis *(Routledge 2017) and* Formless Infinity: Clinical Explorations of Matte Blanco and Bion *(Routledge 2016)*

"Our contemporary world is fraught with many denials of reality and avoidance of sexuality and eroticism in favor of identity quests. This exciting book that highlights the current discontents in our culture leading to new forms of seeking pleasure merits reading by every psychoanalyst and psychoanalytically oriented reader."

Patrick Miller, *a founding member of S.P.R.F (Société Psychanalytique de Recherche et de Formation) and the author of* Le Psychanalyste pendant la séance *(2001) and* Driving Soma: A Transformational Process in the Analytic Encounter *(Routledge 2014)*

"Tsolas and Anzieu-Premmereur have gathered distinguished interdisciplinary scholars to consider the rather neglected topic of the body and its impact on psychic functioning especially in the Subject's pursuit of pleasure. The authors are steeped in the rich and varied European and British traditions. Furthermore, they are immersed in contemporary analytic schools that seem to minimize Soma's centrality to Psyche's capacity for representation. They reach back to Freud to resurrect his energic hypothesis and, with it, the notion of libido, to undergird their contemplation of the vicissitudes of the body's search for pleasure-unpleasure. A difficult task handled with freshness and brilliance. Consider this book a 'Must Read' for those who have been missing the 'Depth' in 'Depth Psychology.'"

Lila Kalinich, *MD, a training and supervising psychoanalyst at Columbia University, Center for Psychoanalytic Training and Research and on the advisory board at the Pulsion Institute, is the co-editor of the Dead Father: A Psychoanalytic Inquiry (Routledge, 2008)*

"We should welcome this book focused on a revision of the concept of pleasure, so crucial to the Freudian economic perspective. In addition to the changes that have occurred in culture since the birth of psychoanalysis, there has now been added the need to reflect on the experiences of living and working during the pandemic, against the background of climatic tragedy to which a war has now been added. Freud pointed out to us in 'Civilization and its Discontents' of 1930 that the purpose of attaining bliss is unrealizable and has also shown us that the substitution of the power of the individual for that of the community is the decisive cultural step, which, in turn, has as its basis the drive's sacrifice with which human beings contribute to the community. But culture has mutated. It is no longer the renunciation of the drive but rather an invitation to the opposite under a promise of well-being that is offered at the click of a button with the numerous technological devices we have at our disposal. The axis of contemporary society seems to be anchored in loving and giving well-being to oneself. And hating and rejecting what is different, if not, it is difficult to understand the direction the whole world is taking. That is why today it is essential to read this book that brings together the contributions of highly relevant authors from different countries who give their personal perspective on the way in which the ways of seeking pleasure have changed in the contemporary world. They also take into account both the uncertainty in which we live and the intolerance to otherness with an increase in the most varied forms of violence."

Virginia Ungar, *the past president of IPA, is a training and supervising analyst at the Buenos Aires Psychoanalytic Association*

A Psychoanalytic Exploration of the Contemporary Search for Pleasure

This interdisciplinary collection of essays explores the malaise of the contemporary individual by returning the economic point of view of Freudian thinking, the concept of satisfaction, libido, and pleasure–unpleasure principle to their rightful place as the motivating forces of human existence.

For Freud, pleasure stands apart from other human experiences, side by side with unpleasure, always a bonus in the search for satisfaction of the pleasure principle and beyond. Along with libido, emotional fulfillment, and the capacities for sublimation and play, pleasure has not been given enough attention in the psychoanalytic literature. The editors of this book address this lack and highlight the importance of examining today's social and individual malaise through these specific lenses of inquiry. It is particularly timely and important today to address this lack, and thereby examine the impact of the social phenomena of the pandemic, the crises of ideals and virtuality on the subject who feels in a state of constant emergency, overwhelmed, addicted, and delibidinalized.

With contributions from across psychoanalysis, this book is essential reading for psychoanalysts in training and in practice who want to understand how the modern world has shaped our understanding of pleasure.

Vaia Tsolas is a training and supervising analyst at Columbia University, Center for Psychoanalytic Training and Research; co-founder and board chair of Pulsion, a psychoanalytic institute in New York City; an assistant clinical professor of Psychiatry, Albert Einstein College of Medicine; a corresponding member of the Hellenic Psychoanalytic Association; co-founder of Rose Hill Psychological Services in New York City; and the editor of the book *A Psychoanalytic Exploration of the Body in Today's World: On the Body* (Routledge 2017).

Christine Anzieu-Premmereur is a psychiatrist and psychoanalyst in New York City. A member of the Société Psychanalytique de Paris, faculty at the Columbia Psychoanalytic Center; an assistant clinical professor in Psychiatry at Columbia University; the chair of the IPA Committee for Child and Adolescent Psychoanalysis, COCAP; and the Board Secretary of Pulsion, a psychoanalytic institute in New York City.

A Psychoanalytic Exploration of the Contemporary Search for Pleasure

The Turning of the Screw

Edited by Vaia Tsolas and Christine Anzieu-Premmereur

Routledge
Taylor & Francis Group

LONDON AND NEW YORK

Designed cover image: © Getty Images

First published 2024
by Informa Law from Routledge
4 Park Square, Milton Park, Abingdon, Oxon OX14 4RN

and by Informa Law from Routledge
605 Third Avenue, New York, NY 10158

Informa Law from Routledge is an imprint of the Taylor & Francis Group, an informa business

British Library Cataloguing-in-Publication Data
A catalogue record for this book is available from the British Library

Library of Congress Cataloging-in-Publication Data
Names: Tsolas, Vaia, editor. | Anzieu-Premmereur, Christine, editor.
Title: A psychoanalytic exploration of the contemporary search for pleasure : the turning of the screw / edited by Vaia Tsolas and Christine Anzieu-Premmereur.
Description: Abingdon, Oxon ; New York, NY : Routledge, 2024. | Includes bibliographical references and index. |
Identifiers: LCCN 2023001007 (print) | LCCN 2023001008 (ebook) | ISBN 9781032471129 (hbk) | ISBN 9781032471136 (pbk) | ISBN 9781003384618 (ebk)
Subjects: LCSH: Satisfaction. | Pleasure. | Psychoanalysis.
Classification: LCC BF515 .P75 2024 (print) | LCC BF515 (ebook) | DDC 152.4/2--dc23/eng/20230501
LC record available at https://lccn.loc.gov/2023001007
LC ebook record available at https://lccn.loc.gov/2023001008

ISBN: 978-1-032-47112-9 (hbk)
ISBN: 978-1-032-47113-6 (pbk)
ISBN: 978-1-003-38461-8 (ebk)

DOI: 10.4324/9781003384618

Typeset in Garamond
by MPS Limited, Dehradun

To all those whose psychoanalytic exploration begins with the drives

Contents

Acknowledgments   *xii*
List of Contributors   *xiii*

General Introduction   1
VAIA TSOLAS

Early Barriers to Pleasure   11
CHRISTINE ANZIEU-PREMMEREUR

PART I
Crises of Ideals, Delibidinalization and Its Discontents
for Our Contemporary World   13

Introduction   15
EVAN MORIARTY

1 Preface to Kristeva's Work: Vitality Against Virality and
  Virtuality   18
  RACHEL BOUÉ-WIDAWSKY

2 "In the Current State of War, It Is Our Most Inner Selves
  That We Must Save"   20
  JULIA KRISTEVA

3 Preface to Contri's Work: Thinking, Drive, Law   24
  MICHAEL CIVIN

4 The Science of Thought: The Thought of Satisfaction   26
  GIACOMO B. CONTRI

5 Three Chapters to Be Remembered and Post-Scriptum   29
GIACOMO B. CONTRI AND RAFFAELLA COLOMBO

6 Dead Mother (Ire)land   33
MATTHEW MCCOY AND MARISA BERWALD

PART II
Delibidinalization and the Malaise of the
Contemporary Subject   45

Introduction   47
SEAN LYNCH AND ANDJELA SAMARDZIC

7 Uncanny Drives: On Nightmares and Wish Fulfillment   50
MONIKA GSELL

8 Ridding Oneself of Reality   66
LAURENCE KAHN

9 On the Roots of Addictive Behavior in Narcissist
   Vulnerability and Lack of Transitional Area   81
CHRISTINE ANZIEU-PREMMEREUR

10 Reaching for the Impossible Jouissance: The Contemporary
   Addictive Female   100
VAIA TSOLAS

11 The Risk of Loss: Anxiety and Depression in Women   111
JACQUELINE SCHAEFFER

12 Enemies of Unpleasure   123
PANOS ALOUPIS

13 Resistance to Psychoanalysis   133
CATHERINE CHABERT

14 "Unjoined Persons": Psychic Isolation and Bodily Symptoms
   in Adolescence   144
MARY T. BRADY

15 Death, Life, Birth and Sublimation in the Pandemic   159
ROSEMARY BALSAM

16 Death and the Use of Pleasure   173
DAVID LICHTENSTEIN

17 Destructive Envy and the Narcissistic Grip 185
DOMINIQUE CUPA

18 "... whatever ..." 197
MICHAEL CIVIN

Afterword *207*
ANAND DESAI
Index *210*

Acknowledgments

Special thanks to Edward Kenny and Luca Flabbi for their exceptional work in translating the corresponding chapters. This book would not come to fruition without the endless hours that Dr. Michael Civin put forward in providing ongoing feedback, conducting some of the translation, and for detailed editorial attention to every chapter and to whom I owe my deep gratitude.

Vaia Tsolas

To all the patients who helped me to think and play with them.

Christine Anzieu-Premmereur

Contributors

Panos Aloupis is a psychiatrist, psychologist, and psychoanalyst (SPP-Paris Psychoanalytic Society) member of the IPA, consultant at IPSO – Pierre Marty (Paris), and a member of the editorial board of Revue Française de Psychosomatique.

Christine Anzieu-Premmereur is the co-founder of Pulsion, the International Institute of Psychoanalysis and Psychoanalytic Psychosomatics, a Psychiatrist, Psychologist, Adult and Child Psychoanalyst, and a member of Société Psychanalytique de Paris. She is on the faculty at the Columbia Psychoanalytic Center and is the Director of the Parent-Infant Psychotherapy Program. She has co-edited with Vaia Tsolas, *the Psychoanalytic Exploration of the Body in Today's World* (Routledge 2017).

Rosemary Balsam is a Fellow of the Royal College of Psychiatrists, London, an associate clinical professor of Psychiatry at Yale Medical School; staff psychiatrist at the Dept. of Student Mental Health and Counseling; training and supervising Analyst at Western New England Institute for Psychoanalysis. Her special interests are in gender and body issues, especially female development. Recent books: *Womens' Bodies in Psychoanalysis* (Routledge 2012) and the co-edited book *Hans Loewald: His Legacy and Promise* (Routledge, in press). She was the winner of the Sigourney Award for excellence in the advancement of psychoanalysis.

Marisa Berwald is a doctoral candidate in psychological anthropology at UCLA. She continues to study with Gifric, The Interdisciplinary Freudian Group for Clinical and Cultural Intervention, which offers a post-Lacanian orientation to psychoanalysis. Her clinical experience and research has specialized in psychosis, depression and anxiety, coming of age issues, gender, and the relationship between political systems, cultural histories, and the psyche. Her research in anthropology examines the contemporary practice of psychoanalysis within the globalizing culture and class contexts of New York City.

Rachel Boué-Widawsky, PhD is a New York Licensed Psychoanalyst in private practice. She is the Chair of admissions at IPTAR (*Institute for Psychoanalytic Training and Research*) and Associate Clinical Professor of NYU Medical School. She is the Editor of the Foreign Books Reviews of *JAPA* (*Journal of American Psychoanalytic Association*). She is the author of numerous articles on French psychoanalysis. Her most recent contributions are "Maternal Eroticism or the Necessary Risk of Madness", in *Eroticism*, edited by S. Akhtar & Rajiv Gulati (Routledge 2020) and "Maternal Eroticism and the Journey of a Concept in Julia Kristeva's Work" in *The Philosophy of Julia Kristeva* (Open Court 2020) in *The Library of Living Philosophers* series. She is also the author of several books in French on literary criticism.

Mary T. Brady is an adult and child psychoanalyst in private practice in San Francisco. She is on the Faculties of the San Francisco Center for Psychoanalysis and the Psychoanalytic Institute of Northern California. She is Editor of *Braving the Erotic Field in the Treatment of Children and Adolescents*, published by Routledge in 2022. Her books, *Analytic Engagements with Adolescents: Sex, Gender and Subversion* and *The Body in Adolescence: Psychic Isolation and Physical Symptoms* were published by Routledge in 2018 and 2016 respectively. She is North American Co-Chair for the Committee on Child Analysis (COCAP) of the IPA. She co-leads a *Psychoanalysis and Film* group.

Raffaella Colombo is a psychopedagogist and psychoanalyst working in Milan, Italy. Previously, she worked as a psychotherapist in the canton Ticino, Switzerland. She is Board Member of the *Società Amici del Pensiero – Sigmund Freud*, Milan, Italy. In addition to her work as psychoanalyst, she provides consulting services to parents, works with young children and teenagers, and trains and supervises social workers. She is the author of numerous contributions, including "Autismo Precoce Infantile o psicopatologia precoce" in M. G. Pediconi and C. Urbinati (eds.) *Non ci sono* (FrancoAngeli, 2019). She has also edited *Hanno pensato* (Pendragon 2013), a collection of writings by Sigmund Freud and Giacomo B. Contri.

Giacomo B. Contri (1941–2022) was an Italian psychoanalyst, president and founder of the *Società Amici del Pensiero – Sigmund Freud*, Milan, Italy. After completing an MD at the *Facoltà di Medicina* of the *Università degli Studi di Milano*, he started analysis with Jacques Lacan in Paris and is a member of his *École Freudienne de Paris* (then *École de la Cause Freudienne*). He introduced Lacan's thought in Italy, also curating the Italian version of Lacan's *Écrits* for the publisher Einaudi. For the publisher Bollati Boringhieri, he collaborated the translation of Freud's collected works. He worked toward a Ph.D. at the *École Pratique des Hautes Études* under the supervision of Roger Bastide, Roland Barthes, and Robert Lefort. He has published numerous contributions and books, including *Il pensiero di natura. Dalla psicoanalisi al pensiero giuridico* (Sic Edizioni, first ed. 1994, last revised ed. 2006), which proposes an original revision of Freud's thought in light of juridical concepts inspired by Hans Kelsen.

Michael Civin is a co-founder and on the board of Pulsion, the International Institute of Psychoanalysis and Psychoanalytic Psychosomatics, a clinical psychologist, psychoanalyst, and the co-founder of Rose Hill Psychological Services, NY. He is in private practice and has worked in a wide range of settings, inpatient, outpatient, addiction, adolescent day care, homes for adults, university-based clinics, and organizational consultation. He is the author of Male Female Email, one of the earliest books on the impact of virtuality on our society and psychology.

Catherine Chabert is a French psychologist and psychoanalyst, a full member of the Psychoanalytic Association of France, and an emeritus professor at Paris-Descartes University (Sorbonne Paris Cité). She has developed her research and teaching in clinical psychopathology from the perspectives of metapsychology and the Freudian method. Her works are focused on femininity, masochism and melancholia. Her most recent writings in French are *Love of Difference* (PUF 2011), *The Young Woman and the Analyst* (Dunod 2015), *We Must Part Ways Now* (PUF 2017), and *Great Expectations: Transference and Waiting* (PUF 2020). Last published: *The Great Story and the Little* (PUF 2022), co-authored with J. André and F. Coblence, and *The Benefits of Jealousy* (PUF 2023), co-authored with E. Louët.

Dominique Cupa is a member of the Société Psychanalytique de Paris (SPP), an Emeritus Professor of Psychopathology at Paris X University, the director of the Psychosomatic Department of the Nephrology Center AURA in Paris, the director of the Center for psychopathology of somatic and identity disorders (Laboratoire de Psychopathologie psychanalytique des Atteintes Somatiques et Identitaires (le LASI), and an expert in the IPA's CAPSA (International Practice and Scientific Activities Committee). She published many books and papers on psychosomatics, and on the Skin Ego.

Anand Desai is on the board of Pulsion, the International Institute of Psychoanalysis and Psychoanalytic Psychosomatics, a Training & Supervising Analyst at Columbia, an Assistant Clinical Professor in the Department of Psychiatry at Columbia University and on the faculty of the Columbia Psychoanalytic Center for Training & Research. In addition to teaching and supervising Medical Students and Psychiatric Residents, he is currently Co-Director of the center's Psychodynamic Psychotherapy Program, where he also teaches and supervises. He practices in New York City.

Monika Gsell is a psychoanalyst and a scholar at the University of Zurich. She studied philosophy and literature at the University of Basel where she completed her doctorate. She received training as a psychoanalyst at the Psychoanalytical Seminar Zurich (PSZ). She received further training in sex therapy at the Zurich Institute for Sexology and Sex Therapy (ZISS). Gsell's research is in the area of gender studies and psychoanalysis. In 2011, she took over the scientific project management of the Judith Le Soldat Foundation. The edition of Le Soldat's works is organized into five volumes. Gsell is responsible for the critical and annotated edition of the estate. The first volume (*Grund zur Homosexualität* (*Grounds for Homosexuality*), frommann-holzboog, Stuttgart-Bad Cannstatt) was published in 2015.

Laurence Kahn is a training analyst at the French Psychoanalytic Association (APF) An Ancient Greek anthropologist before becoming a psychoanalyst, Laurence Kahn is a full member, training and supervising analyst of the Psychoanalytic Association of France, where she has held the roles of Secretary general, Scientific Secretary and

President (2008–2010). Co-editor of the Nouvelle revue de psychanalyse (1990–1995) and editor in chief of l'Annuel de l'APF (2010–2015), she is the author of many books among which Cures d'enfance, Faire parler le destin, L'écoute de l'analyste. The two most recent books have been translated into English: *Psychoanalysis, Apathy and the Postmodern Patient* (Routledge 2018) and *What Nazism Did to Psychoanalysis* (Routledge 2023) as well as a contribution to *On Freud's Moses and Monotheism*, ed. L.J. Brown (2023): "The Probable in Nazi Times: The Opposing Fates of the Mystical and the Law".

Julia Kristeva is the director of the Institute for the Study of Texts and Documents at the University of Paris VII and a Visiting Professor at Columbia University. She is the recipient of France's distinguished *Chevalière de la légion d'honneur* and in 2004 won the Holberg International Prize for her "innovative explorations of questions on the intersection of language, culture and literature [that] have inspired research across the humanities and the social sciences throughout the world". A practicing psychoanalyst, she is a careful reader of Freud, and finds his voice in such contemporary concerns as desire, love, revolution, the poetic, the soul, and faith.

David Lichtenstein, PhD is a psychoanalyst in private practice in NYC. He is a Faculty and Board Member of Pulsion, NY; Faculty Member at the NYU Post Doc. Institute for Psychoanalysis and Psychotherapy, IPTAR, the CUNY Doctoral Program in Clinical Psychology, and Psychoanalytic Institute of Northern California (PINC). He is co-editor of the recent book *The Lacan Tradition* (Routledge 2018) and teaches an independent course entitled: The Clinical Implications of the Work of Jacques Lacan. He was the Founding Editor of *DIVISION/Review: A Quarterly Psychoanalytic Forum*, a Co-Founder of Après-Coup Psychoanalytic Association, and a participant at *Das Unbehagen*.

Sean Lynch is a psychotherapist at Rose Hill Psychological in New York City. His writing and research interests include literary studies, art, and psychoanalysis.

Evan Moriarty is a psychotherapist at Rose Hill Psychological in NYC, seeing adults and couples. He is a graduate of philosophy from the University of Chicago and received his MSW from New York University.

Matthew McCoy is a researcher at the US Department of Veterans Affairs where he works with Los Angeles's homeless Veteran population. Dr. McCoy is trained as a medical and psychological anthropologist. His research interests include person-centered experiences of health and illness, suicide, trauma, substance use, homelessness, and nationalism. He specializes in qualitative methodology inspired by psychoanalytic practice and has conducted ethnographic research with current and ex-paramilitary combatants and victims of civil war in Belfast, Northern Ireland. His work has been published in the Ethos, *Irish Journal of Anthropology, and Pathogens*.

Andjela Samardzic is on the board of Pulsion, the International Institute of Psychoanalysis and Psychoanalytic Psychosomatics, a psychoanalyst and clinical psychologist. She is a member of the Après-Coup Psychoanalytic Association

(New York) and Psychoanalytic Institute Zurich. Andjela is the co-editor with Vaia Tsolas and Michael Civin in the book *Voluntary Servitude. Masochism and Morality by Judith Le Soldat* (Routledge forthcoming). She has published on historical trauma, masochism, jouissance, psyche-soma phenomena, etc.

Jacqueline Schaeffer is a full member and training analyst of the Paris Psychoanalytical Society. She participated in the creation of a "study group" within the International Psychoanalytical Association. In 1986, she was awarded the Maurice Bouvet prize in psychoanalysis. She is a former assistant editor of the "Psychoanalytic Debates" series with the Presses Universitaires de France. She has published several papers and has been the keynote speaker in many conference meetings throughout the world. Her most recent books are *The Universal Refusal: A Psychoanalytic Exploration of the Feminine Sphere and Its Repudiation* (Routledge 2011), currently in its seventh edition in French, *Le refus du féminin. La sphinge et son âme enpeine* (Presses universitaires de France 2022), *Le féminin. Un sexe autre* (in press). She is the editor of *Qu'est la sexualité devenue? De Freud à aujoud'hui* (in press).

Vaia Tsolas is the co-founder of Pulsion, the International Institute of Psychoanalysis and Psychoanalytic Psychosomatics, a psychologist and a training and supervising analyst at Columbia University, Center for Psychoanalytic Training and Research, and on the faculty at Albert Einstein Medical School. She is the director of Rose Hill Psychological Services. She is the winner of the IPA Sacerdoti Prize, Columbia Ovesey and Klar best teacher awards. Dr. Tsolas teaches Freud/Lacan at Columbia Psychoanalytic. She co-edited *A Psychoanalytic Exploration of the Body in Today's World: On the Body* (Routledge 2017) with Christine Anzieu-Premmereur and authored *Sweet Little Deaths of Everyday Life: A Psychoanalytic Study on the Feminine* (VDM Verlag 2008) as well as numerous articles on issues of otherness, body and the drives.

General Introduction

Vaia Tsolas

Living in times of a ravishing pandemic, natural disasters, political upheavals, war and climate change has increasingly accentuated our confrontation with human vulnerability. The need for a potent paternal order that works well to respond to these challenges highlights its defects. In playing with the title and content of James's famous work, *The Turn of the Screw* (1898), this book borrows the metaphor to point to the connection of the consequential changes (the turnings) in the contemporary sexualities (the new screw) to the lack of the paternal order for the psyche in the reigns of a regressive societal primitive maternal superego.

The human body isolated from contact and support from the social order is left even more vulnerable in front of screens, disembodied connections, illusions of being in the world. Humans are resilient and have survived wars, natural catastrophes and pandemics before. But this is the first time that the virtual has come as a solution to the disastrous consequences of the pandemic, offering to some a platform to continue work and "connection" (quite literally) with each other. This solution of viral connection as a substitute has brought the individual even more intensely either to face or to defend against facing the reality of social isolation and group fragmentation in which the distinction between a tweet and a truth has become obscured. Depression, suicide and violence are on the rise as the desperate attempts to find pleasure with others and to share meaningful encounters catapult into a crisis.

This multidisciplinary edited work addresses the contemporary search for pleasure in a world of uncertainty, illusions, trauma and social isolation. In addition, this edited book attempts to address this exploration by bringing Freud's economic point of view to its rightful central place of metapsychology by collecting a number of psychoanalysts and social theorists who share the importance of this approach.

Freud's (1915) precise definition of metapsychology included the economic alongside the dynamic and topographical: "I propose that when we have succeeded in describing a psychical process in its dynamic, topographical and economic aspects, we should speak of it as a metapsychological presentation" (p. 181). Libido as the psychic energy and infantile sexuality have been the most significant and most isolating principles of Freudian theorizing. Sexuality has been left behind, losing its metapsychological magnificence in Freud's theorizing, restricted and confused with

DOI: 10.4324/9781003384618-1

sexual behavior and genitality. Freud's warning that the scandalous revolutionary discovery of sexuality at the center of the psyche was to be rejected from his contemporaries, is in our days the unwanted "xenos", discredited now to have a significance that is outdated and invalid.

> But the silence which my communications met with, the void which formed itself about me, the hints that were conveyed to me, gradually made me realize that assertions on the part played by sexuality in the aetiology of the neuroses cannot count upon meeting with the same kind of treatment as other communications. I understood that from now onwards I was one of those who have "disturbed the sleep of the world," as Hebbel says, and that I could not reckon upon objectivity and tolerance.
>
> (Freud, 1914a, p. 22)

Green (2018) points directly to the undermining of psychosexuality and the drives in contemporary psychoanalysis in favor of object relations. He writes that

> we see the sexual here reduced to a specialized function, subordinated to other criteria, included now in the frame of object-relations, now in that of personality theory. What clearly disappears here, in this instance—but we can observe this disappearance elsewhere as well—is the Freudian concept of libido, which is alone capable of accounting for variations, transformations, extensions, coverings-up, fixations, regressions, time-lags, enmeshing and unraveling. The reference to the pleasure-unpleasure principle also disappears, deprived of its status as the regulatory system of the psyche—especially so since Freud himself placed a "Beyond" alongside it, something even more difficult to comprehend.
>
> (p. 27)

This interdisciplinary collection of essays returns the economic point of view of Freudian thinking, exactly along the lines of Green's warning, and to restore its significance to a rightful place as the motivating force of human existence. In so doing, it aims collectively to explore the malaise of the contemporary individual desperately trying to survive and to secure some satisfaction in combating the overwhelming, overpowering climate of ethical and political impotence.

In the Civilization and its Discontents, Freud (1930) writes

> our possibilities of happiness are thus limited from the start by our very constitution … Suffering comes from three quarters: from our own body, which is destined to decay and dissolution, and cannot even dispense with anxiety and pain as danger-signals; from the outer world, which can rage against us with the most powerful and pitiless forces of destruction; and finally from our relations with other men.
>
> (p. 21)

The vulnerability of the species (phylogeny) and the inescapability of mortality (ontology) are undoubtedly, the basic ingredients of what makes us human. The omnipotent mind housed and unceasingly challenged by the limited body is confronted with needs, pain, illness and extinction: "The biological factor is the long period of time during which the young of the human species is in a condition of helplessness and dependence" (Freud 1926, p. 138). Freud reminds us that the intra-uterine existence of humans is short in comparison to most animals. He points out that the human is sent into the world in a less readied and more vulnerable state.

> Moreover, the dangers of the external world have a greater importance for it, so that the value of the object which can alone protect it against them and take the place of its former intra-uterine life is enormously enhanced. The biological factor, then, establishes the earliest situations of danger and creates the need to be loved which will accompany the child through the rest of its life.
>
> (Freud 1926, p. 155)

Language, thought, psyche, human evolution in the advances of civilization wage war against this discord between the omnipotent mind and limited human body always at risk, faced with danger from within and without and dependent on for survival. The Freudian concept of the drive as the borderline concept between the mind and the body captures human nature and human imperative of the incompatibility of a mind that knows no limits and of a body that only knows limits, being born too prematurely to satisfy its needs as compared to other primates. As humans, standing upright means that we have separated perceptions from those of animal instincts. ... speaking is an inborn consequence of the human as a speaking being just as much as it reflects humanity's evolution from nature to culture. It is in this imperative where the separation of the drive from instinct guides the psychic apparatus into the symbolic sphere of language and thought, according to Freud, constantly seeking to satisfy the need to decrease internal tension and bring pleasure. Pleasure though according to Freud as it operates within and beyond the pleasure principle is always a bonus, a plus as it can never eliminate the tension of the constant push (of the drives) and can never duplicate the first experience of satisfaction, that first inscription of satisfaction that had no a priori.

The problematics of searching for satisfaction, a prerequisite of human nature, have undoubtedly evolved over time and from one generation to the next. In keeping with these changes, our libidinization of others and the world at large as the means of reaching fulfillment of our needs and desires has also changed.

> A strong egoism is a protection against falling ill, but in the last resort we must begin to love in order not to fall ill, and we are bound to fall ill, if, in consequence of frustration, we are unable to love.
>
> (Freud, 1914b, p. 85)

Before we proceed to the introduction of the individual contributions, it is important to touch briefly on the concept of pleasure. Pleasure in its meta-psychological meaning, not merely as a sensation or experience, has been undertheorized in psychoanalytic literature despite its position as one of Freud's main fascinations in his inquiries into human psyche. In the Laplanche and Pontalis dictionary (1973), pleasure does not have a separate entry; we find, however, the pleasure principle defined as the governing and directing principle for the avoidance of unpleasure: "Inasmuch as unpleasure is related to the increase of excitation, and pleasure to their reduction, the principle in question may be said to be an economic one" (p. 322).

Lacan was the pioneer in developing further Freud's inquiries of the "beyond the pleasure principle" with his notion of jouissance. First, referring to the enjoyment of a sexual object to jouissance as orgasmic pleasure, Lacan in 1960 differentiates jouissance from pleasure by alluding to the Hegelian/Kojevian distinction between Genuâ (enjoyment) and Lust (pleasure) (Kojève, 1947). Put simply, jouissance as a quantitative excess of excitation, is what the pleasure principle tries to prevent. The pleasure principle, by dictating to enjoy as little as possible, justifies why Freud originally named it as the unpleasure principle. On the other hand, jouissance constantly threatens to go beyond the pleasure principle, disrupting and traumatizing. The term jouissance refers to pain as the consequence of this transgression, to the painful pleasure, the suffering of the symptoms (Freud's primary gain of illness). For Lacan (1992) since it is the drives that always push beyond the pleasure-principle prohibitions, every drive is a death drive: "The function of the pleasure principle is to make man always search for what he has to find again, but which he will never attain" (p. 68).

The multidisciplinary contributors to this volume approach the contemporary version of the evolution of our search for pleasure, especially heightened now by the pandemic and other crises, resulting in the psyche's present-day malaise and contemporary symptoms.

This book features, within the common denominator of thinking within Freud's economic point of view (drives), arrange of disciplines, clinical and theoretical approaches and generational differences. More specifically with respect to the latter, this book offers the bonus of exposure to the views of younger psychodynamic-oriented and trained clinicians (Moriarty, Lynch and Samardzic) in their own "digestion" of the wide span of psychoanalytic, social and philosophical thought presented in the sub-introductions to Parts I and II.

In the first section of this book that foregrounds *the crises of ideals, delibidinalization and its discontents,* we include essays by Julia Kristeva, Giacomo Contri, Raffaella Colombo, Matthew McCoy, and Marisa Berwald.

Julia Kristeva approaches the human problematic in the search of satisfaction in a world of social isolation and crises as it pertains to the pandemic directly in her interview, "In The Current State of War, It is our Most Inner Selves that We must Save". Kristeva writes on the role of psychoanalysis facing the pandemic and the hyper connection in the news and social media, leading to depression and isolation. Thus, although

> we know how to foster palliative care, manage nursing homes, study the biology of the mechanism of apoptosis, the continuous process of cell death and

regeneration. But we seem unable 'to pay' the ultimate price of old age, no doubt because, in our secularized societies, death, the ultimate boundary of human experience, is hidden …. It seems to me that, more insidiously and more violently, this viral surge that we have just experienced has revealed to us the inescapable vulnerability of the human condition, beyond old age. I'm talking about the vulnerability that is in us, that lives in us, and which our ideologies of performance and win-win turn out to be incapable of assuming.

She argues that it is the inner self that beckons for us to save given the war against viral social networks that seduce us from the fundamentals of our sexual being. To be able to be "sur-vivants" [those who continue to live] … it is important to soak up this inherent vulnerability (the capacity for solitude, the mortality inside of us, limits and their negotiation through inter-diction) that has the potentiality "to prepare humanity for more tenderness in the competition, endurance …. "

Giacomo Contri, the first translator of Lacan's *Ecrit* in Italy, in Chapter 4, "The Science of Thought: The Thought of Satisfaction", reveals a pessimistic view of contemporary society's achievement of satisfaction. In large part, he sees a movement in the direction of an eclipsing of sexual difference and, at the same time, a social orientation to the superficial, the statistical. As Civin writes in his introduction, Contri philosophy and clinic of psychoanalysis are built on articulation of Freud's Science through the triangular foundation of Drive, Thinking and Law. We and our relationship to sexual differences differ from other creatures because (1) we are, from birth, thinking subjects; (2) we think we have drives in addition to the instincts that govern other creatures; and (3) we have laws that locate the subject within the larger society by legislating rules that govern the drives, speech, action and reaction. Contri develops his notion of the phonic drive, a drive that from the earliest moments of life directs the infant toward the complexity of speech and the creation of a complex grammar. This phonic drive situates the subject in a world of potential partnership with other speaking subjects, hence toward fulfillment. The life of the speaking subject, in fact, is directed only toward drive, and drive follows its only Law— fulfillment. Consistent with the overarching themes of this book, Contri views civilization (built on the Laws that govern the drives) to have adopted new ways of behaving that are a manic deviation from the seeking satisfaction. Based on this, Contri concludes that the pleasure principle is not about hedonism, but rather about the individual's ability to further the Law of Fulfillment and this fulfillment requires the partnership with other thinking/speaking subjects. He feels that until now humanity has managed to achieve little satisfaction of this law of fulfillment.

Raffaella Colombo, the President of the Società Amici del Pensiero – Sigmund Freud (SAP), employs Giacomo Contri's final writings, penned just six days before his death, as a springboard to illustrate that "Contri showed how, with Freud, the concept of human being enters the history of thought". In Chapter 5, Colombo demonstrates how Contri elaborates to the changes he sees in contemporary society by adding Faith to his triangular canon of Thinking, Drive and Law. Colombo outlines the ways in which these interlinking constructs have served as the basis for the constitution of the Society that Contri founded. She addresses Contri's view of the importance of "profit" in human partnership, even in the partnership with God. In Contri's own Chapter 4, we see that this form of partnership is threatened in the contemporary turns of the search for fulfillment. This partnership-based profit is *the sine qua non* of Contri's Faith, in which God profits from the subject and the subject profits from God. It is on these final thoughts of ultimate partnership that Contri left for us to reflect.

In Chapter 3, on "Resurrecting the Dead Mother in Ireland: The Work of the Negative in Irish Republicanism", McCoy and Berwald explore from an anthropological point of view the individual crisis of satisfaction within the social context of the erosion of the paternal metaphor by focusing their research on the community of Irish Republicans in Belfast, Northern Ireland. This chapter traces the generational shifts in an Irish paternal metaphor represented by rebellion, a metaphor that functions to maintain a connection to the nation as a maternal figure it serves to protect: The authors argue:

> Illustrating the transition to the contemporary moment in Northern Ireland where the impotence of an Irish rebel movement has failed to overcome the effects of colonialism, the nation no longer provides an illusion of paternity to new generations of Irish Republicans ... an absence observed in enactments of cultural death evidenced by high rates of suicide in Northern Ireland and performed perceptually as drug-induced *zombie* states of the Irish youth.

In the second section of this book, "Delibinalization and Malaise of the Contemporary Subject", we include essays from Monika Gsell, Laurence Kahn, Christine Anzieu Premmereur, Vaia Tsolas, Jacqueline Schaeffer, Panos Aloupis, Catherine Chabert, Mary Brady, Rosemary Balsam, David Lichtenstein, Dominique Cupa and Michael Civin focusing from different angles on the contemporary malaise of the psyche desperately trying to sur-vive (in Kristeva's terms) existential anxieties and to find new ways to satisfy itself isolated in front of screens. How does this social isolation, compounded by fears of contamination of viral threats and the epidemic of virtuality, impact our libido, emotional health and creativity?

Monika Gsell writes on "Uncanny Drives – On Nightmares and Wish Fulfillment".

In Cédric Kahn's 2004 film adaptation of Georges Simenon's homonymous thriller *Feux Rouges,* Helen and Antoine are on their way to pick up their children from summer camp. It is the end of the summer holiday and they are stuck in traffic jams. Both are irritable. The provocations and arguments escalate. Helen decides to continue the journey by train and disappears into the night. In her stead, an escaped violent criminal shows up and continues the ride with Antoine. When Helen and Antoine reunite in the morning, both will have experienced traumatic events. Nevertheless, they continue their journey together—both with a blissful smile on their lips, as if newly in love after a deeply satisfying night. What are we to make of this puzzling ending? The psychoanalytic reading of the film offers an answer to this question and not only brings to light an uncanny drive, but also provides some interesting insights into the contemporary unconscious meaning of masculinity and femininity.

Laurence Kahn, in her chapter "Ridding Oneself of Reality" differentiates, when the reality of the contemporary sick body and the infection has been put under the cover of the perversion of theoretical, polemical and political statements. She digs the trap doors of such liberation: if one frees oneself from the neurotic complex (and compromises) caused by the constraints of psychic reality, then the field of projection is completely invaded; and if we free ourselves from the constraints of material reality, then as Freud says the psychotic risk (autoplastic modification) is upon us. She illustrates this with brief clinical examples by questioning the question of whether these are borderline cases.

Anzieu-Premmereur banks on her extensive experience with babies and parents to observe that babies dependent upon self-soothing objects, of the compulsive use of technology such as the new use of adult-size "dolls" for comfort without any partner, show the lack of mutuality in relationships and the increasing need for therapeutic interventions centered on the creation of a transitional space. Addiction cannot give long-term satisfaction nor a source of structure for the psyche. Mastering the object is the only way to avoid feeling the pain. This is further developed in an application of the transitional object concept to contemporary psychosocial trends along with a look at some relevant aspects of infant-parent relations.

Tsolas, in her chapter on "Reaching for the Impossible Jouissance – The Contemporary Addictive Female", focuses on the daemonic nature of the addictive impossible jouissance further elaborating on Michel De M'Uzan's notion (2013) that certain individuals are *Slaves of Quantity*, "condemned to a destiny dominated by the quantity of excitation that cannot be psychically elaborated". The primal representation of the first experience of the surface of our erogenous body, the skin ego, as the initial source of sensations and feelings in exchanges with the maternal environment, holds together the psychic contents and provides unity, holding, containment and separation of inside/outside, thus becoming the psychic envelope of the ego. What is the role of instinctual excitation that throws a different light on understanding the daemonic nature of repetition with non-neurotic female patients? The recent pandemic and subsequent social unrest in the United States undoubtedly placed another straw on the camel's back of the psychic envelope. Bombarded by infinite echo chambers of information, the subject in a state of unbearable tension, attempts to achieve some measure of relief and gratification by evacuating via addictive behaviors. Clinical material of a female patient abusing medication will illustrate both these desperate attempts of seeking relief and the challenges in working with such patients.

Schaeffer's chapter focuses on depressive states in women. Falling into depression differs between women and men, as are their anxieties about loss. With a focus on sexual difference, this chapter explores how in women a state of depression is associated with the experience of dependency and with the maternal link. There is a relationship between anxiety of narcissistic loss and anxiety of objectal loss that can shed light on feminine castration anxiety. How are the midlife depressions transformed to become a source of psychic elaboration? Depression, loss of pleasure and narcissistic suffering are rarely examined from the perspective of sex differences. Schaeffer proposes to explore the above via the Freudian economic point of view.

Panos Aloupis' chapter on "the Enemies of Unpleasure" will explore the intertwining of pleasure and pain in our contemporary world, where we have witnessed social phenomena in which hyperactivity, mass denial and destruction of thinking are emphasized and privileged. Aloupis launches his analysis with a reminder that Freud founded psychoanalysis on the pleasure principle. There is attraction through the object for wish fulfillment and rejection of unpleasure. These two movements endure throughout human life. The acknowledgment of pleasure and the identification of unpleasure leads to expectation and patience, which become the essential/primary masochistic position. Its evolution signifies the psychic investment in unpleasure and pain following the vicissitudes of the fusion between eros and death drive. The refusal of unpleasure leads to the construction of defenses with the aim of avoidance; the more psychic they are the less they need discharge through the body or through action. This subjective position oriented by the pleasure/unpleasure principle orchestrates the work of negative (Green), constantly enriching the unconscious basically through the mechanism of repression. However, the psychic apparatus has at its disposal more defensive tools, such a negation, splitting, unbinding, denial or foreclosure in order to neutralize the object aggressions. The human being is characterized by the evolution of the psychic apparatus (mentalization), the capacity for thinking and the acquisition of language. Individual life is intimately linked to social life and civilization. The subject grows up between his/her drive demands and social imperatives in the midst of conflicts and quests. Both subjectively and socially the avoidance of conflicts and pains may result in a life of struggling against passivity and thought. The author will study these aspects through clinical material and with the help of the theoretical works of the Psychosomatic School of Paris.

Catherine Chabert's chapter on "Resistance to Psychoanalysis" explores via the case of a woman with compulsive destructiveness, the negative therapeutic reaction as it relates to the female superego and stands as a refusal of cure. This, in extreme moments, means very precisely the rejection of the benefits of the cure, the toxic, diabolical dimension which it denounces in order to maintain, against all odds, pleasure seeking through the bodily-psychic suffering of moral masochism. There is no question here of contradicting the aims prescribed by the destiny of forces behind which hide the tyrannical injunctions of parental figures. With Ms. G resistance was embodied not only in the reference to a seductive father, but also to a controlling mother, powerful and jealous of his power, not supporting any sharing, rendering the child subservient to her requirements alone. Chabert poses the central question of her argument, that the bonus of pleasure of this abusive attraction comes side by side with being indispensable for the mother and the analyst as the motivational factors for the psyche.

Mary Brady's chapter specifically focuses on psychic isolation in adolescence, estrangement and loneliness in our contemporary world. The author conceives of psychic isolation in adolescence as an affective state with important developmental underpinnings which include shifting (conscious as well as unconscious, internal as well as external) object relations and senses of the self. However, psychic isolation combined with the intensity of adolescent experience can leave adolescents unable to articulate their experience. In turn, this difficulty with articulation and symbolization can leave them vulnerable to breakdown into concrete bodily symptoms. The paper uses Bion's conceptualization of containment and the balance of psychotic versus non-psychotic integrative parts of the personality to examine the emergence of concrete bodily symptoms in adolescence. At times, the transitional space of an analysis, where new experiences can be dreamed together with the analyst, allows adolescents to find joy and feel that they are no longer "unjoined persons" but "members of the wedding" (McCullers, 1946).

Rosemary Balsam's chapter explores the links of death and life, birth and sublimation in the pandemic which has razor-sharpened many contrasts in living into a warring fractiousness within class, race, politics, nature and science. The diminished physical mobility and control of quarantine households forces individual energies toward intrapsychic channels that often culminate in demanding expression—anything from illicit societal actions to transgressive fantasies. Processes of sublimation are dynamically brought to the fore. In using Hans Loewald's 1988 work on *Sublimation*, Balsam explores these issues and poses the question as to what can be further understood from our patients and ourselves about this aspect of the mind given the opportunity to study these contemporary pressures. The role of the power of the biological body and nature's forces will specifically be studied in textured psychic responses—including intense pleasure as well as fear—to the pandemic confrontation and frequent inner helplessness in the face of nature.

Lichtenstein explores the clinical implications of the death drive. When Freud proposed a logic of motivation beyond the pleasure principle, he opened questions about what the motivating principle of that alternative logic might be. Lacan suggested that the French term *jouissance* might convey the meaning of this other motivation. It is a term that evokes the complex enjoyment of use as such, an enjoyment that may be pleasurable but may also be painful. It is a term that suggests that there may be a paradox, an unresolvable contradiction at the heart of human motivation. How this idea might explain certain clinical phenomena as well as the process of addressing them in psychoanalytic work is the focus of this chapter.

Cupa examines the relations between destructive primary envy and narcissism, its disturbances, and the responses they arouse. Drawing on the clinical work with a female patient, it is suggested that envy is a primary affect belonging to the projection of the primitive hatred that is constitutive of the external object in combination with the introjective movement of the hallucinatory satisfaction of the wish for libidinal contributions. Specific to the primary narcissistic relationship, it is especially violent in that the mirror reflects an envious negative image, as is the case between Lola and her mother. The child's envy is therefore made more complicated by the mother's envy. The toxic activity of envy undermines the narcissistic foundations and leads to disturbances in the establishment of primary identity and of the oedipal organization. It distorts feelings like jealousy and greed. It can spread from one generation to another. The father, as the mother's lover, will help to loosen the vice of envious narcissistic mastery.

In his chapter, " … whatever", Michael Civin suggests that the echo of "whatever" and "it is what it is", inside and outside the consulting room, reflects a turning of the contemporary search for pleasure. The virtual extinction of striving and prohibition signify a disaffected retreat toward Thanatos at the intersection of drive (life or death, love or destruction) and impossibility accompanied by blank depression, a depression devoid of both thought and affect. Two clinical vignettes illustrate this trend and some of the clinical challenges that emerge from it.

In the Afterword on the decline of sexuality in our days, Desai elegantly depicts the dramatic contemporary changes in the search for pleasure. The data supplied by Desai bears witness to the dramatic turning in the role of sexuality today.

References

De M'Uzan, M. (2013) *Death and Identity: Being and the Psycho-Sexual Drama*. London and New York: Routledge. Kindle edition.

Freud, S. (1914a) On the History of the Psycho-Analytic Movement. *The Standard Edition of the Complete Psychological Works of Sigmund Freud* 14:1–66.

Freud, S. (1914b) On Narcissism: An Introduction. *The Standard Edition of the Complete Psychological Works of Sigmund Freud* 14:67–102.

Freud, S. (1915) The Unconscious. *The Standard Edition of the Complete Psychological Works of Sigmund Freud* 14:159–215.

Freud, S. (1926) Inhibitions, Symptoms and Anxiety. *The Standard Edition of the Complete Psychological Works of Sigmund Freud* 20:75–176.

Freud, S. (1930) Civilization and its Discontents. *The Standard Edition of the Complete Psychological Works of Sigmund Freud* 21:57–146.

Green, A (2018) *The Chains of Eros. The Sexual in Psychoanalysis*. Translated by Luce Thurston. New York and London: Routledge (Originally published 2001).

James, H. (1898) *The Turn of the Screw*. 2nd ed., D. Esch & J. Warren (Ed.). New York: Norton (Original work published 1898).

Kojève, A. (1947) *Introduction to the Reading of Hegel*. Translated by James H. Nichols Jr., New York and London: Basic Books (1969).

Lacan, J. (1992) *The Seminar. Book VII. The Ethics of Psychoanalysis*, 1959–60. Translated by Dennis Porter, London: Routledge (Originally published 1986).

Laplanche, J. & Pontalis, J. B. (1973) *The Language of Psycho-Analysis* 94:295–374.

McCullers, C. (1946) *The Member of the Wedding*. Boston, MA/New York: Houghton Mifflin.

Early Barriers to Pleasure

Christine Anzieu-Premmereur

If we remember the 1965 Rolling Stones' "(I Can't Get No) Satisfaction", and the next step in disillusion with the 1970s punk movement, we observe that our time of disconnection and pessimism is not so new. This multidisciplinary book addresses the shifting forms of enjoyment in our contemporary world. Our first title was "The turning of the screw: bodies in crisis".

The search for pleasure seems to have evolved from the alias of sexual pleasure to enjoyment in either addictive or masochistic adventures.

Following Freud, we label the energy as libido: Life energy, or life drives, "preserve the cohesion of living matter". Eros, psychosexuality, used to be central in psychoanalytic thinking and we are to reconsider its importance now: to understand the transformations of the experiences in pleasure seeking, and the role of regulation of the psyche in quantity as in the quality of pleasure–unpleasure.

We think with Freud that the desire is the engine of the psyche, the movement which tends to reinvest the sensory memory of the first satisfaction.

The major Freudian concept of principle of pleasure–displeasure is an economic model of the psyche, centered on acquiring pleasure and withdrawing from what causes displeasure. The primary process, with the hallucinatory satisfaction, is in the immediacy of the circulation of energy, with the discharge of displeasure and of excess. The primitive narcissism enjoys the ego-pleasure of the beginnings of life. It is beyond the principle of pleasure that taught us how much the traumatic phenomena manifest the tendency to repetition of experiences of displeasure.

The nascent psyche of the infant is in search of a lost object: the painful experiences of loss of an object already invested, that can threaten the cohesion of the ego.

It can cause affect discharges, consuming libidinal energy. The relation to the object will be altered, as far as the process of disobjectalization.

The hallucinatory satisfaction takes place at the forefront of all other processes. The loss of the object of that satisfaction stresses the capability for representation and symbol formation. Feelings of emptiness and withdrawal from others are easily observed in our patients now. Autoeroticism is the search for pleasure sometimes associated with the fantasy of the other, but in our time more an action of discharge without a fantasy about a love object, leading to addictive compulsion. Then

DOI: 10.4324/9781003384618-2

psychosomatic symptoms can appear as a mode of anchoring in order not to be overwhelmed by affective experiences that could not give rise to representations.

We will add the notion of Après Coup, deferred action, into which past representations and experiences are reprocessed and we will explore the consequences of the analytic technique when facing resistances and complex issues with the feminine.

This book addresses the shifting forms of enjoyment in our world of uncertainty, trauma and social isolation.

Crises of Ideals, Delibidinalization and Its Discontents for Our Contemporary World

Introduction

Evan Moriarty

In a recent session, an adolescent patient says, "I can't escape the fact that the world's dying." He goes on to describe aligning himself with the decaying of the world by various means, including social and sexual isolation, repetitive drug use, and continual retreat into social media and virtuality. This is just one person's report, and one manner of responding to its content, but it stands to exemplify the broader contemporary pull to follow the arc of the Nirvana principle toward zero tension and psychic death. As he put it, "Sleeping is the ultimate euphoria." In the manner of a *reductio ad absurdum,* this micro-vignette reminds us why Freud (1924) found it necessary to pull the pleasure principle apart from identification with the Nirvana principle, such that he no longer considered it the fundamental aim of the mind "reducing to nothing" or "keeping as low as possible … the sums of excitation which flow in upon it" (p. 159). If the two principles were left theoretically fused, one would be forced to describe this young person's life as paradigm case of pleasurable living rather than an example of present-day delibidinization and discontentedness. While the second section of this volume addresses clinical phenomena of this sort "beyond" Freud's initial formulation of the pleasure principle by focusing primarily on the individual subject, the present section explores how contemporary society's crisis of ideals plays a role in shaping this subject.

Kristeva highlights how our very existence as speaking beings, beings capable of "remaking" ourselves, constituting what we are by virtue of what we take one another to be saying, as opposed to beings merely adaptable to (and so entirely at the mercy of) changes in circumstances (i.e., zombies), depends on what she calls the "mutuality of speech." This is speech composed of "words of the flesh" rather than "word-foam," speech fundamentally addressed to and reliant on another for its elaboration and substance. Kristeva pinpoints an abiding temptation made all the more alluring during the Covid pandemic: the temptation to block out an awareness of our limitedness in favor of omnipotence. Up against nearly intolerable excesses of excitation, it appears possible to save ourselves by retreating within. But this disinvestment in the flow of our drive energies out into the world of others—the only place where they can find meaning and significance—leaves our "inner selves" so radically impoverished as to be unrecognizable, incapable of building together "the day after."

DOI: 10.4324/9781003384618-4

Contri's first contribution relies on the fundamental difference between drive and instinct to elaborate what is distinctively human about the search for, in his vocabulary, satisfaction. For the human creature, drive excites thinking, which in turn has the potential to produce "the law of the body's motions" toward satisfaction. In this, humans represent an "exception to nature": our psychic lives are seats of robust causal power rather than yet more inert material through which energy flows, as is the case for those creatures subject to instinct, in whom excitement is a direct cause of determinate bodily motion. The capacity for "thinking," in this particular sense, shows the self-legislating character of our being, that which makes us both free and responsible. Thinking is, as Contri puts it, "one of the forces in the field." "Civilization" is another—one with the potential to shut down or inhibit an individual's thinking by infringing on one's authority to act in accordance with a law given to oneself, by eroding "thinking's imputability." Contri's second contribution, published with a synoptic postscript by Raffaella Colombo, stresses the necessity that our partners in thinking—those with whom we create "the realm of appointments"—be themselves out for the profit at which thinking aims. In the friendship founded by genuine thinking, we stand to profit only from those who stand to profit from us.

Drawing on the conceptual resources of Andre Green's "dead mother complex," McCoy and Berwald trace the origins of drug addiction in young men born into Belfast's Irish Republican community back to a generational loss of signification. They illuminate the challenge facing young Irish Republican men, whose social existence as such depends on their fulfillment of a largely abandoned political cause and inoperative cultural ideal, describing how (at least some) of their drug use—aimed at blocking out experience—represents, in negative form, the death of this ideal. Although situated within a particular social context and so not readily exportable to other cultures without careful consideration and amendment, this study fashions a vocabulary for acknowledging the precariousness of our shared forms of life and drives home the imperative to recognize and work through their collapse and reconstruction.

At least since Nietzsche's pronouncement of God's death, we have been unable to determine our societal values and ideals by reference to something supernatural. American philosopher Richard Rorty's recently published 1996 University of Girona lectures, collected as *Pragmatism as Anti-Authoritarianism* (2021), push the point even further, arguing that our beliefs and judgments can not be settled by reference to Reality or anything else non-human. This detour through philosophy emphasizes the extent to which we are primarily responsible *to one another* for creating, sustaining, and developing what counts as a good life in our societies, unable to rest on our laurels from one generation to the next, taking for granted the "givenness" of a set of values by virtue of their bearing some particular relation to the eternal, to the non-human. When we succeed in shouldering this responsibility, it is done in something like the way the individual matures by projecting their ego ideal up ahead into the future again and again. Of course, the individual does not always mature. As Chasseguet-Smirgel demonstrates in detailing the "bipolarity" of the ego ideal (1976, p. 356), this maturational trajectory is often neglected in favor of a return to fusion with the mother under the regressive pull of primary narcissism and the seductive but illusory promise of omnipotence. This same fork in the road between maturation and regression exists in the societal realm. Whether the current crisis of ideals can be a productive one depends on our ability to embrace castration and lack (rather than perversion and completeness) as a precondition for both personal intercourse and political discourse.

References

Chasseguet-Smirgel, J. (1976). Some thoughts on the ego ideal a contribution to the study of the 'illness of ideality.' *The Psychoanalytic Quarterly*, 45(3), 345–373.

Rorty, R. (2021). *Pragmatism as Anti-Authoritarianism*. Eduardo Mendieta, (Ed.), Harvard University Press.

Chapter 1

Preface to Kristeva's Work
Vitality Against Virality and Virtuality

Rachel Boué-Widawsky

As an introduction to the article "The Day After" by Julia Kristeva, it is important to understand the context of its publication (May/June 2021) in *L'Arche*, a Jewish cultural magazine, during the pandemic.

The context (pandemic and religious magazine) reveals how much Kristeva's thinking goes beyond the clinical space of our consulting rooms, or rather on zoom nowadays.

This article/interview not only illustrates how Kristeva's psychoanalytic thinking is relevant to the outside social, political and biological reality but also the tools psychoanalytic theory has to address the irruption of the unknown, the unpredictable and the unacceptable in our lives, namely our daily mortality. The beginning sentence of the article is significant of her approach to the crisis brought on by the pandemic: "the inability to foresee, to plan, is one of the scandals that pandemic has revealed. Ever since the beginning of humanity, religions have taken up the question of human finiteness, of mortality, but it's not part of today's general discourse."

In this article, Kristeva demonstrates her apt and acute sense of observation of anthropological shifts in our societies that her book, *Passions of Our Time*,[1] had already highlighted on various contemporary issues. In her view, the pandemic revealed a void in the secular discourse of today through its incapacity to address the human vulnerability, subsequent to our mortality which religions used to address in their prophetic narratives.

Additionally, Kristeva holds neoliberal ideologies of hubris responsible for the mismanagement of the pandemic in their avoidance of taking into consideration the weakest, and more specifically the eldest. She perceives delusion in our ideology of power and in our hyperconnected global economy, a dangerous denial of human vulnerability and mortality.

However, if the denial of our mortality can also be recognized as a vital necessity, it must preserve, according to Kristeva, the eminence of the subject at the center of our social contracts: "We urgently need to change the paradigm and put the individual personhood at the center of our data. At the essential levels of the social pact: the ethical, educational, religious, political levels."

The singularity of the human subjectivity has always been the focal point of Kristeva's work in her search for an articulation between the singular and the

DOI: 10.4324/9781003384618-5

universal. This "in between" (sic) is an intermediate mental place, a transference, where an "inter-diction" (sic) can occur between our inner self and the other. Being hospitable to this otherness in the core of our thinking selves is where a reliance[2] is built. For Kristeva, reliance is the process of humanization, which not only provides the maternal foundation for future human relationships but also operates as the regulator between libidinal and destructive drives.

According to Kristeva, the pandemic and its lockdowns have revealed the deficiencies of this human reliance in the era of virtuality, where hyper-connections have hidden, profound loneliness as well as social and emotional disjunction. The desocialization, promoted by the necessary social distanciation and needed to repel the viral attack, brought to the forefront the vacuum of internet connections. The latter have disembodied the fabric of human ties – beyond individual relationships – which Kristeva unearths with her patients in listening precisely to the "flesh" of their words, referring to the emotional, affective, semiotic vitality of language.

In being the prototype of the most primary human link and generating the emergence of language in human history, reliance is, for Kristeva, the first ethical space where singularity and otherness meet. For her, this "between two and within oneself" space delineates limits, that consumerism and accelerated technological developments have baffled at the detriment of our inner lives, our bodies and our planet.

While Kristeva praises the genius of the human mind capable of producing prodigious biological solutions, such as the RNA-based treatments for Covid vaccines, she also advocates for a humble acknowledgment of human vulnerability in its universal mortality. As essentially a humanist, Kristeva sees the future, "the day after," in the recovery of our sense of limits, lodged in this "in-between" space, as the only guarantee for the preservation of our planet and for the survival of the human mind.

Notes

1   Julia Kristeva, *Passions of Our Time* (2013), New York: Columbia University Press, 2019.
2   Julia Kristeva, "Reliance, or Maternal Eroticism", *Journal of the American Psychoanalytic Association* (62, vol. 1:69–85), 2014.

Chapter 2

"In the Current State of War, It Is Our Most Inner Selves That We Must Save" *

Julia Kristeva

Paule-Henriette Lévy (*L'Arche*)

A significant number of elderly people died during this pandemic. What should one think of a society which, in the event of a crisis, has not planned to bother with the fate of its elders?

The inability to foresee, to plan, is one of the scandals the pandemic has revealed. Ever since the beginning of humanity, religions have taken up the question of human finiteness, of mortality, but it's not part of today's general discourse. So, yes, we know how to foster palliative care, manage nursing homes, study the biology of the mechanism of apoptosis, the continuous process of cell death and regeneration. But we seem unable "to pay" the ultimate price of old age, no doubt because, in our secularized societies, death, the ultimate boundary of human experience, is hidden. A health provider from a nursing home recently became angry on TV when he spoke about how, "there are no staff to *talk* with our elders ... "

I would like us to go one step further. It seems to me that, more insidiously and more violently, this viral surge that we have just experienced has revealed to us the inescapable vulnerability of the human condition, beyond old age. I'm talking about the vulnerability that is in us, that lives in us, and which our ideologies of performance and win-win turn out to be incapable of assuming.

The question of accompanying and supporting old age directly challenges the model of neoliberalism. Some say this health crisis is tipping liberal neo-capitalism into digital capitalism, which would mean organizing *direct* budget support from the government and finding digital tools capable of "tailoring" cost decreases while increasing remuneration in certain undervalued professions, in particular in health, education, or security. And so on ... But this human disaster that the pandemic is causing seems to me such that it cannot be resolved with political, economic and health measures only, essential as they are. **We urgently need to change the paradigm and put individual**

---

* Appeared originally in the special edition of *L'Arche*, no. 681, May/June 2020 entitled "The Day After." Reprinted with permission.

DOI: 10.4324/9781003384618-6

personhood at the center of our data. At the essential levels of the social pact: the ethical, educational, religious, political levels. That is where issues of old age, mortality, and boundaries become the main topics for "the day after."

This crisis has taught us a lot about isolation

For obvious health reasons, the government has compelled everyone to stay home, but what is left of "home," of the "self"? Quarantine has revealed the ravages of loneliness into which anthropological acceleration has led us, driven by unrestrained neoliberalism and hyper-globalized networks. The latter would have us believe that we are not *isolated* as long as we are *connected*. Mistake. Hyperconnection has not made *loneliness* disappear, far from it. The virtual screen has only compressed and trapped it in social networks. Messages, likes, emojis—this implosive and explosive "word-foam" has, on the contrary, revealed and emphasized emptiness. It has not restored what I, listening to my patients, call "the flesh of words." That is to say the affects and passions, desires for love, life and death desires that are shared in the transference between the analyst and the analysand, such that sharing the primary affects that the one can offer to the other allows the latter, in confidence, to put them into words, into a narrative, into history. To elucidate, evaluate, and recast *their ties-to-others.*

Analysis and containment: a major agenda!

In pre-Covid times, we used inevitable smartphones as "barrier gestures": tools for distancing ourselves from impulses, avoiding close physical contact, protecting ourselves from regression and trauma. We feared that quarantine would further empower these devices. But instead, the pandemic has unleashed fears so acute that they call for unexpected inner resources, at least among the men and women who have wagered that it is possible to rebound. That is how I define the women and men who have undertaken an analysis. And so, a breach breaks through their quarantine. This same object, their smartphone, set down, as if forgotten, on a table or the bed pillow of a stressed and stuck internet surfer, in fact facilitates the need and the desire to strip down, to drop one's mask, to speak "one on one," "for real." There follows the unlocking of guilt, of pretense, of worldly defenses. Each person discovers their "intimate/extimate," "inside/outside" dug up from the fragile zones of their lives, calling out to the analyst's vitality. As we wait for a vaccine, it is not an antibody that thus develops, but rather a genuine *psycho-somatic* buttress that can repel the collapse fomented by viral attack and confining desocialization. A kind of *ethics,* transversal to the moral borders and prohibitions it remains aware of, but which in our specialized analytic language is an "*inter-diction*" [an "in-between-what-is-spoken"]. In my work, I call "reliance" this nuclear mutuality of speech that constitutes the speaking being and that we must rediscover. **In a new world to be invented, we need to be able to push the links between words** all the way to the "flesh of words," failing which survivors will be zombies who in the end will be able to adapt but will no longer be humans capable of remaking themselves.

We have also faced the impossibility of experiencing many of our religious rituals. How will they regain meaning now that they have been replaced?

I am a child of the Enlightenment, "of unbelief and doubt" (this is my Dostoyevskian side),[1] and I think religious facts are rich in meaning, provided they are reassessed, and that we raise questions about them with respect to today's problems and disasters. But it is Freud, a Jew without God who enlightens me on this path, because he took up, it seems to me, the essence of this religious experience which is precisely the nuclear duality of the same and the Other, as revealed in speech where the mutuality constitutive of the human is invented. The transferential relationship bequeathed to us by the inventor of the unconscious and which solicits each of two protagonists (the analysand and the analyst), participates in this ongoing transvaluation of religions; it is one of the remedies for religions' loss of speed in the contemporary world. There are undoubtedly others, but I privilege the capacity of analysis to rebuild our "inner self" as that which holds up and recasts two pillars of biblical and evangelical religion: *otherness* and *singularity*. Thus is the "in-between" and "inter" expressed: between two and within oneself. Only from there is it possible to grasp *the meaning of the limits* (prohibitions, purifications, retreats, etc.) advanced by religions and to accept that necessary rituals can evolve. Indeed, beyond its health value, spatial quarantine is a normative social and *moral* constraint, whose subjective and *ethical* scope of consent should be elaborated, this free choice that each individual person makes between two.

Evoking limits, we today have come to understand how our technological and consumerist, relentlessness, without limits, has harmed our planet. If we do not reevaluate the sense of "in-betweenness" and limits that are part of religious and moral history, if we do not rebuild human "innerness," our planet, even if cleaned up through ecological rigor, risks being delivered over to the cruelty of its first inhabitants, namely the viruses. *It is the inner self that we must therefore save, given the current state of war.*

Do you believe in "the day after"?

Yes, and including what it will require from us. Just a few months ago, the metaphor of things going viral was widely used. I used it myself. It could be broken down thus: seduction, explosion, destruction. Social networks are viral. They seduce you, blame you, and then destroy you. The Yellow Vests, too, who reveal nameless desires, get going and then ransack Paris with the Black Blocks. Was this external virality foretelling what is happening to us today from inside? The pathogenic agents are no longer external to us; they live in the genetic tissue of humanity. There are more bacteria in the human body than there are cells. Some are infectious, others are not! Long live virology! We accuse scientists and politicians of being "uncertain." But these viruses that befall us reveal the abysmal uncertainty of the boundaries between life and death. (Are these parasites concepts, molecules, or living beings?) We must therefore be ready to live with these threats that are present inside our bodies and with which we have lived for millennia, but which will become more and more invasive. If nothing is done to curb them, politico-economic virality risks turning back on us in boomerang as part of what is now an inevitable global warming. An apocalyptic observation … but I am an energetic pessimist, because I know that we have the resources needed to face these challenges. I am not here to make an apology for melancholy and claustration. I listened with great interest to information about the projects of Stéphane Bancel, Director of the biotech company *Moderna Therapeutics*, which specializes in RNA-based treatments that are not about injecting attenuated viruses but allowing our cells to produce antibodies. **The apocalypse also stimulates the genius of the human mind.** Perhaps it is because I have experienced three wars—I was born a day after World War II was declared; I was a child and adolescent during the Cold War; and now I am immersed in this world health war—I consider myself a "survivor," and I tend to approach, listen to, and love humans as "*sur-vivants*" [those who continue to live] But to be able to be one, it is important to soak up this inherent vulnerability that I mentioned at the beginning of the interview (the capacity for solitude, the mortality inside of us, limits and their negotiation through *inter-diction*). By forcing us to integrate them better, would that the viral challenge prepare humanity for more tenderness in the competition, endurance, and enthusiasm that we will have to reinvent in order to rebuild after Covid. Precisely to be *sur-vivants*.

Note

1   See Kristeva, Julia, *Dostoïevski*, coll. "Les auteurs de ma vie" (Buchet/Chastel, 2020); Kristeva, Julia et Marie-Rose Moro, *Grandir c'est croire* (Bayard, 2020).

Chapter 3

Preface to Contri's Work
Thinking, Drive, Law

Michael Civin

Giacomo Contri passed away in 2022. The first translator of *Ecrit* into Italian, he was widely considered to be one of Italy's foremost scholars of the works of Jacques Lacan. Contri built upon Lacan's thinking while departing from much of the latter's later writing. He was the founder of *Società Amici del Pensiero – Sigmund Freud*, a society dedicated to the development and fulfillment of Contri's own thinking. Not unlike Lacan, Contri's texts can be quite complex and subject to multiple interpretations. In this introduction I am trying to convey, in as straightforward a manner as possible, my understanding of Contri's thought in this chapter.

Contri philosophy and clinic of psychoanalysis are built on articulation of Freud's Science through the triangular foundation of Drive, Thinking and Law.[1] We and our relationship to sexual difference differ from other creatures because (1) we are, from birth, thinking subjects; (2) because we think we have drives in addition to the instincts that govern other creatures; and (3) we have laws that locate the subject within the larger society by legislating rules that govern the drives, speech, action and reaction.

Contri begins with the notion that man (and man's relationship to sexual difference) has distinguished himself from other evolutionary elements because of man's capacity to think about motoric responses to excitement, rather than simply to react motorically (instinct). Artificial intelligence can reproduce a great deal, if not eventually all mental functioning, but it cannot reproduce our capacity to formulate rules (law/legislation), and most specifically the law of the drives. From birth, and without waiting for adult maturation this capacity for thought means that excitement cannot be equated with "stimulus" nor can reaction to excitement be equated with "instinct." Even the most "primitive" man is distinguished by this capacity for thinking. Only Freud's psychoanalysis recognizes this foundational Truth. From its earliest days, the infant (in the context of a transgenerational order) establishes unique thought through language, drives through thought and a relationship to the Laws of Sexual Difference (e.g. castration, penis envy and the Oedipus) through thought, the drives and their vicissitudes.

In this essay, Contri develops his notion of the phonic drive, a drive that from the earliest moments of life directs the infant toward the complexity of speech and the creation of a complex grammar. This phonic drive situates the subject in a world of

DOI: 10.4324/9781003384618-7

potential partnership with other speaking subjects, hence toward fulfillment. The life of the speaking subject, in fact, is directed only toward drive, and drive follows its only Law—fulfillment. Based on this, Contri concludes that the pleasure principle is not about hedonism, but rather about the individual's ability to further the Law of Fulfillment and this fulfillment requires the partnership with other thinking/speaking subjects. He feels that until now humanity has managed to achieve little satisfaction of this law of fulfillment.

Contri is highly critical, even fearful of the turns of contemporary "psychology." Freud inaugurated the Science of Thought as it pertains to all stimuli, not merely superficial phenomena, but rather all the currents and cross-currents of human drives, even those that live in the deepest, unknowable recesses of our psyches. Cognitive theories ignore this, attending only to the superficial.

Using this superficiality, we can't talk about psychopathology in our days in terms of the inhibition of thought, in terms of anguish: society has substituted the superficial, the statistical. Consistent with the overarching themes of this book, Contri views civilization (built on the Laws that govern the drives) to have adopted new ways of behaving that are a manic deviation from seeking satisfaction.

It is only Freud's Science of Thought (psychoanalysis), not the science of statistics, that applies to the treatment of psychopathology and the psychoanalyst is the means, the partner, for the correction of psychopathology, for the thought attached to the motion of the drives. That primary production of language and thought that precociously allows the subject, through the collective order, to select the motion of its drives and, thus, the partner. The partnering is a function of the subject. The universality of the environment allows the subject to make use of the partner through the assumption of his own ambition. This unique foundation of the subject, in the context of the Social World, forms the partnership of the psychoanalyst.

Finally, sexual difference (not its erasure into an entity as Contri sees the contemporary world doing) introduces the forwarding of the complexity of thought/drives. However, in terms of the recognition of sexual difference, Contri sees the Western world peppered by its traumatic erasure.

Note

1   Contri's final writings, the last of which is presented in this book, locate his philosophy on a related triangular base of Thought, Science and Faith.

Chapter 4

The Science of Thought

The Thought of Satisfaction

Giacomo B. Contri

Translated by Luca Flabbi, Glauco M. Genga, and Maria Gabriella Pediconi[1]

Excitement is a cause: it causes not the motion (of the body, what else?), but of the thought that elaborates the law of motion of the body:

It is an exception to nature.

Thought is a legislator, which decays in artificial intelligence.

It is in this that the biological entity called "man," immediately man and woman, detaches itself, more or less mysteriously, from biological evolution: excitement is not a stimulus of the body and motion is not instinct, and this until from the newborn.

Intellectualism connotes man even the most "beast" (I do not know scientific works intended to draw the intellectualism of the aforementioned "beast," or of what has been offensively called "ox people" by the aristocracy, as well as I do not know works on the correlative intellectualism of the aristocracy).

"Desire" designates the excitement, and "satisfaction" the outcome of the excitement in an end point, contrary to the trend of natural causality that has no end.

Life is directed towards the sense of motion, and no other ... sense.

The sense is that of motion which has only one duty immanent to its law, that of being conclusive.

The question is legitimate: how much satisfaction has humanity been able to produce? The balance sheet is not exciting.

This is what we call the "pleasure principle": individual competence in promoting the final point of the law of satisfaction.

This is not about hedonism.

Freud inaugurated the science of thought in general, as this is susceptibility to arousals, all of which are sensory.

DOI: 10.4324/9781003384618-8

Educational theories ignore this as their premise.

Since the motions of the body have effects, the discovery of the imputability of thought as a legal (legislating) agency is essential: in military language we should speak of thought as a force in the field.

Freud called thought, always individual, as the law of motion "drive."

However, what I have been calling for years the "phonic drive" has not been recognized, which I introduced by saying that at two years of age the child has surpassed Mozart twice: for having built the harpsichord himself (the assembly of the organs of the phonation), and for having built up grammar by himself (with thought), well before education:

thus (self) gifted ("drive" and language), the child would seem to start his adventure well in the sense (of motion): we know that this is not the case, and the Greeks got away too easily with "destiny."

It would be time to talk about psychopathology, including perversion, starting from thought inhibition and anguish, but Culture no longer does so under the new pretext of statistics:

the inhibited thought (Civilization) takes new avenues of action, even in excess to the point of mania, distracting itself from satisfaction.

The science of thought finds application in the treatment of psychopathology, to the point of reserving – as I suggest – the word "psychoanalysis" only for this application and no longer for this science.

In this application the psychoanalyst is the means, or partner, for the correction (pathology) of the thought of the motion of his subject.

In the primary production of language by the subject itself, that is to say, of thought, therefore precociously not fantastical, the subject procures the thought of the collective order, without waiting for adulthood, in which to select the partner or means of its motion.

The universal environment in which the child obtains a partner makes him ambitious, which soon exposes him to the saying of Brutus: "I loved Caesar, but he was ambitious and I killed him."

Finally, the sexes: which in the excitement of thought propose themselves exclusively in their difference and not in their entity.

The Talibanism that has just traumatized the world rejects this truth on a social scale, but we cannot say that in our democratic Westernism we are in good standing on the sexes.

Note

1   Luca Flabbi, Ph.D., is Professor at the University of North Carolina – Chapel Hill and member of the board of the psychoanalytic society Società Amici del Pensiero – Sigmund Freud (SAP), based in Milan, Italy. Maria Gabriella Pediconi is Assistant Professor at Urbino University, psychoanalyst, and member of the board of the psychoanalytic society Società Amici del Pensiero — Sigmund Freud (SAP). Glauco M. Genga, Physician, Psychiatrist, Psychoanalyst. Forensic Psychiatrist at the Institute of Aerospace Medicine of the Italian Air Force and member of the board of the psychoanalytic society Società Amici del Pensiero — Sigmund Freud (SAP).

Chapter 5

Three Chapters to Be Remembered and Post-Scriptum

Giacomo B. Contri and Raffaella Colombo

Translated by Luca Flabbi, Glauco M. Genga, and Maria Gabriella Pediconi[1]

To Be Remembered

I wish to be remembered for the juridical conception of love and for the science of thinking (unconscious).

(Letter to the members of the *Società Amici del Pensiero*
– *Sigmund Freud*, December 16, 2021)

Three Chapters: Contributed by Giacomo B. Contri

I would like to add a link between the two chapters of my December 16th talk—entitled "The Juridical Conception of Love and the Science of Thinking"—and faith.

We have always been wrong in linking faith to God, I do not believe in God. No one has faith in God. God has never given us any reasons to believe him, i.e. to consider him reliable,[2] nor to love him.

It is not as if everything is left to be done, but, indeed, all is left to be done. what I call the juridical thinking of love, or the love's profit. In order to love God, God would need to have "an axe to grind,"[3] a personal interest to which we could contribute.

That is what Muhammad, who has no Allah-God, understood, as he gave the name "Allah" to Akbar, that is to the pure fact that "the Greatest" is supposed to exist. Or better, to the pure supposition that the Greatest exists. In other words, I name "Allah" the Greatest one, exactly as I name an object. Nothing personal.

What was to be built is the reliability (juridicity, partner) that the Christians had missed. It is from the juridical that comes reliability since reliability is a judgment, i.e. faith as a judgment about reliability (profit).

There is no faith, there is no reliability, if there is no profit of the other. And there is no love of God without my grinding the axe of God.

From God, I want that he gains from me and I gain from him.

Therefore, my concluding chapters are three: Law, Science, Faith.

DOI: 10.4324/9781003384618-9

Post-Scriptum: Contributed by Raffaella Colombo

Giacomo Contri has carried out an act of such novelty that those who have grasped its importance like to spread the news. He has founded a Society—not an association—open to anyone who wishes to assume its statute. The Statute of this Society supports the friendship for thinking as initially discovered by Freud.

Does not seem much? Contri showed how, with Freud, the concept of human being enters the history of thought. Until Freud, the definition of man was based on the Aristotelian ontological category of animal. Human beings as rational animals. Starting with Freud, we can say "if there was no thinking, there would be no man" (Article 2, Statute of the *Società Amici del Pensiero – Sigmund Freud*). This is Freud's discovery: Freud "did not discover the unconscious (common mistake): he discovered thinking, not a portion of it, in its congenital faculty to assert, to pose, un-tamed despite the hostility to it" (Article 3), and in discovering thinking he posited it by "redeeming the thinking from the servitudes-divisions-partitions of traditional philosophy" (Article 3).

The friendship for and of thinking is the fundamental norm of this Society, and it is a positive norm, not the prerequisite of a Constitution. Just as for any State's Constitutions that presupposes a fundamental norm but, for that reason, it is left in weakness (Article 2, note 12); also for the individual's Constitution, the fundamental norm is its foundational implication. But here is Contri's innovation: since it is a principle of law that "whatever is not expressly forbidden by law is permitted," it follows from that principle that:

1   Every act that takes place within the scope of that permission is not autonomous with respect to law but it is law itself: a first law with respect to the second one, the law of the State;
2   "We do not argue from pompous benches about the theoretical possibility of a First law: we simply posit it, as it is done by every thinker whose act posits a realm of appointments with its own norm" (Article 2).

Freud never spoke of a realm of appointments. "Freud inaugurated friendship for thinking, but he could not do, nor think, its Society, stopping himself at an Association about which he later complained" (Article 3). However, the humanity described by Freud suffers exactly of the lack of capacity to live by appointments. Freud has discovered and described thinking in the critical conditions in which it is typically found, right after the very first years of life: it is thinking impoverished, inhibited, inconclusive, repressed, occupied by a usurper (the super-ego), prone to destroy what it has built, prone to avoid satisfaction for fearing of losing love, a love that is not at all real. In short, thinking becomes the enemy to itself. In conclusion, it is thinking in a pathological state, even if not clinically sick. But with consequences that go so far as to become actually clinical (symptoms) and economically oriented to failure.

Contri relaunches the real possibility of the realm of appointments as the normal individual constitution founded on the friendship for thinking and he poses its fundamental norm. "With the modest means at our disposal, today we found a Society of Friends of Thinking, or for the defense of thinking, based on a three-sided fundamental Norm that distinguishes three species of imputations:

I   The friendships for thinking;
II   The hostility to thinking;
III The indifference with respect to thinking (Article 2).

The friendship for thinking—the principle of a Constitution that makes us human being— provides the benefit of a law for production, for satisfaction, and for enjoyment of the fruits of such production, without anguish. It is up to the single subject to cultivate interest and passion in it." [...] "The aim (of the Friends of Thinking Society) is designable once again as the Freudian 'reclamation' or the 'favorable conditions' (recalling Leopardi's words). The desire to be a Member with access to this supplementary benefit cannot be supported by proselytism nor be a source of militancy. The only duty of a Society's Member is constituted by the obedience to the three-sided fundamental Norm, not as a limitation, but as the norm of friendship itself, without limitations for thinking. [...]

Since the psychoanalysis, and Freud's thinking before it, are both derived from the friendship for thinking, the application to the Society does not need to include any certification about one's own psychoanalysis. It is not a matter of dispensation nor of fungibility. This is an opportunity to emphasize that for this same reason the Friends of Thinking Society is not a psychoanalytic Society. Not even among psychoanalysts there is a social tie that is not mediated by the friendship for and of thinking.

(Article 10)

This Society has not the aim to make the revolution, Contri says in the Introduction, but to have the thought of the revolution, "because thinking means to care, in all its meanings" (Premise).

Drawing up a Statute for thinking not as a theory among many but as juridical statute, i.e. as a statute made for real people, has been Contri's conclusive act. It was the act of a layman because it is the free—sovereign—individual conviction that produces a doctrine of law (see Kelsen).

His last paper, *Three Chapters to be Remembered* (January 15, 2022, six days before dying), resumes his conclusive act: Contri dissolved any uncertainty about the science of thinking founded by Freud. He has also dissolved the millennial deception of love as equivalent to "falling in love" of which many authors have written the apology: Dostoevsky with *The Idiot* being a good example among many. Finally, he has also dissolved the most viral of ambiguities, the one related to faith: nothing to do with the "the greatest," the inscrutable, the omnipotent, in a word, God. Faith is a judgment of trustworthiness that includes the profit as a proof for truth. Profit for the subject and for the other.

Notes

1   Luca Flabbi, Ph.D., is a Professor at the University of North Carolina-Chapel Carolina – Chapel Hill and a regular member of the board of the psychoanalytic society Società Amici del Pensiero — Sigmund Freud (SAP), based in Milan, Italy. Maria Gabriella Pediconi is Assistant Professor at Urbino University, psychoanalyst, and member of the board of the psychoanalytic society Società Amici del Pensiero — Sigmund Freud (SAP). Glauco M. Genga, M.D., Physician, Psychiatrist, Psychoanalyst. Forensic Psychiatrist at the Institute of Aerospace Medicine of the Italian Air Force and member of the board of the psychoanalytic society Società Amici del Pensiero — Sigmund Freud (SAP).
2   Translator Note: The original Italian is *affidabile*, which shares the same root with *fede*, i.e. faith.
3   Translator Note: The original Italian idiomatic expression is *portare acqua al proprio mulino*, which literally means "to draw water to your mill."

Chapter 6

Dead Mother (Ire)land

Matthew McCoy and Marisa Berwald

Generations of Irish Republicans reside in *An Trá Ghearr* ("The Short Strand"), a social housing district of 3,000 people surrounded by a series of "peace" walls and environmental buffers, the infrastructural legacy of a century of colonial and sectarian conflict. These walls function to isolate and contain in space and time multiple generations of Irish rebel movements. We argue that these generations are connected via the transmission of a distinctively Irish paternal signifier, that of rebellion, which orients Irish Republicans toward the aim of uniting the paternity of the state and the maternity of the land as an Irish nationalism. However, as we will illustrate via analysis of ethnographic data, the meaning of this signifier of Irish paternity has lost potency over time and results in a cultural psychic blankness among a generation of young men who inherit it.

To orient our discussion, we map two aims of rebellion as a social movement: one that functions to constitute an ideal of masculinity as willing to sacrifice life to protect a motherland, and the other, which navigates the loss of that same motherland as this ideal loses meaning. The first, "bloody" aim (Green 1986), we depict as successive failed rebellion movements of Irish Republicans whose meaning is eroded by eventual acquiescence to British colonial power. The other, navigating the loss of the "motherland," neglects to (re)instantiate a sense of potent masculinity intergenerationally in the face of these failures, and through this potent masculinity, a new form of viable motherhood. We contend that this neglect opens to an experience of an "abject" (Kristeva 1982).

In this chapter, we analyze ethnographic data gathered by Matthew between June 2015 and July 2017 in Irish Republican working-class social housing districts in Belfast, Northern Ireland (McCoy 2020). We treat Irish nationalism as a form of life whose vitality has depended upon the ability of rebel movements to establish a relation, even if oppositional, between the affective motherland and the paternal laws of a "unified" Irish nation state separated from British rule. This form of life was lost, in the experience of Matthew's more radical Irish Republican interlocutors, when in 1998 Sinn Féin, the political wing of the Provisional Irish Republican Army (henceforth IRA), became party to a complex set of peace agreements which, in the end, allowed for the continued existence of Northern Ireland as part of the United Kingdom. At this point, generations of Irish uprisings during the 20th century

DOI: 10.4324/9781003384618-10

(begun in 1916 and repeating sporadically until a prolonged period of conflict between 1969 and 1998 called "the Troubles") are revealed to have failed to achieve their aims. While the aims themselves, succession from British rule and establishment of a 32-County Irish Republic, were never meant to be realized immediately, they functioned to create a rite of passage verifying an Irish manhood premised upon the ability to rule over an Irish motherland in an imaginary future. When this relation between Irish masculinity and femininity, as united in law and land, was abandoned, passage toward manhood as rebellion against colonial rule became a defunct paradigm.

Why blankness? We explain the emergence of a psychic blankness, felt as a stripping of experience, as a cultural symptom via analogy with André Green's "dead mother complex" (Green 1986). We compare Green's mother – a present mother who withdraws from her child due to a maternal depression – to a motherland that loses its ability to birth Irish sons. We depict the transition within the history of Irish rebellion from a potent to now defunct paradigm for nationhood, wherein motherland transforms from an active ideal to something lost that cannot not be revitalized. This loss of motherland as an object of love results in a kind of affective flattening or disaffection (Berlant 2015), which reflects the inability of Irish youth to orient toward a future imagination of what life *could* be like, either as an imagined nation (Anderson 1983) or otherwise. In this example, an Irish cultural unconsciousness, established over multiple generations of rebel movements, "cruelly" structures the now impossible relation of care between motherland and the state as a forgotten, absent (yet present) (im)possibility (Berlant 2011).

Irish Torso

On the night of Good Friday 1916, a car of four Irish Volunteers drove to retrieve a shipment of arms for use during the already-planned Easter weekend's rebellion against British rule. Their car careened off a pier into the River Laune at Ballykissane. Three of the four men drowned, including Charlie Monahan, the first casualty of the Easter Rising from Belfast. Monahan's headless torso washed up six months later.

In East Belfast, 100 years later, within the small memorial grounds of *An Tine Bheo* ("the living flame") of *An Trá Ghearr*, a predominantly Catholic and Irish Republican social housing area, a drama is staged to commemorate Monahan's sacrifice. The street play, *Johanna Monahan*, part of Sinn Féin's *1916: Our History, Our Future*, was one of the numerous Easter Rising Centenary celebrations planned across the Republic of Ireland and Northern Ireland. The playwright of *Johanna Monahan*, Laurence McKeown, is a well-known writer and former IRA volunteer. He participated in the 1981 Hunger Strike in which ten Irish Republican volunteers died for the sake of attaining political prisoner status from then-UK Prime Minister Margaret Thatcher and her government. McKeown survived 70 days without food, the longest stretch of any hunger striker who lived.

Today, he stands in the street with residents of the *An Trá Ghearr* community and watches the play he wrote for a community that suffered many losses during cyclical periods of conflict, the names and portraits of their volunteers lost on active duty emblazoned on the memorial garden wall. The symbolic effect of the play is to link these former generations of rebellion to the current one, via the trope of mothers mourning lost sons. *Johanna Monahan* is about Charlie's mother, Johanna. And while Monahan represents a middle generation of Irish rebellion, the majority of the faces memorialized are those who died on active duty during the latest period of conflict, the Troubles.

The actress playing Johanna speaks directly to the audience in the front of the headwall of the memorial garden wearing a plain woolen skirt, crimson overcoat, and white scarf. She recites the poem "Mother" by Pádraic Pearse, one of the main revolutionaries and planners of the Easter Rising, subsequently executed by firing squad by the British Army. Then, she compares Pearse's mother's experience to her own:[1]

Lord, thou art hard on mothers:
We suffer in their coming and their going;
And tho' I grudge them not, I weary, weary
Of the long sorrow – And yet I have my joy:
My sons were faithful, and they fought.

Johanna soliloquizes,

Pádraic Pearse wrote that for his mother but it's as if he wrote it for me because I watched my own two sons, Charlie and Albhie, take the path of bloody protest for a glorious thing. Unlike Pearse's mother one of my sons, Albhie, was returned to me but not Charlie. I think of them often and speak their names to my own heart in the long nights. I think of the time they grew up here. Simple times. We had nothing. We were poor. Everyone was poor then. But we shared what we had. The community shared. That's what community is about.

The depiction of this ideal of a long mourning Irish mother is not unusual in the well-renowned history of 20th-century Irish drama.[2] Particular to this staged play, the actress depicting Johanna Monahan links herself to Pearse's mother, Margaret, and to the community's mothers, some of whom watching the drama also lost sons during the Troubles. Further emphasizing this link, Johanna gently touches an image of her son, Charlie, on a memorial wall that includes the faces of other sons from the community who died on active duty (Figure 6.1).

In this play, encountering Johanna means to disorient oneself from the individual, Johanna or Charlie, and to reorient oneself to the social conditions out of which this mother-son dyad emerges in the first place. Johanna constitutes the very community as one in which losing sons to fight dispossession is shared. Through mourning such loss, the community becomes ever more tightly bound, less individuated, and oriented toward a future for the sake of which all Irish mothers and sons shall have been redeemed – a future defined by a melancholic relation to a future Irish state.

Figure 6.1 Johanna touching Charlie.
Source: © Matthew McCoy.

The play of *Johanna Monahan*, just one of many Irish dramatizations, habilitates mother Ireland via a memorialized enactment of a scenario premised on absence – a future yet to come in which Irish paternity is reinstated and mothers no longer sacrifice their sons. The staging of this specific drama, wherein the appearance of Charlie's ghost speaks to the social ties of responsibility those in the district have to their martyrs, provides only one portrayal of what it means to be a man and woman in Ireland. Yet, it serves a very specific function within the contemporary context of Irish colonialism. Charlie's ghost haunts the present scene as a kind of uncanny reminder of what the community has sacrificed, a *staged* return of the repressed. While the community witnesses this sacrifice, Charlie's ghost enacts the other side of this relationality, as Charlie also witnesses and surveils the living to ensure that they continue to do their part as circumscribed by Sinn Féin. Through the dead's witnessing, the living are called to account.

But to account for what? For what remains of the Irish Republican movement is a technocratic political process worked out in British institutions. For dissenting, anti-peace agreement Irish Republicans, a united Ireland is further away than ever. Charlie, at the same time he is made grievable (Butler 2004), makes iconic the sacrifice of male life for a future. If this future is not "yet to come," but "never to come," or already given up on, then for what is such a sacrifice made? To make the future imaginary of a nation state alive and well in the minds of the Irish, it must be a possibility. This possibility, given up in the 1998 peace accords, is now mostly defunct. Charlie appears less as a ghost and more like a zombie, becoming eerie to mourn so long as Northern Ireland exists without a vibrant Irish Republican movement to bring about a united Ireland.

Irish Neck

One street away from the memorial garden lies a currently unoccupied ground floor flat. On a small coffee table sits cold brown tea with the tea bag still in the cup, blotted cigarettes in an ashtray. Oilibhéar, the inhabitant of this flat, lies in a hospital bed in a communal recovery room with several other patients in the "mother of the sick," the Mater Infirmorum Hospital, on the Crumlin Road. He recovers from a neck surgery to replace a cervical vertebra, a wound 40 years old. In his early 20s, in active combat with the IRA, Oilibhéar describes being lifted vertically like a battering ram by British soldiers and plunged headfirst into a moving Saracen. Amid this excruciating pain, he understood what it meant to "see stars," as his sight went dark. His artificial cervical vertebra continues to cause him pain, perhaps "phantom pain." He calls his neck "his cunt" every time it hurts.

Though Oilibhéar incurred this injury while defending the district as an IRA operator in the early 1970s, his name will not be remembered on the walls of *An Tine Bheo*, and no one will stage a play for him in the future. He left the IRA/Sinn Féin as a dissenter against the Sinn Féin-backed peace agreement. In his youth, Oilibhéar was an operator, prisoner, and victim of British torture schemes, but he was also tortured by the IRA, his former comrades, after falling out with the organization. The position of Oilibhéar whose willingness to sacrifice himself for the possibility of an Irish nation state will not be memorialized, at least according to the logic of Oilibhéar's account, reveals a cover up.

Oilibhéar has a theory that Irish mothers are estranged from their children, and that Irish parents (though not grandparents) lack the capacity to empathize. He developed this thought as a child, seeing his devout Catholic mother birth six other children in the span of a decade. He said she was prone to periods of sadness, especially after childbirth. Other women in his family reached upward of 20 children birthed under the weight of Catholic expectations, and Oilibhéar said that she described her contributions to birthing children as meager. In the late 1960s, doctors performed a hysterectomy on Oilibhéar's mother, under the pretense of curing her depression. Having failed at achieving a cessation of her sadness, the doctors then gave her electroconvulsive therapy, treating what today the National Health Service (NHS) might consider an anxiety order called postnatal post-traumatic stress disorder (PTSD), also known as "birth trauma."

Davoine and Gaudillière (2004) create a clinical and historical formulation of the "conditions of possibility for an analytic approach to symptoms that reveal a rupture of transmission along the fault lines of the social link" (2004, 6). We wonder if the hysterectomy of a depressed mother – the removal of her child-bearing possibilities –

reveals one of these types of ruptures, and if so, how this factors into the psychic life of not just Oilibhéar, but the community and culture of which he was a part in Ireland. In the case of Oilibhéar's particular mother, we might presume she faced depression in the wake of a pessimistic future for her sons, one in which their lives were dedicated to fighting a battle they were unlikely to win. One of her sons, Oilibhéar's brother, was in fact murdered by a pro-British Loyalist paramilitary. This sentiment places her firmly in the first generation of Irish rebellion, the one that contains the possibility of mourning.

Yet, what if this is not the end of it? A transition happens at the moment in which instead of recognizing her depression as viable and meaningful, the reason for the depression itself is removed via hysterectomy (removing the possibility of having children), and electric convulsive therapy (removing the possibility to think and remember). This latter loss, the removal and erasure, rather than the mourning and rehabilitation of the Irish womb, marks the current generation of Irish sons and daughters as existing within a cultural void rather than a cultural future yet to come. Fathers can no longer fight for a motherland that has no womb. The rebellious rite/right of passage is lost, via the loss of a possible paternity. Irish mothers birth bastard sons, the sons of British colonialism.

Maybe it is this loss of his mother, first depressed, and then as Oilibhéar describes "absent, not present," that caused Oilibhéar to hold onto at the least a pessimistic vision of what his life could mean fighting for an Irish future, instead of submitting to colonial rule and absence. Oilibhéar describes his mother after the hysterectomy, and electric convulsion therapy (ECT), wherein:

> She hid her emotions more. And she had this glazed look in her eyes, like absent not present. And it got a bit better as I got older. She became more, she actually became more verbal, but for awhile she made noises, but she didn't really talk. She was really docile. My mother would have been a very strong person verbally and emotionally and she was very present when I was a kid. And that changed. Like when she fought with my dad, she was well-able to hold her own if you know what I mean. But after that, she couldn't … Women used to be viewed as a certain thing. Back then, the idea of virgin, mother, whore.

If we use Oilibhéar's story to tack back and forth between the individual and social scales, we can also see the ways in which what happened to Oilibhéar's mother could indicate a moment of historical erasure, a "rupture in transmission" in the words of Davoine and Gaudillière, in which Irish psychic culture shifts from a paradigm of mourning and the uncanny (Freud 1955) and toward what Kristeva describes as absence and the "abject" (Kristeva 1982).

If this is the case, then the staging of the play *Johanna Monahan* no longer functions to constitute mourning. Instead, its (re)staging after "peace" symbolizes absence. In this scenario, the symbolic sacrifice of the lives of sons represented by Charlie's washed-up torso as a metonym for mother Ireland becomes a mute possibility, which emerges in the wake of the sacrifice of *real* rather than imaginary mothers to a peace agreement. Signing away the future of an Irish state disables mothers from bearing symbolic sons. Mothers lose their wombs and the staging of this play prevents them from remembering *that*.

Irish Personthing

Through Oilibhéar's eyes and ears, we piece together what happened and is happening to a current generation whose motherland appeared, over a period of six days during the failed Easter Rising of 1916, reappeared between 1969 and 1998, and then abruptly disappeared with a peace agreement. We use Green's dead mother complex as a theoretical tool that assists us in making sense of the intergenerational psychic effects of this cultural transition from depressed to absent motherhood on a current generation of Irish, as they appear via Matthew's ethnographic research.

As described by Green, the mother of a child suffering from what he calls the dead mother complex experiences a "sudden bereavement" that causes her to "become abruptly detached from her infant." The infant, in turn, experiences this as a "catastrophe; because without any warning signal, love has been lost at one blow" (1972, 150). This results in a situation where "the subject, who is prey to the repetition compulsion, will actively employ the decathexis of the object who is about to bring disappointment" (1972, 151). The infant responds by acting as if a love object in the form of the mother no longer matters. This exclusion of the mother as self-constituting shields the infant/subject from disappointment and consequent breakdown that attachment to a new object could induce if the object were to suddenly disappear. However, to protect against cathecting with a new object, the infant, and infant turned child, and then adult, compulsively repeats this (dis)identification with the dead mother by treating all new love objects as something toward which it is impossible to connect. In this way, the adult symptomatically enacts the memory traces left by the original trauma in their inability to form new relationships based on a premise other than the impossibility of the love object.

Using the logic of the dead mother complex to create an analogy between the male infant who reels from the sudden loss of its mother, and the male Irish Republican who reels from the sudden loss of the imaginary motherland, we make a theoretical transition from the individual to the group. Following this logic, we argue that the play *Johanna Monahan* enacts the absence of the motherland rather than, as culturally narrated, acting as a binding ritual of communal mourning. The play enacts this loss by putting a now null and void story of rebellion and mourning in the place of what has now become a new Irish aggrievement, caused when the sons of Ireland gave away the maternal womb to British colonialism. The enactment of the play pretends as if there were no reason to need, and thereby to grieve this womb, or otherwise saying – it pretends that Ireland can live without mothers who birth sons who can protect a motherland.

Since he was imprisoned in the mid-1970s for IRA activities, Oilibhéar has had vivid, often nightmarish dreams. During the initial outbreak of the COVID-19 pandemic in Belfast, he sent Matthew a cryptic text message. The text read: "Bad dreams man." It was the late evening for him. His chronic insomnia gave way to a dream where he was invited to a film casting by a British actor in the likeness of Jason Isaacs who played the British Dragoon, Colonel William Tavington, in *The Patriot*. Oilibhéar explained later on a phone call, "then there was a skirmish round the house and volleys of gunshots and I got out – realized only as I left as one does in dreams I was set up." And then his bad dream segued into "sure I was not alone in my bedroom … just the personthing in my dream seemed so real." Transitioning into waking life a formless shape greeted him, the "personthing." Perceptual experience could not get a grasp of this informable entity. He then says with a sardonic croak, "we all have our demons." In his case, of course, he sometimes does experience actual demons.

What Oilibhéar describes here, the "personthing" in the dream, maps rather cleanly onto a Lacanian conceptualization of *Das Ding*. Daniel Wilson, in his explanation of *Das Ding*, describes it as

> a scene of experience about which the Other knows nothing. This set of unconscious experiences constitutes the Thing as a lost object that appears nowhere in reality, and as an unconscious orientation that insists as the excluded center of the subjective experience.
>
> (2015, 134)

It follows that the "personthing" in Oilibhéar's transition out of his dream of being "set up" by the British Army constitutes a repetition of the lost object, represented in the cultural unconscious as a motherland.

Of another dream, Oilibhéar says:

> then I had these small negative type frames. But some of them were depicted in enamel weird kind of tech things. Futuristic and sinister, showing battle scenes I had been involved in here, and it was freaky. Anyhow it got worse and worse, then I wakened with dry mouth so drank some apple cider vinegar in water and went online.

In these futuristic visions, Oilibhéar sees battles he's already been involved in, as if he were destined to relive his life over again (McCoy 2019).

For a new generation of Irishmen, however, the question of death presents very differently from it does for Oilibhéar. Oilibhéar would sacrifice his life for the motherland. He remains attached to this vision and especially after the peace agreement between his former organization and the British government, he harbors within him a future, even if bloodsoaked, for a united Ireland. For a new generation of Irishmen, one that does not consciously remember the loss of their motherland, as Oilibhéar does, this ability to sacrifice life for a greater cause appears generationally impossible. Rebellion is not passed on, and only absence comes in its place. We argue that the erasure of this historical memory reveals itself through the emergence of something far creepier than the ghost of Charlie, and even of the personthing in Oilibhéar's dreams. It appears as a zombie-like and at least somewhat ubiquitous symptomology of a current generation of Irish male youth, acted out not in dreams, but in reality.

Irish Zombies

"Tablets," the catchall name for drugs prescribed for anxiety or depression, have long since been used in Belfast throughout the conflict to treat "the nerves" (Sluka 1989). Oilibhéar uses painkillers and patches to cope with his physical and psychological wounds. This intergenerational practice of taking prescription tablets continues with the youth, but new prescriptions are used in a different way *not* experiencing the world at all. Switching over from experiencing to not-experiencing, humans transmute into partially other-than-human entities. Epileptic drugs are most popular. Lyrica is known as "bud" or "Budweisers," similar in effect to being intensely drunk, but mind-wiping. Lyrica is often ground then snorted. Matthew observed framed photographs of dead loved ones kept in home altars, flipped horizontal, glass upward, the proper surface for a "wee sniff." The images of the dead are chosen perhaps at random, or perhaps because one sniffs something of their death as well. Now instead of honoring the dead on the memorial garden walls, the dead are snorted.

One effect of the buds mixed with "allsorts" of other drugs and alcohol is becoming what locals call "Lyrica zombies" or just "zombies." Temporarily undead, individuals will stand on a footpath or in the middle of a street barely moving, eyes glazed or droopy, for upward of an hour. Videos circulate on Facebook. Some express keyboard empathy for the zombies, posting "god love them." Others ridicule: "SCUM." Scum, the frothy offscourings of humanity, as well as the foam that might be found around a zombie's mouth. Tablet or Lyrica zombies are a common sight in Belfast, especially during the weekend evenings when rescue boats in the River Lagan keep on suicide watch.

On one of these evenings, Matthew stumbled across one of his participants, Francis, leaning uneasily against the "peace walls" – 30-foot-tall concrete and metal structures continuing to segregate Protestant and Catholic working-class communities. The wall is also a physical representation, as many other walls throughout nationalist histories have been, of a division between life and death, the citizens of a country, and those "quarantined," whose corruption is "contagious" – those found beyond the pale. Though Matthew tried to coax Francis, prone to ending conversations with suicidal undertones of finality, to move away from the wall and walk over to his mother's house several yards away, he did not move from his spot. Perhaps he found a much-needed repose from dodging drug debt punishments. "A minute, mate," Francis said, or so Matthew interprets. Francis's eyelids sunk and fixed, Matthew may have mistakenly imputed meaning to unintelligible sounds.

At first euphoric, and then deadening, Lyrica zombies often linger in clumsy stasis. Recently, primary school-age children mimic a lesser form of zombiehood, taken to ordering nitrous oxide in palm-sized metal canisters from Amazon, inhaled through a balloon, causing an anesthetized laugh. Asking Francis and his friend Fergal, in their early 20s, why they become zombies, they respond:

Francis says, "They have nothing for people our age … There's two ways. You either take drugs or you don't. There's that many different drugs people are taking … Depression has affected all of us."

Francis gestures to Fergal and continues,

> We're both on for depression. Both of us alone are on medications for depression at our age. And it's not right. And it's 'cause, I read that up to 50% of people that live on the peace line grow up with post-traumatic distress.

Fergal replies, "Aye."

This generation, rather than enacting the uncanny, the return of the repressed, as in the vignette of Monahan's play, dramatizes what Kristeva describes as the abject. In this case:

> Essentially different from "uncanniness," more violent, too, abjection is elaborated through a failure to recognize its kin; nothing is familiar, not even the shadow of a memory. I imagine a child who has swallowed up his parents too soon, who frightens himself on that account, "all by himself," and to save himself, rejects and throws up everything that is given to him – all gifts, all objects … Even before things for him *are* – hence before they are signifiable – he drives them out, dominated by the drive as he is, and constitutes his own territory, edged by the abject.
>
> (1980, 6)

Abjection does not recognize the familiar, but rather subsumes it in the vicissitudes of its own jouissance – in the images *not* of men in battle, men signing declarations, men with their photos on a wall, or even as ghosts, but of men tripping over their own bodies on the streets.

Irish Rebirth

Arguing that Green's dead mother complex applies to a group of people (and of course would not do so uniformly), and can result in a kind of cultural symptomology risks stigmatization. Following ideas from psychoanalytic anthropology (Garcia 2008; Pandolfo 2018; Stevenson 2014), we look at structural and historical violence not only to explore the relation between the psychic and the social, and to dislocate what we diagnose as mental illness from the individual and reread it into the political, but also to create a model for conceptualizing how these psychic phenomena emerge on a group level. In this case, by conceptualizing drug addiction in Irish male youth as a rupture in the social link (Apollon 2010), we are able to connect it to a historical transmission of cultural signification in which a sense of viable motherhood and potent masculinity is lost. Here we target the social psychologically, rather than the psychological socially.

Although early Irish Republican movements foreground an Irish identity based on the realization of a cultural heritage, later Republicans negate this cultural heritage via the constitution of a non-relation between the signifier "Irish" to a motherland, revealing how this relation in the first instance was perhaps too complete. As long as the signifier "Irish" is established upon a paternal order constituted by British colonialism, even if in resistance to it, the Irish can revel in a kind of enjoyment that emerges from the phallic jouissance of resistance and rebellion. However, once this type of jouissance is lost, another emerges, one that further premises itself on absence, death, and hatred. This culturally mediated form of jouissance, while different from a phallic jouissance, engenders an enjoyment in which there is no future.

Davoine and Gaudillière contend that via a historical psychoanalysis it is possible:

> to weave a social bond that was impossible up until then and to make a "text," a memory, and thus a possible forgetting. For the madness that speaks to itself – or to everyone, that is, to no one – shows outside of temporality what no one wants to know anything about and what is not inscribed as memory.
>
> (2004, 13)

For this purpose, we want to remember Oilibhéar's mother, her depression, the hysterectomy, and her absence, so that we can forget a trauma repressed within a new generation of Irishmen, for example, within the play *Johanna* Monahan. We wonder if in this transition, what Matthew has described as a provisional time (McCoy 2020) constituting an Irish nation-state yet to come, could shift to an apocalyptic time, in which our sense of nationhood itself no longer conforms to that established under colonialism. An apocalyptic time could reveal the possibility for what the zombie states of young Irishmen submerge, a new Irish imaginary of what it means to be Irish premised on a different type of signification, one not dependent on the unification of mothers and fathers via a nationalistic statehood. Rather than premised on an existential form of rebellion, a more radical vision of a future could emerge, rooted in a more human and less racist form of social organization then the nation-state implies.

The emergence of zombie states among Irish youth describes what can happen in the wake of historical trauma, and in particular as ideals of masculinity and femininity, paternity and maternity, man and woman, associated with nation-states break down. In this world, increasingly non-"subjective" forms of human experience emerge, at least where that includes a sense of self-reflection, morality, and progress. For the future, if we are not as a society or as societies to break down into the abject as nationalism falls around us, as technology flattens our sense of the other, as we lose a sense of motherland as nation-state, then we can think critically about these issues as Oilibhéar does when he reflects on what happened to his mother as a symptom of deteriorating Irish ideals. In this sense, like Oilibhéar, we desire a future that has yet to come and that has many times already been signed over. We desire a future where nations and motherlands are no longer connected. Instead, we see the necessity to invent a new sense of motherhood out from a pessimistic understanding of the failure, the blankness, of current ideals.

Notes

1   In Pearse's final letter to his mother written from Kilmainham Prison on the day of his execution (May 3, 1916), he refers to this poem, his last creative act for the sake of his

mother: "You asked me to write a little poem which would seem to be said by you about me. I have written it, and a copy is in Arbour Hill Barracks with other papers and Father Aloysius is taking care of another copy of it." Remarkably, the voice of the poem is his mother speaking to him, the writer of the poem, as Pearse trades places with his mother to consider what she, and any mother, might be experiencing upon the death of her son.

2   For example, W.B. Yeats and Lady Gregory's *Cathleen Ni Houlihan* is a play about the folkloric old Irish woman asking young men to fight against colonial rule, a personification of Ireland herself.

References

Anderson, Benedict. *Imagined Communities: Reflections on the Origin and Spread of Nationalism*. Verso Books *(Reprinted London: Karnac, 2006)*, 1983.

Apollon, W. "The Limit: A Fundamental Question for the Subject in Human Experience." *Konturen* 3, no. 1 (2010): 103–118. doi:10.5399/uo/konturen.3.1.1391

Berlant, Lauren. *Cruel Optimism*. Duke University Press, 2011.

Berlant, Lauren. "Structures of Unfeeling: Mysterious Skin." *International Journal of Politics, Culture, and Society* 28, no. 3 (2015): 191–213.

Butler, Judith. *Precarious Life: The Powers of Mourning and Violence*. London: New York: Verso, 2004.

Davoine, Françoise, and Jean-Max Gaudillière. *History beyond Trauma: Where of One Cannot Speak, Thereof One Cannot Stay Silent*. Other Press, LLC, 2004.

Freud, Sigmund. "The Uncanny." In *The Standard Edition of the Complete Psychological Works of Sigmund Freud, Volume XVII (1917–1919): An Infantile Neurosis and Other Works*, 217–256, 1955.

Garcia, Angela. "The Elegiac Addict: History, Chronicity, and the Melancholic Subject." *Cultural Anthropology* 23, no. 4 (2008): 718–746.

Green, André. "The Dead Mother." (K. Aubertin, Trans.) In *On Private Madness* (pp. 142–173). London: Karnac (*Reprinted London: Karnac, 1997*), 1986.

Kristeva, Julia. *Powers of Horror*, Vol. 98. Columbia and Princeton: University Presses of California, 1982.

McCoy, Matthew. "Dreams, Death, and the Irish Question." *Irish Journal of Anthropology* 22 (2019): 104–113.

McCoy, Matthew. "Unsettling Futures: Morality, Time, and Death in a Divided Belfast Community." Dissertation. University of California, Los Angeles, 2020.

Pandolfo, Stefania. *Knot of the Soul: Madness, Psychoanalysis, Islam*. University of Chicago Press, 2018.

Sluka, Jeffrey A. "Living on Their Nerves: Nervous Debility in Northern Ireland." *Health Care for Women International* 10, no. 2–3 (January 1989): 219–243.

Stevenson, Lisa. *Life beside Itself: Imagining Care in the Canadian Arctic*. Oakland, California: University of California Press, 2014.

Wilson, Daniel. "The Freudian Thing and the Ethics of Speech." *Konturen* 8 (2015): 133–154.

Part II

Delibidinalization and the Malaise of the Contemporary Subject

Introduction

Sean Lynch and Andjela Samardzic

The contemporary world, imbued with and benumbed by incalculable threats (pandemics, racial discords, political populism, climate change, ubiquitous virtuality, etc.), has birthed new forms of enjoyment and desire. Each turn of the contemporary screw leads not to a hard-won feeling of fulfillment, a journey traversed by the force of Eros, but to a tidal discharge of raw affect. Somatizations, suicide, and violence are on the rise as the desperate attempts to find pleasure with others and to share meaningful encounters catapult into a crisis. What defines contemporary pleasure, in and out of the consulting room, in the midst of these crises? Clearly, Fechner's principle of constancy of pleasure—is no longer viable. Our society has moved toward a new beyond of the pleasure principle as Freud devised in 1920, and perhaps we are wondering what suffering has to offer, a radical question that places limitation not as hindrance to but constitutive of pleasure itself.

In this collection, the authors explore the malaise of the contemporary subject, desperately trying to survive and secure some satisfaction while combating the overwhelming climate of ethical and political impotence where tweet and truth have become fungible. Via the lens of Freud's theory of the drives, particularly the economic model, what emerges is an examination of the nature, cause, impact, and prognosis of these changes on the individual. The authors emphasize the notion of libido as psychic energy, accounting for variations, transformations, extensions, coverings-up, fixations, regressions, time-lags, enmeshing and unraveling, a concept buried in the depths of psychoanalytic Pompei to date.

Addiction acts as a signifier in the contemporary dialectic of jouissance, where Thanatos takes precedence over Eros, allowing for a narcissistic enjoyment, a pseudo fortress of impenetrability and invulnerability.

Vaia Tsolas evokes a daemonic nature of addictive jouissance, developing Michel De M'Uzan's notion (2003) that certain individuals are Slaves of Quantity, "condemned to a destiny dominated by the quantity of excitation that cannot be psychically elaborated." There is a decathexis from an Other but a hypercathexis of the Pharmakon (in Greek *poison* and *cure*) echoing the death drive's nirvana principle, a re-establishing of the lost state of equilibrium and of its toxic character.

Catherine Chabert and Dominique Cupa examine the relations between destructive primary envy, narcissism, and addiction. Christine Anzieu-Premmereur, drawing from

DOI: 10.4324/9781003384618-12

her extensive experience with babies, contends that babies dependent on self-soothing objects or the compulsive use of technology show a lack of mutuality in relationships. Addiction cannot give long-term satisfaction nor a structure for the psyche.

Negating the other, and feeling "complete" on one's own, touches on both narcissistic defenses, disavowal, fetishism, and ultimately a regression to an earlier psychosexual stage, pre-castration, into the arms of the archaic phallic mother (Melanie Klein).

Jacqueline Schaeffer explores the contemporary repudiation of the depressive position, inadequacies, losses, presence of evil, ageing, and death, which is essential for humans "emerging from existence itself" (Dante's Great sadness). Schaeffer makes an appeal for "the commitment to a psychoanalytic process [with] a new objectal and narcissistic investment oriented towards consolation, the acceptance of limitations, and the renunciation of illusions," which will give way to new psychic life and pleasure via objectal and narcissistic reorganization (p. 6). She emphasizes sexual difference as the neglected key to understanding the particularities of the human condition, depression, and the psychic and social "refusal of the feminine," which is of the flesh and the same for both sexes, while femininity is the body and prone to masquerade. When the bedrock of phallic defenses and organization breaks down, depression arises as an attempt to mourn and repair the loss, which positions the receptivity of the feminine in opposition to the solution of omnipotence and negative solipsistic narcissism. Sexual difference, in this sense, stands as the prototype for all difference, the difference of the other, and, as Schaeffer writes, "because the phallic is the same for everyone ... the other sex, whether one is a man or woman, is always the female sex" (p. 8).

Laurence Kahn in "Freeing Oneself from Reality" draws attention to the liberation movement against the other/others, for if one frees oneself from the neurotic complex (and compromises) caused by the constraints of psychic reality, then the field of projection is completely invaded and, as Freud says, the psychotic risk (autoplastic modification) is upon us. Linking this to the modern rise in political despotism, he positions truth as outside the maneuvers of control of the group, whose aim is to expand the "we" no matter what relation to reality is needed to do so. He wonders about the proliferation of alternative descriptions of reality we see in our days and the short step that might be made from this to alternative facts.

Furthermore, Mary Brady's chapter on psychic isolation in adolescence, estrangement, and loneliness argues that the transitional space of analysis allows adolescents to find joy and feel that they are no longer "unjoined persons" but "members of the wedding".

Another aspect of contemporaneity is the pandemic and virtuality, which seem to open and preclude or even transcend our enjoyment into yet another beyond the pleasure principle.

Michael Civin, in his chapter "... Whatever ...," problematizes on a case-by-case basis a widespread tendency in the contemporary Western world to drift progressively further away from a binding of the drives in the service of Eros; instead, the delibidinalization of our technocentric digital world is dragging society in the direction of the frozen depths of Thanatos, creating or witnessing an "impotential space."

Similarly, Panos Aloupis explores the intertwining of pleasure and pain in our contemporary world, where we have witnessed social phenomena in which hyper-activity, mass denial, and destruction of thinking are emphasized and promoted. Both subjectively and socially, the avoidance of conflicts and pains may result in a life of struggling against passivity and thought.

Some authors argue, however, that the pandemic and virtuality have brought forth new forms or sublimation and pleasure. Rosemary Balsam contends that both her elder and younger patients retreat into phantasy worlds that are limitless, youthful, deathless, and stark contrasts from the virus' fatal reality. Monika Gsell introduces in her chapter a new drive phenomenon, a desire to experience a violent deadly strike that most likely, if it were real, would lead to death. Gsell draws on the elaborate drive theory by Judith Le Soldat who has formulated another pulsation beyond the principle of constancy, the Hammerstrike desire (Hammerschlagwunsch).

David Lichtenstein's contention is similar. "The psyche is driven by something beyond the principle of internal balance" (p. 2), Lichtenstein writes, linking beyond the pleasure principle with the death drive as a redefinition of the pleasure principle. Lichtenstein further refines Lacan's concept of jouissance as it is connoted in Avgi Saketopoulou's essay on the drive to overwhelm: beyond the pleasure principle is a "pleasure that is suffered" (p. 18). He weaves the notion of play and jouissance together where horror, loss, aphanisis, surprise, and joint pleasure/pain come together in a repetitive modus. Lichtenstein notes that jouissance is juridical and attached to the notion of usufruct, or use of an object, which involves absence, destruction but also reappearance, and a birth of something new.

How can we generate something new if we retreat into a pseudo completeness, anti-otherness, anti-loss, and anti-thought cocoons? Too much pain, too much pleasure, too much death since our physical body may break under too many turns of the screw of our omnipotent mind. And yet, a limit is imperative when enjoying, as Lichtenstein writes, "the one who enjoys (the subject of jouissance) comes into being also as the one who accepts the limits to enjoyment" (2021, p. 11). We must find a solution toward Eros while not interrupting Thanatos, as they bind together, en-capsulating an Other, an object that is always and has always been, lost in order to be re-found.

Chapter 7

Uncanny Drives
On Nightmares and Wish Fulfillment

Monika Gsell

Translated by Nils F. Schott

Introduction

Cedric Kahn's *Feux rouges* (*Red Lights*), based on the crime novel by Georges Simenon published in 1953, was released in 2004.[1] This film presents the psychical forces involved in a particular drive process with a precision I have rarely encountered in cinematic or literary works. It is thus well-suited to illustrating some characteristics of the psychanalytic theory of the drives. At the same time, I would like to draw attention to the work of Swiss psychoanalyst Judith Le Soldat, which remains largely unknown in the English-speaking world. Le Soldat, who died in 2008, was a great theorist of the drives. Her entire oeuvre testifies that the theory of the drives remains an indispensable tool for gaining an adequate understanding of certain psychical phenomena. Le Soldat further developed Freud's drive theory and on that basis articulated a new, revolutionary theory of the Oedipus complex. One important aspect of her theory concerns the concept of "passive wishes" and the role they play in the psychosexual development of women *and* men. One such very specific passive wish is at the heart of *Red Lights*.

The movie begins by zooming in, from a bird's eye perspective, on a Paris district (Figure 7.1). It is hardly a coincidence that the name of the area is *La Défense*. The primary meaning of *défense* is the same as that of the English "defense." Yet it also translates the psychoanalytical term "Abwehr." Since Freud, the expression names psychical processes whose purpose is to restrict and repress everything that might endanger the psychical equilibrium. "Generally speaking," Laplanche and Pontalis write, "defence is directed towards internal excitation (instinct [*Trieb*])" insofar as this excitation is "incompatib[le] with the individual's equilibrium" and thus "un-pleasurable for the ego" (Laplanche and Pontalis 1973, 103).

And that, precisely, is what is at issue in *Red Lights*. The drama unfolding before our eyes is a life and death struggle; the names of the antagonists in this struggle are drive and defense. Put differently: I decided to read the film as presenting inner processes, namely the inner events of Antoine, the figure at the center of the film. This means that I do not read the *other* protagonists as individuals with motives and emotions of their own but as representations of different aspects of Antoine's mental life as the drive-process unfolds. I thus do not treat the film in a way different from I would the dream or the session material of a neurotic patient.

DOI: 10.4324/9781003384618-13

Figure 7.1 Place de La Défense, Paris - "défense" translates the psychoanalytical term "Abwehr." Screenshot from the film *Feux Rouges (Red Lights)* by Cedric Kahn, dir. (2004; DVD: Paris, Wild Side Vidéo/MGM Home Entertainment France [distrib.]).

The Plot

Let's begin with a summary of the plot, of the manifest dream-text, as it were, with what we see and hear. After the programmatic zoom onto *La Défense*, we follow the turn of the camera to enter a modern office building and end with Antoine. Antoine, our hero, seems a bit tense (Figure 7.2). He is writing an email: "Meet you as planned at 5 p.m. I feel like a young man in love on his first date. I can't wait for us to get on the road." He hesitates for a second, clicks "send," and tells his colleagues that he is off to drive with his wife to pick up the kids from summer camp. One of his coworkers shouts "Be careful!" Why this warning? We find out right away: in the bistro where Antoine is waiting for his wife and downing his first beer, an announcer on TV warns of the traffic expected for that night and the following days. It's vacation time, everyone in France is on the road. A year ago, the announcer says, there were 200 fatalities on the highways. These news—together with Antoine's continuous alcohol consumption—accompany the action going forward.

Finally, Antoine's wife Hélène shows up. She is late, the mood is one of irritation. By the time the two are finally on the road, Antoine has had three beers and a double Scotch. They are stuck in traffic; Antoine can't stand it any longer and suddenly decides to leave the highway. Later—Antoine having nearly caused two accidents, driving ever more aggressively after every whiskey pit stop, missing the right turn, and Hélène drily noting they are lost—an argument breaks out (Figure 7.3).

Figure 7.2 Antoine: "I feel like a young man in love on his first date." Screenshot from the film *Feux Rouges (Red Lights)* by Cedric Kahn, dir. (2004; DVD: Paris, Wild Side Vidéo/MGM Home Entertainment France [distrib.]).

Figure 7.3 Antoine showers Hélène with reproaches. Screenshot from the film *Feux Rouges (Red Lights)* by Cedric Kahn, dir. (2004; DVD: Paris, Wild Side Vidéo/MGM Home Entertainment France [distrib.]).

Antoine says sarcastically that he'll behave from now on, "without getting off the tracks": "You know which tracks I mean? You get my meaning? ... I felt like a train on that highway. I had to get off the tracks". And then, unsolicited: "Do all these guys ask their wives before getting a beer?" Hélène clearly knows he's had more than one beer.

Antoine: You think I'm drunk, is that it?
Hélène: In any case, you talk like you've been drinking … you hate me … .
Antoine: I don't hate you. I just wish you'd treat me like a man sometimes.
Hélène: And let you stop at every bar along the road?

Antoine defends himself: he is not an alcoholic, gets drunk twice, maybe three times a year at most.

Hélène: So what's got into you?
Antoine: Dunno. I'm in a tunnel tonight. It's your fault. If only you didn't treat me as the lowest of the low as soon as I feel like stepping out of line.

The argument is interrupted as they reach an intersection; Hélène indicates which way to go. She turns on the radio. A news flash reports a spectacular escape: "The fugitive, highly dangerous, was last seen in a stolen car." Antoine stops at a bar. Hélène warns him: "If you get out of this car, I'm going on alone." Antoine gives her a glare, takes the key from the ignition, and enters the bar. While he empties his whiskey, he stares at a screen behind the bar showing scenes of violence and destruction—bullet holes on a prison wall? Police roadblocks, a burnt-out car, another car burning. When Antoine finally leaves the bar, Hélène is gone. There is a note on the driver seat: "I'm taking the train." Antoine panics. He races to the Tours train station where he learns that the train to Bordeaux has just left. Desperately, Antoine tries to overtake the train to catch Hélène at the next stop, Sainte Maure. He races down the street running in parallel to the tracks, runs a red light at 100 mph—only to be stopped by a line of cars waiting to be checked by police searching for the escaped criminal. Antoine finally reaches the empty train station at Sainte Maure—much too late, the train has long left. Antoine is looking for the closest bar. An obtrusive flashing arrow points the way (Figure 7.4).

Figure 7.4 Eros's arrow: neon advertisement of the bar at Sainte Maure station. Screenshot from the film *Feux Rouges (Red Lights)* by Cedric Kahn, dir. (2004; DVD: Paris, Wild Side Vidéo/MGM Home Entertainment France [distrib.]).

Figure 7.5 Antoine offers the stranger standing next to him a drink. Screenshot from the film *Feux Rouges (Red Lights)* by Cedric Kahn, dir. (2004; DVD: Paris, Wild Side Vidéo/MGM Home Entertainment France [distrib.]).

Antoine downs a beer, orders a whiskey, and jovially pats the stranger standing next to him on the shoulder, offering to pay for a drink and beginning to talk nonstop (Figure 7.5). Most importantly: for the first time, we see Antoine with a relaxed smile on his face. The next time he looks up, the stranger has left. The barman points out that the man had a tattoo—Antoine seems not to care, but viewers immediately suspect the guy to be the criminal being sought. When Antoine leaves the bar, the man is suddenly standing next to his car; he wants a ride. With his new companion, Antoine now appears totally happy and relaxed (Figure 7.6)—until the next police checkpoint.

Antoine is just as afraid as his companion that the police will pick them out. They pass the checkpoint without trouble; Antoine breaks into cheers. At the next checkpoint, he wants to take no risks: he closes his eyes, hits the gas, and almost runs over a policeman. He then stops at a gas station, buys a bottle of whiskey, empties half of it, and stores the bottle under the driver seat. When his companion falls asleep, Antoine seizes the opportunity to drink what's left. In trying to put the empty bottle back under his seat, he takes both hands off the wheel—and drives the car into the ditch. A tire has blown and needs to be changed. Antoine is too drunk to do it, he collapses. The other man drags him a short distance up a grassy slope (Figure 7.7), where Antoine falls asleep. He is dreaming. In his dream, he is lying on the floor, in the same position as on the side of the road, but at home. Behind him a Christmas tree is lit up. Hélène drags him by the arms along the floor, exactly like the man did earlier, but gently (Figure 7.8). Then Antoine joins Hélène on the bed. Relaxed and laughing, she is smoking a joint, he tenderly caresses her hands, both look happy and in love.

Figure 7.6 Antoine with his new companion: "like a young man in love on his first date". Screenshot from the film *Feux Rouges (Red Lights)* by Cedric Kahn, dir. (2004; DVD: Paris, Wild Side Vidéo/MGM Home Entertainment France [distrib.]).

Figure 7.7 The man drags Antoine, completely wasted, up the slope. Screenshot from the film *Feux Rouges (Red Lights)* by Cedric Kahn, dir. (2004; DVD: Paris, Wild Side Vidéo/MGM Home Entertainment France [distrib.]).

Antoine awakes. The man is standing over him, brutally slapping him. Antoine barely manages to crawl to the car and is shoved onto the backseat. His companion takes the wheel. We hear Antoine's voice coming from the back:

Figure 7.8 Antoine's dream: It's Christmas, the time when we receive gifts and wishes are fulfilled. Screenshot from the film *Feux Rouges (Red Lights)* by Cedric Kahn, dir. (2004; DVD: Paris, Wild Side Vidéo/MGM Home Entertainment France [distrib.]).

To think, hundreds of 'em are out looking for you, howling your name on every TV program. You screwed 'em good. You don't give a shit about their laws … . If men weren't scared shitless, if they were real men like you, we wouldn't need courts and cops and red lights at every intersection. You're above all that. You're a lord, a prince. Tonight, I feel happy. Happier than I've ever been in my life … . You're a brother. You could've left me back there to die like a dog. If you didn't do it for fear I'd turn you in, you're wrong. I'm no snitch. I have a sense of honor. I'm a man, too. You misjudge me. That hurts me … . Hélène misjudges me, too. She doesn't think I'm a man, either.

The other man does not utter a word. Antoine carefully reaches for the empty whiskey bottle under the driver's seat and hides it in his pocket. The criminal turns off the main road. Antoine protests loudly, is beaten brutally, and collapses on the back seat. The car turns onto a forest road and stops. Antoine: "If you're gonna kill me, do it fast and clean." While the other man goes to the trunk and takes out the jack, Antoine manages to hide in the brush. He takes out the bottle, smashes it. The other man jumps on him, Antoine shoves the broken bottle into the attacker's eyes, grabs the car jack and hits him again and again. He runs to the car. The wheels spin, Antoine gets out and places rocks under the tires. When he is back at the wheel, the other man is standing before him, covered in blood. Then a blackout.

Antoine wakes up behind the wheel, on the side of the road, the back right wheel has come loose. A farmer gives him a ride to the next village. While the car is being towed and repaired, Antoine feverishly tries to find out Hélène's whereabouts. From a bar, he makes calls to the summer camp, to police stations and hospitals. Finally, he finds her. She's in a hospital. A police officer accompanies him to her bedside. But she is still in shock, cannot talk to Antoine (Figure 7.9).

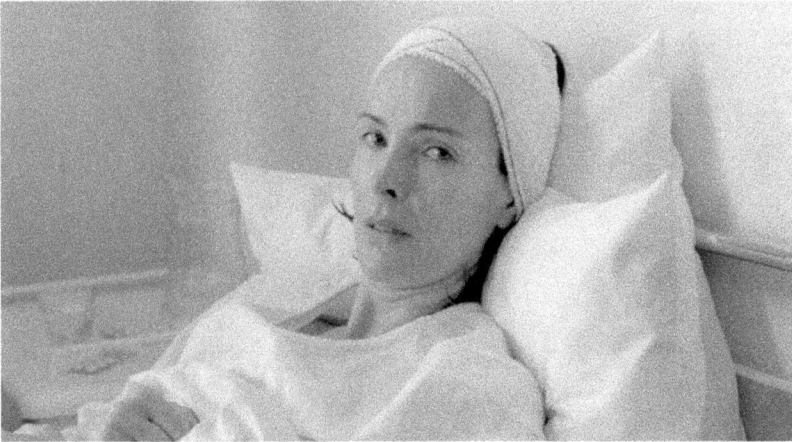

Figure 7.9 Antoine finds Hélène in the hospital. Screenshot from the film *Feux Rouges (Red Lights)* by Cedric Kahn, dir. (2004; DVD: Paris, Wild Side Vidéo/MGM Home Entertainment France [distrib.]).

The policeman brings Antoine to a meeting room and begins an interrogation: first a verification of identities, then a detailed reconstruction of events up to the point at which Hélène disappeared. The officer shows him photographs of the dead body of the criminal, one eye gouged out. The policeman explains that it is the escaped convict who was found dead. Only now does Antoine learn what happened to his wife; witnesses saw the escapee at the station in Tours. He followed Hélène and boarded the train to Bordeaux behind her. The train was practically empty, he was undisturbed as he attacked and robbed her. He got off the train in Sainte Maure—and was seen in the bar after midnight. The officer concludes his report by saying that a DNA sample has been taken and adds: "It wasn't just to rob her that he attacked your wife." When Antoine later returns to the hospital, Hélène is doing much better and lovingly takes his hand. Antoine is finally able to tell her what was going on with him. He confesses that he had been drinking beer and whiskey even before their departure and had kept drinking:

Antoine: I wanted to feel strong. Without anything holding me back.
Hélène: You hated me.
Antoine: [*nods*] I railed against you. In a drunken rage, I wanted to sully everything.

At the end of the film, we see Antoine and Hélène continue their journey: relaxed and happy like lovers after a blissful night (Figure 7.10).

Figure 7.10 United again: Antoine and Hélène, like lovers after a night of bliss. Screenshot from the film *Feux Rouges (Red Lights)* by Cedric Kahn, dir. (2004; DVD: Paris, Wild Side Vidéo/MGM Home Entertainment France [distrib.]).

Interpretation

I already mentioned that *Red Lights* is about a dynamic of drive and defense. What drive is at issue here? How does it present itself? And why and how must one defend against it? Allow me to give a first answer to these questions in the form of thesis, which I will then support in detail via the film. The thesis is: The drive-wish at issue in the film is the one for which the Zurich psychoanalyst Judith Le Soldat coined the term *Hammerschlag-Wunsch.*[2] This "hammer-blow wish" includes the phantasy of a violent, sexual overpowering—overpowering in a passive sense. This means that one "wants" to *be* overpowered. I use quotation marks because where drive-wishes are concerned, it is strictly speaking not possible to say that *we want* something: a drive-wish, rather, is a demand addressed to us—to our ego. The special feature of the hammer-blow wish is that it is a drive-demand that cannot, by definition, be fulfilled: the fulfillment is thwarted by the fear that inevitably comes with this drive-wish. The fear results from the violence we imagine the hammer-blow must be executed with for the act to be as satisfying as our phantasy depicts it: the hammer-blow would have to be so violent that we must fear not surviving it (Le Soldat 2015, 175–77). But we do not want to die; we only want to experience the supreme, the most intense satisfaction imaginable. For this reason, because the expectation of supreme pleasure and supreme fear keep each other in check, this drive-demand cannot be fulfilled. The only way for us to get close to fulfilling this drive-wish—which, importantly, is a wish we all have, according to Le Soldat, and one that results from a perfectly normal psychosexual development—the only way to approximate satisfying it is to sublimate it. And the least dangerous kind of sublimation is watching a thriller.[3]

Now, *Red Lights* is a special kind of thriller. It is a thriller that diehard fans of mainstream thrillers find boring. *Red Lights* wasn't a box office hit. The problem—or, precisely, the stroke of genius—of *Red Lights* is that it constantly confronts us with the result of the enormous defense action provoked by the hammer-blow wish. And the result is just this: unpleasure.

The unpleasure this film prompts in us, however, is also Antoine's unpleasure. On this hot summer day, a drive-demand wanting finally to be fulfilled is making its way through this Antoine. Its first, still hesitant expression is the email Antoine writes to his wife. This message only yields two bits of information: Antoine is excited and the source of his excitation is something sexual. The first, still tentative expression of the defense is the short, barely perceptible moment of hesitation before sending the email and the face Antoine is making—one that is so unlike anything we associate with a man in love on his first date. Then the warnings come in: Be careful! There will be casualties! These warnings are curiously ambivalent: we might hear in them the voice of the super-ego, which for its part is already alarmed and comes to the aid of the defense. However, the warnings also contain a promise: all the "red lights" we will encounter along Antoine's horror trip and which he runs heroically are enticing for that part in Antoine that is fiercely decided to give the drive-wish its due, siren-like signposts that only seem to stimulate and to feed his impulse … like the news of the escaped, highly dangerous felon and like the obtrusively flashing blue neon arrow that will drive Antoine directly into the arms of this convict.

But let's return to the beginning so we can observe the play of forces between drive and defense. The next expression of this play is the antagonism between the alcohol and Hélène. The alcohol is, unmistakably, an agent of the drive. That means: it works in the service of the drive. Its task is to weaken Antoine's defensive structures, to allay fears that come with the strengthening of the drive. Hélène, by contrast, is the agent of Antoine's ego, more precisely: of the ego's defensive functions, and thus the antagonist of the alcohol. The more the alcohol weakens Antoine's defense, the more Antoine delegates his ego functions to his wife: Hélène's task is to prevent the drive-impulse from breaking through or at least to ensure that there is no catastrophe. That, precisely, is what Antoine reproaches his wife with: he (his drive) wants to break out and take off, wants to leave the straitjacket of rigid tracks (the congestion of traffic here is also an expression of a congestion of drives). Hélène (his ego structure) tries to stop him in this breakout. If we read the film as presenting social realities, we would suppose that Antoine suffers from the coolness and control of the woman at his side. If by contrast we read the film as presenting an inner world, it becomes clear that Antoine needs this woman exactly as she is—if he loses her, he loses his well-structured ego and is helplessly exposed to his drive-wish. And that is precisely what happens now: the moment Hélène capitulates and decides to continue on by train, Antoine's reaction is anything but one of relief. On the contrary: he panics and tries desperately to get his defensive functions (that is, Hélène) back.

Appearing in Hélène's stead is the felon who assumes her place at Antoine's side. What aspect does this figure represent in Antoine's inner world? In the moment of the first encounter and up to the point at which the dynamic flips over, it is none other than Antoine's love object—more precisely: the longed-for object of Antoine's acute hammer-blow wish (Figure 7.11). In the figure of the convict, Antoine's fantasy creates the object capable of completely fulfilling the hammer-blow wish: the escaped prisoner is big and strong and has already been described beforehand—via the radio

Figure 7.11 Antoine's longed-for object of desire. Screenshot from the film *Feux Rouges (Red Lights)* by Cedric Kahn, dir. (2004; DVD: Paris, Wild Side Vidéo/MGM Home Entertainment France [distrib.]).

news—as ruthless. All this endows the criminal with a resplendent and fascinating aura. It is also striking how his hard, sharply drawn features recall Hélène's cool beauty. Yet: what Antoine's drive demands in this moment is something that is quite simply impossible for his wife to provide (which is also the reason for Antoine's disdainful behavior toward Hélène that night). Le Soldat notes: "The hammer-blow wish presupposes a man as its object. A woman as object of the general hammer-blow drive-wish is impossible" (Le Soldat 2015, 78).[4]

With the promise incarnate of fulfilling his most secrete wishes sitting right next to him, Antoine is happy: the struggle between drive and defense has been resolved for a moment, the expectation of imminent satisfaction is stronger than the fear of the consequences. A dreamlike, enraptured sequence shows Antoine smiling blissfully, adoring the object promising him satisfaction: he has finally reached the realm of his longings.[5]

When a police checkpoint abruptly pulls him from this trance, his panic re-awakens. This panic now is not an expression of defense, not a fear of the drive and its consequences; rather, it is fear that the drive might not be able to reach its aim. To prevent the love object required from being taken away from him, he goes full speed at the policeman at the next road block.

From now on, Antoine deploys all kinds of means to rid himself of what remains of his ego control: he keeps drinking, falls asleep, finally let's go of the wheel. Waking consciousness and thus ego control have been suspended completely: Antoine falls asleep and dreams. Considering what has been said so far, there is little need to go further into the function of the dream: evidently, it stresses the analogy between Hélène and the felon *as* love object.

Let's focus on what happens after the dream: on the one hand, Antoine is "happier than [he's] ever been"—he's lying, completely passively, on the back seat of the car, expecting the grandiose fulfillment of his drive-wish. The convict is at the wheel and thus in the active position—just as the hammer-blow wish demands of its object. On the other hand, it dawns on Antoine that what is at stake is not the fulfillment of a drive-wish but his life. This first shows in his wise precaution to arm himself with the whiskey bottle. This whiskey bottle will ultimately save his life the moment he succeeds in getting out of the passive position, beating to death the one whom Antoine is now able to recognize for what he actually is: a violent guy out for his life.

Let's try to get a better grasp of Antoine's switch from the *passive*-aggressive drive position to the *active*-aggressive position. Can we still speak of a drive-wish being at work in the *active*-aggressive position? We could do so if the aim of Antoine's deed (his beating the felon to death) were to generate pleasure. That, however, is obviously not the case: Antoine does not kill the other man to satisfy an active-aggressive drive-wish but exclusively to save his own life. In German, we would speak of a *drive* of self-preservation (Selbsterhaltungs*trieb*). And although the translation into English of Freud's concept of *Trieb* by "instinct" has done a lot of damage, in our case, the English term "*instinct* of self-preservation" (Laplanche and Pontalis 1973, 22, 215, 380) is, for once, more precise: because the instinct of self-preservation is not a drive in the psychoanalytic sense of the term, which constantly seeks discharge or satisfaction (Nagera 2014 [1970], 21). Rather, it is a biologically inherited behavioral pattern that is activated under specific conditions and is known in trauma theory as "fight or flight" mode.

Let's move on to the second part of the film. It is essentially concerned with what has happened to "Hélène." Since we are reading Hélène as an aspect of Antoine's inner world, the question arises: Why must it be a raped female figure who now enters the scene of Antoine's inner world—a figure, moreover, that is overpowered and raped by the same criminal whom Antoine will run into a short time later? My claim is that "Hélène's" storyline as reported in the second half of the film is a representation of the core aspect of the hammer-blow wish. This core aspect concerns the wish not only to be brutally overpowered by a potent, phallic object but very specifically to be *sexually* overpowered and *genitally* penetrated *like* a woman. In other words: The hammer-blow wish essentially is a libidinous-*genital* wish with a *passive* aim and fused with a large quantity of *aggressive* energy. In *Red Lights*, all this is expressed in the raped female figure.

Two issues must be addressed at this point. The first issue is: does Antoine *want* to be raped? The answer is very clearly no. Nobody wants to be actually raped—and this includes those who enjoy *phantasies* of being raped. There is a categorial difference between the (conscious, yet often also unconscious) phantasy as expression of *my* currently acute drive-wish and the actual rape, which is *never* an implementation of *my* drive-wish but *always* constitutes a destructive attack on the integrity of my ego as well as my body and therefore can only result in trauma.

The second issue concerns the association of passive-genital drive-wish and femininity. You will have noticed that the film (and my interpretation) "casts" the active (aggressive) position with a male character and the passive-genital position with a female character: the male figure of the criminal serves to represent the kind of object Antoine's drive-wish demands, the female figure of Hélène serves to represent what Antoine "wishes" to happen to *him*. This "casting" might have set off the alarms and you may wonder what this is all about—haven't we left the stereotypes of active-male and passive-female behind? Of course. We agree that there is no gender-specific difference in the way people move actively or passively in the world and which mode they prefer—these are individual differences and tendencies. That is why stereotypes and other norms that posit such a gender-specific distinction are rightly unacceptable today; they demonstrably lead to gender-specific discrimination—of women and of men.[6] Le Soldat's theory even goes a step further: she assumes that *every* human being, independently of their gender, is endowed with a drive-wish to penetrate actively and to be penetrated passively. She articulated this assumption based on her clinical observations. And there is theoretical support in the axiom of drives' bipolarity already formulated by Freud: every drive has a passive and an active pole (see, for instance, Freud 1913, 181–82; Freud 1933, 96).

Why, then, should our unconscious phantasy represent a passive-genital wish as feminine or in the figure of a woman, or an active-genital wish as masculine or in the figure of a man? As far as I can see, there is only one reason: the *unconscious* coupling of *masculine* and *active*, and of *feminine* and *passive*. This coupling takes place precisely *because* both sexes (all human beings) develop both forms of the genital drive but always are capable of satisfying only one of them: because of anatomical preconditions, men can physically satisfy only the active-genital drive—that is, enact a penetration—and women can physically satisfy only the passive-genital drive, that is, let themselves be penetrated.[7] If the unconscious represents an active-genital wish, it can do so only in concrete terms, for example via a male character; in the case of a passive-genital wish via a female character. If then—to take a simple example—a gay man says to his lover, "Let me be your girl," he generally does not express a female gender identity but quite simply the wish to be "taken," to be penetrated. "Girl," in this case, is the expression of the passive-genital wish. We find a somewhat more complex example in *Red Lights*: Antoine's repeated reproach that Hélène does *not treat him like a man*. This reproach is a classic neurotic symptom, a compromise between wish and defense. The passive drive in Antoine *demands* that he *not* be treated like a man but "like a woman." The defense turns the demand into a reproach: Antoine blames Hélène for his own, frightening wishes, which he experiences as "feminine," meaning: *If you treated me like a man, I would not be so helplessly exposed to my own passive wishes.* A further expression of the defense against the passive-"feminine" pull is Antoine's flight into defiant macho behavior: exaggerated masculinity as defense against his own "femininity."

Let's return, though, to the problem of gender stereotypes. Personally, I'm convinced that the unconscious coupling of *masculine* and *active* and of *feminine* and *passive* contributes massively to the stubborn persistence of the corresponding gender stereotypes. There is, however, an additional problem that complicates our societal and theoretical engagement with these stereotypes and constantly causes confusion: the expressions *passive* and *active* have fundamentally differing meanings in different contexts. In everyday speech, we usually employ the words *active* and *passive* to name character traits: active then means enterprising, go-getting, and assertive; *passive* means that someone tends toward inactivity, lacks motivation, and prefers watching to intervening. Furthermore, activity is connoted with the subject status, passivity with the object status. In this phenomenal-descriptive sense, passivity in our society has decidedly negative connotations. This has consequences, among other things, the feminist reception of Freud, who has frequently been reproached for denying women a subjective desiring of their own by allegedly reducing them to (passive) objects of male (active) desire. With regard to a few remarks by Freud, this reproach might be justified; with regard to others, however, it is not. In the latter case, it is based on misinterpretations, just as the wholesale condemnation of Freud as misogynist theoretician is due to misinterpretations and often quite simply to unfamiliarity with his work and thought.[8] It is of utmost significance, therefore, to be aware that the everyday, phenomenal use of *passive* and *active* has nothing to do with the meaning these concepts acquire in the context of the theory of the drives. In that context, *active* and *passive* name the direction of the drive-aim: does the subject of the drive want to penetrate its object (active-genital drive-aim) or does the subject want to be penetrated by the object (passive-genital drive-aim)? In both cases, we are dealing with the "desiring" of one and the same subject. A passive drive-aim does not make me the object of desire: I remain the subject of my passive drive-aim and might have to engage in considerable activity to achieve its fulfillment (Freud 1933, 96)—"activity" here understood in the everyday, phenomenal-descriptive sense but "passive" in the drive-theoretical sense. Our hero, Antoine, is a great example: he really does everything for his acute passive-genital-aggressive drive-wish to come true.[9]

Summary

We enter onto the stage of Antoine's inner world via *La Défense*, the defense. I read the accurately trimmed lawns filled with people enjoying themselves as a representation of Antoine's—usually—well-structured ego. Next, the drive-demand enters the stage, disguised in the form of a harmless-erotic email. It will thoroughly shake up Antoine's well-structured ego in the course of the coming night. We now also understand why Antoine makes such a frightened face as he writes the email. From the beginning, we are being told that Antoine is getting himself into something dangerous. The alcohol Antoine consumes in large amounts is to numb the tension and weaken the ego control that so far has successfully kept the drive in check. Hélène, in the first part of the movie, the antagonist of the alcohol, is to counter it and ensure that Antoine does not derail completely. The drive gains the upper hand and replaces Hélène with an object that is perfectly suited to satisfying the drive: the escaped prisoner who has all the attributes of a potent, cold, aggressive, ruthless, and at the same time fascinating drive-object. What kind of drive-demand it is that drives and torments Antoine gradually becomes manifest. The demand first appears as an aggressive demand with a passive aim: Antoine "wants" to be brutally overpowered. The genital-sexual component of his passive-aggressive wish finally comes to be represented in the fate of Hélène. Now, Hélène no longer represents Antoine's ego but a key aspect of his drive-wish. What is represented via Hélène is that Antoine has not just a passive-aggressive but, more precisely, a passive-aggressive-*genital* drive-wish. Following Le Soldat, I've called it a "hammer-blow wish." On the manifest level of plot, Antoine and

Hélène are victims of the same perpetrator. I read this unity of the perpetrator (in our case, of the drive-object) as unity of the drive-subject: what happens successively in the narrative chronology—first the rape of Hélène (which we learn about only later), then Antoine's encounter with the perpetrator—is to be seen as representing two crucial aspects of the same subjective drive-wish. This wish is not satisfied in reality—and, by definition, cannot be satisfied in reality. This, too, the film represents with great precision: as long as Antoine is driven by his own drive, blue light filters dominate. The moment the line is crossed and bare, instinctual survival is all that is left, red tones take over (the forest the convict is driving into is tinted blood red). The drive-process is interrupted when things tip over and naked horror takes place.

And yet some kind of drive satisfaction must have been achieved. Otherwise, Antoine's blissful smile at the end of the film is incomprehensible. What, then, does this satisfaction result from? In my view, it does not follow from the real events but from the pleasurable cathexis of the drive-related phantasies: "Already the excitation—that is, the energetic cathexis—of phantasies is experienced as pleasurable" (Le Soldat 2015, 64n17). Which is true for Antoine as well as the viewers.

Notes

1   Kahn, Cedric, dir. (2004). Feux Rouges, DVD (Paris: Wild Side Vidéo/MGM Home Entertainment France [distrib.]). - I would like to thank both the director, Cédric Kahn, and the film distributor, Studiocanal, for their kind permission to reprint the screenshots and to use quotes from the film dialogues.

2   Le Soldat introduced the concept "hammer-blow wish" in 1994 as part of her Oedipus theory, built on the basis of a theory of the drives (see also Le Soldat 2015, chapter 7). The term "Hammerschlag-Wunsch" takes up the name of the Hammerschlag family. Samuel Hammerschlag was Freud's religious studies teacher; his daughter Anna was Freud's patient, the "Irma" of psychoanalysis's inaugural dream, "Irma's injection."

   I suspect that Saketopoulou's concept "the draw to overwhelm" essentially means the same thing as Le Soldat's hammer-blow wish, although Saketopoulou frames it in completely different terms (see Saketopoulou 2019).

3   Less harmless forms of sublimation are extreme sports or risky sexual practices; see also Saketopoulou (2019, 151).

4   Things are more complicated, though: "I must, however, immediately revise this last condition. A woman obviously cannot be considered 'as a hammer' because of her anatomy. Yet the psychical sometimes does not conform to anatomical textbooks. Sometimes a woman appears to it not as a woman, and a man not as a man. The psychical has its own laws according to which it considers a woman as a woman, or sometimes as a man as well, and a man as a man or as a woman. These criteria are by no means to be sought in the appearance, in the conduct of the object but solely in the observer's subjective wish phantasies" (Le Soldat 2015, 78).

5   It is certainly no coincidence that Antoine first encounters the criminal in Sainte Maure: the name of the town is pronounced *sainte mort*—"sacred death." This recalls Bataille's philosophy of transgressive eroticism. It is also a perfect allegory for the paradigmatic object of the hammer-blow wish, which Le Soldat named "Apollo," after the cruel Greek god (Le Soldat 2015, chapter 7).

6   See the research by Alice H. Eagly, for instance in Miller, Eagly & Linn 2014.

7   See Le Soldat 2015 (123–29) for the basic conflict between monosexual bodies and active- and passive-genital drive-wishes respectively.

8   For a detailed discussion of justified and unjustified criticism of Freud's ideas on femininity, see Gsell/Zürcher 2011; a comprehensive summary of the article in English is available in Teusch 2013, 265–69.

9   It is interesting to see how Saketopoulou, too, is struggling with the concepts where *passive-aggressive drive-aims* are concerned: she sidesteps the issue by referring to Lyotard's concept of "passibility" and Ghent's notion of "radical receptivity" and stresses that "surrender" (i.e. passive drive-wishes) "cannot be demanded or exacted by the other" (2019, 137). No matter how we go about it: if we want to talk about passive drive-aims—and all the more if we want to talk about passive-aggressive ones—we must explain precisely what we mean by that and what we precisely do not mean. Most often we are misunderstood anyway. This is due to the special defense that weighs down on passive drive-aims and that causes the persistent bad reputation of the concept of passivity.

Illustrations

All illustrations are screenshots from the film *Feux Rouges (Red Lights)* by Cedric Kahn, dir. (2004; DVD: Paris, Wild Side Vidéo/MGM Home Entertainment France [distrib.]).

References

Freud, Sigmund (1913). "The Claims of Psycho-analysis to Scientific Interest," trans. James Strachey, in *The Standard Edition of the Complete Psychological Works of Sigmund Freud* 13, ed. James Strachey et al., 165–190 (London: Hogarth, 1958).

Freud, Sigmund (1933). "Anxiety and Instinctual Life," trans. James Strachey, in *New Introductory Lectures On Psychoanalysis and Other Works*, ed. James Strachey et al., *The Standard Edition of the Complete Psychological Works of Sigmund Freud* 22, 1–182 (London: Hogarth, 1964).

Gsell, Monika, and Markus Zürcher (2011). "Licht ins Dunkel der Bisexualität. Bisexualität, anatomische Geschlechtsdifferenz und die psychoanalytische Bedeutung von männlich und weiblich." *Psyche* 65, no. 8: 669–729.

Kahn, Cedric, dir. (2004). *Feux Rouges*, DVD (Paris: Wild Side Vidéo/MGM Home Entertainment France [distrib.]).

Laplanche, Jacques and Pontalis, Jean-Bertrand (1973). *The Language of Psycho-Analysis*, trans. Donald Nicholson-Smith (London: Hogarth, 1973).

Le Soldat, Judith (1994). *Eine Theorie menschlichen Unglücks. Trieb, Schuld, Phantasie*, Frankfurt a.M; (2020): *Raubmord und Verrat. Eine Analyse von Freuds Irma-Traum*. Kritisch revidierte Neuausgabe von Eine Theorie menschlichen Unglücks (1994), Stuttgart-Bad Cannstatt (= LSW 3).

Le Soldat, Judith (2015). *Grund zur Homosexualität. Vorlesungen zu einer neuen psychoanalytischen Theorie der Homosexualität*, Stuttgart-Bad Cannstatt (= LSW 1). – Open Access: https://openresearchlibrary.org/content/f992f4f1-c771-414a-ab34-e66351edc4e0

Miller, David I., Eagly, Alice H., and Linn, Marcia C. (2014). "Women's Representation in Science Predicts National Gender-Science Stereotypes: Evidence From 66 Nations." *Journal of Educational Psychology* 107, no. 3 (October): 631–644.

Nagera, Humbert et al. (2014 [1970]). *Basic Psychoanalytic Concepts on the Theory of Instincts*. London: Routledge.

Saketopoulou, Avgi (2019). "The Draw to Overwhelm: Consent, Risk, and the Retranslation of Enigma." *Journal of the American Psychoanalytic Association* 67, no. 1: 133–167.

Teusch, Rita (2013). "Selections from Two German Journals." *Psychoanalytic Quarterly* 82, no. 1: 245–269.

Chapter 8

Ridding Oneself of Reality

Laurence Kahn

Translated by Edward Kenny[1]

That the reality of *facts* is vulnerable is not something new. It was thought, in France at least, that Historical negationism, the denial of historical facts,[2] was the extreme end of disengagement from a shared discourse involving real facts. After World War II, this position was accompanied by an antisemitism that, while perhaps less noisily apparent than among the partisans of Marshal Pétain during the Vichy government, remained absolutely active. Subsequently, upon this was grafted a prevalent hatred of foreigners, especially so-called Arabs, even if they are French citizens in all respects. In fact, giving form to the invisible enemy, that is, lending a face to the hateful part at the bottom of our souls that never accepts to be silenced and that ensures the channeling of the destructiveness at work in all of us, has always been part of the strategies of projection which are violently exploited by populism. For example, Emmanuel Macron was represented as the Jewish henchman of the Rothschild bank where he once worked: An iconic caricature depicted him with a crooked nose and a top hat, trimming his cigar with a red sickle, paired with the caption, "The truth about the galaxy of Macron" (Rescan & Lemarié, 2017). *The Daily Stormer* relayed this image (Anglin, 2017), which will not surprise any American: A cruel echo of certain pages from *Völkische Beobachter*, the association of Macron with fraudulent Jewish finance, restoring to vogue *The Protocols of the Elders of Zion*, reimagined by American white supremacists and improved upon by the Proud Boys (cf. Roudinesco, 2020).

Nonetheless, at the moment when the relationship to truth appears to be fragile, one point merits attention. As Kimiko de Freytas-Tamura explained in an article in the *New York Times*, George Orwell's *1984* became the bestselling book in America at the time of the inauguration of Donald Trump as president of the United States (De Freytas-Tamura, 2017). Did this clarify the spirit of the chief asset of Trump, the secret of his phenomenal exploits, to have succeeded in disconnecting public debate from the reality principle?

In this situation, in the name of what legitimacy does a psychoanalyst lean into the question? What is her particular competence? Is it one of reflection on the individual psychic processes that govern the relationship with reality? Is it the exploration of the collective phenomena that push the masses down the path of destruction? There is no

DOI: 10.4324/9781003384618-14

doubt that Trump's success among his supporters stems from "his uncanny ability to appeal to their long-standing feelings of anger, exclusion, humiliation and victimization", as Bill Glover and Kerry Sulkowicz have written (Glover & Sulkowicz, 2021). But what do we say when we consider that if "Trump's supporters identify with him, consciously or unconsciously", this is because he has known how to "(give) voice to grievances that he has promised to solve, but he has done so with lies, deceptions and false promises"? Shall we consider the economic situation, the social distress, and the anger that results from this as the key to the support of the crowd for the word of the leader? Certainly, as Glover and Sulkowicz wrote, "Psychoanalysts understand the impact of words on individual and group psychology as reflecting the power of transference to authority, and there are few leaders with more authority than the President". But what inner megaphones does this voice from outside find in the psychic interior so as to drive citizens to deny what still seems to be evidence, and from this point to divert the judgement of these individuals?

In these cases, identification with the leader seems to have invaded the entire territory of the ego and the ego ideal – causing, at the exact hinge between the individual and the collective, between internal authority and external authority, a double collapse of judgement: The collapse of judgement of reality and the collapse of ethical judgement. But the problem remains, beyond the effect of injustice and the dysregulation of society, how to understand the consent that is given to this. What role does the superego play in the claim the crowd makes to exercise its freedom to speak its "truth" in opposition to the proofs of the truth? On what authority does the revolt against a rule accused of being "freedom-killing" depend, whereas the rule takes into account a piece of reality? Is it reality itself that kills freedom? In this case, what reality are we talking about? For example, from what reality is the mob that climbed the Capitol steps on January 6, or the rabble that ransacked the Arc de Triomphe during the Yellow Vest demonstrations, trying to rid itself? Internal? External?

Regarding the American demagogues and in the light of the study on *The Authoritarian Personality* conducted after the Second World War, Theodor Adorno observed that their propagandistic rhetoric always relies on a promise of "a general American revival" thanks to their "great movement" (Adorno et al., 1950). In doing so, "The glorification of action, of something going on, simultaneously obliterates and replaces the purpose of the so-called movement", the propaganda functions in itself "as a kind of wish-fulfillment" (Adorno et al., 1994, p. 163). Making use of memes and simulacra of combat against sinister powers, these leaders drum up moments of collective fervor. But these moments of "mass hypnosis" depend primarily on conscious manipulation: "There is always something self-styled, self-ordained, spurious about fascist hysteria" (Adorno et al., 1994, p. 165) that prohibits considering it as the simple product of a contagion that is passively suffered. Is this not simply the golden rule of the leaders, "to avoid any formulation to which they might have to stick later" (Adorno et al., 1994, p. 164)? As a remarkable strategist, the leader is careful to guarantee nothing, so as to avoid any limit which a political agenda would impose. This allows Adorno to reflect that, "the ego plays much too large a role in fascist irrationality to admit of an interpretation of the supposed ecstasy as a mere manifestation of the unconscious" (Adorno et al., 1994, p. 165). The effects are calculated. And even if on first impression we can imagine that the "mental confusion" of the leaders resembles that of their partisans, "they have learned, from vast experience and from the striking example of Hitler, how to utilize their own neurotic or psychotic dispositions for ends which are wholly adapted to the principle of reality" (Adorno et al., 1994, p. 165. *Realitätsgerecht* in German in the original). Said another way, the invocation of the humiliation of the people and the mobilization of their anger says very little about the internal mechanisms in the partisans that cause the paralysis of authoritative prohibition.[3] How are narcissistic collapse, the assemblage of ideals of grandeur and the gagging of the superego all combined to permit the drives to break the barriers of repression?

As Anna Ornstein has written,

> With the introduction of post-Freudian psychoanalytic theories, we no longer question that there is a complex and powerful intertwining of history, society and the psyche. In other words, ethnicity, religion, race, culture in all their varied dimensions, are important aspects of one's conscious and unconscious mental life; they are essential shapers of one's identity.
>
> (Ornstein, 2020, p. 227)

However, even if our political heritages were constructed in an intersubjective and interpersonal way and modeled according to the psychological and social internalizations from our surrounding world, Ornstein cites here Amanda Hirsch-Geffner (Hirsch-Geffner, 2004), according to her, this heritage does not lead to a direct transmission. The action of intrapsychic forces and their resulting internal conflicts also play their part.

It is doubtless here that the reading of *Group Psychology and the Analysis of the Ego* proposed by Adorno is precious. Freud maintains that "the psychology of groups is the oldest human psychology" (Freud, 1921, p. 123) because from the outset, individual psychology takes shape in the family and finds itself to be a social psychology. This is the reason for which understanding the fates of identifications in the nuclear family allows grasping the phenomena at work in the masses, and inversely, the observation of crowds allows elucidating certain individual psychic mechanisms. Thus, apropos of manic and melancholic alternations, Freud gives the example of the Roman Saturnalia, those moments of "excess permitted by law", where prohibitions and limitations commanded by the superego are lifted. Freud spells out that just as we do not stably tolerate the separation of the ego and the repressed – because unconscious fantasies sometimes brutally erupt into consciousness – just so, "it is quite conceivable that the separation of the ego ideal from the ego cannot be borne for long either, and has to be temporarily undone" (Freud, 1921, p. 131). The erasure of the superego can therefore constitute, as such, a grandiose feat for the ego. The feeling of manic triumph corresponds with the congruence of the ego and its ideals, and with the disappearance of the feeling of guilt inherent in the moral conscience, the authoritative prohibitions then dissolve into the ego.

This hypothesis that depends on a collective fact allows us, according to Freud, to elucidate the seesaw between mania and melancholy on the level of the individual. But conversely, in what way do individual clinical cases – in which their structure is forged in the heart of the social psychology of the family – permit us to throw light on the collective phenomena?

Madame M requested a consultation with me following a diagnosis of evolving schizophrenia that was just established for her sister, following two successive psychotic episodes. At first overwhelmed during our initial meeting, she showed an intense agitation while trying to explain the reasons for her sister's collapse: Their father, a consummate authoritarian, had "psychologically laminated" and "sexually laminated" them both[4]: He flattened them out. Psychologically, by believing that he could achieve adherence from his daughters to his expectations of exceptional success only by threatening to cut them off financially.[5] Sexually, by making them intense, intimate accomplices in his relationships with his mistresses. If Mme M was able to escape from it, it was because she had been a ferocious militant. Affiliated with movements of the extreme left, she had supported the Red Army Faction because, according to her, only this movement had the courage to really act against the lies and the treacherous silence of the established German powers. However, she had never personally participated in a real operation, which was the theme of a lancinating internal indictment: She was nothing but cowardice.

Between the weight of the ideal demands and the fragility of her narcissistic organization, the beginning of the treatment was fraught with high tension, oscillating between her unworthiness for having been only a verbal support for the Baader-Meinhof gang and the affirmation of her "program"of well-being thanks to the analysis. Her guilt at having abandoned her sister to her fate was overcome, more or less, thanks to the promise of a future revolutionary. Her self-reproaches set off great moments of depression that were succeeded by revivals of energy in which little by little I measured the dimension of grandiosity. During our sessions, she needed to "say everything" in an incessant and disordered stream, without losses or discoveries, and in wresting out a maxim of action to be achieved to counter her cowardice – this overflowing was intended as much to avoid annihilation as to neutralize contact. The totality of it was drowned in a "positive" adherence to the analysis which was "helping her to liberate herself".

Nevertheless, sometimes, Mme M fell asleep during our sessions, dreamed and, greatly astonished, told me her dream – which, despite everything, assured the analytic process a double anchoring, both narcissistic and transferential. So it was that one day she dreamed she was with a young man whom she was preparing to kiss, when all of a sudden he transformed into a woman: A "whore" who showed all "her whore's junk",[6] garter belt and genitalia. They began to make love together. Upon awakening, anger invaded her: Even if she remembered the militant era when she considered psychoanalysts "people who made you pay for tricks", she was not there on the couch to think about prostitutes, even less prostitutes with whom she would make love. That kind of thing was just good for her father.

However, she began to think about it constantly. She spoke about it to her husband as she spoke about it to me, vehemently taking a position against the alienation of these women who sold their flesh. This did not pacify the internal earthquake because, she had to admit, she had sold herself to her father by taking advantage of the apartment he bought for her. Like the mistress of her father, she had let herself be corrupted and, just like her mother who never said anything, never openly rebelled. The confrontation with her father thus took an extremely violent turn. The intense scenes of family fights multiplied, in her relentless battle against this man who "even in dreams forced her". Session after session she recounted the detailed and feverish narrative.

In the context of this extremely troubling exaltation, I could just about see how Mme M was in the grips of two incompatible tyrannies: The demands of her ideals and the power of the transferential homosexual bond about which, at this moment in the treatment, nothing could be said, neither on the side of the extreme sexualization – the "junk" of the prostitute suggesting the phallic and bisexual character of this figure – nor the side of the desperate call for a maternal shelter. But I saw especially that her hostility did not penetrate our relationship; her furious aggression was entirely directed outwards. I was only summoned as a witness to a successful liberation of which the enthusiastic reunion with a formerly loved militant became the concrete proof. The narcissistic transference found in the lateralization the means to fill the visible cracks in the idealization of the analyst since the prostitute had sexually erupted. Inflamed by this passionate liaison, she took hypomanic flight, resulting in a triumphant victory against the constraints of the superego which represented the hateful demands of the father and of the society which he identified with. Her rupture with her husband was very brutal, under the argument that this man condemned her to a miserable little bourgeois life. To rid herself of this bond which shackled her and to regain the force of the group of political comrades, this was the new program.

As for me, bizarrely I remained the marvelous analyst who, no matter what I did or said, understood her: So little disappointment and no hatred! That is, up until the moment where, too busy with her lover, her work, and her political meetings, she began to miss many sessions. It was then that the conflict with me burst open, and, I would say, "finally". Because my inflexibility regarding payment for the missed sessions and my disregard vis-à-vis the most diverse reasons she gave to justify these absences burst the fantasied bubble of our complicity. I fell from my pedestal and faced the turnaround from love to hatred in the transference: I was from the same mold as her father and she hated me, as she told me session after session. Probably it was the thunderous, booming expression of this hatred that permitted the treatment to continue: Isn't hatred a more solid bond than love? And probably it was thanks to the self-preservative function of hatred, noted by Freud beginning with *Instincts and their Vicissitudes* (Freud, 1915, pp. 138–139) that Mme M escaped from the melancholic reversal of destructive wishes towards herself. The rebellion against the internalized paternal figure found in the forms of the analyst and also in the lover, who revealed himself not to be any better, what was needed to maintain the fight against the exterior mortal enemy: The tyrant, fantastically still capable of "cutting off her means of living" and who threatened to crush her.

For my part, I was carefully vigilant not to "cut off her means of living". But the debt continued to accumulate, forging a mute but very solid bond, while Mme M came to experience the extreme dread of being ruined: Financial ruin, the terror of not being able to assure her survival, and emotional ruin because gradually she was seeing to what extent she was affected by the separation from her husband. Pain broke in, not strictly speaking because she had lost this man, but because her "dream to build a beautiful family", exactly the opposite of what her father had done, was now nothing more than rubble. She cried in session, insisting that I erase her debt, threatening to stop treatment. I was uncompromising, asking her what she wanted me to make disappear: Should I erase her absences and her loss? Should I erase her enthusiasm? Should I erase the real consequences of her life experience and make as if it had never happened? When she was surprised that I was so "mean" – it was no longer the shrieks of hostile exaltation – I asked her why she sought to recreate the system of subjugation against which she had so greatly struggled.

"I don't see the subjugation", she retorted.

"But yes!", I told her, "You put yourself under my all-powerful guardianship since you act as if the cancellation of the debt, your absences, and the past relied entirely on my good will, as if we were not both subject to our initial contract, as if the breach of the rule depended entirely on my power".

"Still, you are really the one who makes the law here!", she said.

I responded, "I am subject to it too, for example when I wait for you".

The working through in the transference of the unconscious search for such a subjugation permitted a relative release from her furor against the paternal figure. Little by little, it became clearer to her that the thing she was fighting against was made of the same clay as the weapon with which she was fighting. Her love for this father, so powerful and so detested for this same power, was in the field of the transference.

That's when shame and anguish surged up, attached on the one side to the violence of the prostitute dream, and on the other to her unfathomable guilt vis-à-vis her sister. At the same time that she slowly became conscious of the re-sexualizaton of the homosexual bond that made of me simultaneously a man and a woman under the form of the prostitute, we encountered, from the depths of infantile distress, the opacity of the silence of her mother and her inert wanderings. Mme M called her "the shroud of the house". She vacuumed, erasing everything in her path. She swallowed words and feelings without any trace appearing on her face. This mother had covered the little girl with all this indifference, but did so in clinging to her, in "glueing to her", in simulating admiration, punctuating all these behaviors with a single comment:

"*Phenomenal!*" she said, the grandiosity conveyed by this empty expression without standards was the narcissistic paradox around which Mme M must have organized herself.[7]

In this treatment, whereas the narcissistic lockdown seemed to me to be at its peak, the regression permitted me as a result to enter into contact with the infantile organization sedimented within the superego and the ego ideal. If the maternal vacuum had been filled by an intense love for the father, the only protective power, it was this idealized figure that was also internalized as a violently coercive form of the superego. That is, until this love was transformed into hatred in an attempt at separation and disaliena-tion. In this way, during the process of transference, I had initially been in the grips of narcissistic elation and its effect of dissolving the oppression of the superego, a little Saturnalia at the individual level. After this, I was confronted with the violence aroused by my position regarding payment for missed sessions, which she experienced as lim-iting and constraining. This violence emanated from the unfolding of the constitutive strata of the introjected prohibiting figure, and notably from this fact: If at the heart of the identificatory mechanism the severity of the superego was fed also by the aggression that the child would have liked to have exercised against authority and its coercion, this internalized aggression could again find the path to expression against the external parental figure, embodied in the transference (cf., Freud, 1930, p. 129).

The adherence of Mme M to the positions of the Red Army Faction, and her attempt by this means to free herself from reality, expressed this complexity. Against the establishment powers, their silence regarding numerous massacres and the suf-focation of guilt, the highest morality had been summoned. The extortion used to obtain truth and respect for a moral sense, all mattered little: It was a sign of courage, as were all forms of emancipation from the fraudulent norms. The virulence of the rebellion took root in the bond to the figure who had originally ordered the pro-hibitions, while the grandiosity of the ideal narcissistically appropriated the grandi-osity of the figure of authority. Thus, if one admits that the feeling of guilt is basically only "a topographical variety of anxiety" (Freud, 1930, p. 135), can one grasp how the inalterable remainder of the voice that formerly uttered the prohibition still remains capable of mobilizing the terror of loss, even obliteration. When the most appealing speech or the most brutal tirade of a leader restores the remnants of the power of this internal tyrant, the outside resonating voice – borrowing the paths of these identificatory inscriptions – combines with the voice that resonates internally.

Now, the play of identifications is the hinge for the formation of the mob. Could one imagine that the collective attempt to free the self from reality also proceeds in unison with the attempt to disalienate the self and through the search for subjugation?

If, on the individual level, the group phenomenon is constituted of the sole fact that the individuals, having all put a same, single object in the place of their ego ideal, have surrendered their individual characteristics and conduct themselves as if they were all of a similar form (Freud, 1921, pp. 102–103), we can imagine that a group can, in a unified manner, enact a same unconscious fantasy. Especially since its state of being enamored of a leader is comparable to the state of being in love, which is just a "normal psychosis"[8] (Grubrich-Simitis, 1993, p. 153) so that the leader is able to take away reality testing. In addition, the individual having made his own the col-lective ideal incarnated in the leader, draws the immense narcissistic profit brought by membership in a vast homogeneous group. However, in *Group Psychology and the Analysis of the Ego*, Freud specifies that the ego often preserves the auto-satisfaction from the previous period, which in fact facilitates the choice of the leader. In fact, it is enough that the leader possesses the typical qualities of these individuals, in creating the impression of a larger potency and libidinal freedom, such that the group attributes to this man an omnipotence that he may not otherwise have claimed.

In rereading Freud, Adorno sees here a sign that permits grasping how a particular sort of monumental figure can be fabricated, a "great little man" (Adorno & Bernstein, 2001, p. 142). In fact, the leader can simultaneously be a person haloed with the omnipotence that the child attributed to parental figures and also be at the same level as his supporters. Therefore, he is not only omnipotent; one can also recognize oneself in him, the leader being simply a larger version of oneself. According to Adorno, from there comes the realization of this "social miracle": "The leader image gratifies the follower's twofold wish to submit to authority and to be the authority himself" (Adorno & Bernstein, 2001, p. 142).

One can say that Adorno saw Trump coming from very far, just as Freud, starting in 1921, saw Hitler coming. However, as Anna Ornstein pointed out,

> One of the greatest dangers in Germany was not to have taken Hitler seriously and dismiss him as a madman. Nobody could believe that what Hitler wrote in *Mein Kampf* could actually happen in the 20th Century in the middle of Europe in the most literate and most highly educated country in the world.
>
> (Ornstein, 2020, p. 230)

Moreover, if Freud made the error in 1921 of assigning the proof of reality to the ego Ideal (a mistake he later recognized), it is only a partial error. Not only does it coincide with the most essential part of the analyses of Arendt regarding the onion structure of totalitarian regimes (Arendt, 1956, pp. 411–412) when these succeed in the miracle of abolishing the relationship of the group to reality, but it corresponds to the importance accorded by Freud to the strict relationship between truth and correspondence with the world outside. This "correspondence with reality – that is to say, with what exists outside us and independently of us" (Freud, 1933, p. 170) is a determining factor in our construction of the world.

> If what we believe were really a matter of indifference, if there were no such thing as knowledge distinguished among our opinions by corresponding to reality, we might build bridges just as well out of cardboard as out of stone, we might inject our patients with a decagram of morphine instead of a centigram, and we might use tear-gas as a narcotic instead of ether.
>
> (Freud, 1933, p. 176)

Freud cried foul when the "intellectual nihilists" (Freud, 1933, p. 175), exploiting the theory of relativity of modern physics and through skillful sophism, tried to push science to abolish itself. The vehemence of the last pages of the *New Introductory*

Lectures on Psychoanalysis is commensurate with what Freud already perceived as a menace weighing on the relationship of the social community to reality. In 1933, had not Hitler just attained the chancellery of the Reich? That every man may freely establish his convictions in enjoying equal rights to the truth, it is here

> a view of this kind is regarded as particularly superior, tolerant, broad-minded and free from illiberal prejudices. Unfortunately it is not tenable and shares all the pernicious features of an entirely unscientific *Weltanschauung* and is equivalent to one in practice. It is simply a fact that the truth cannot be tolerant, that it admits of no compromises or limitations.
>
> (Freud, 1933, p. 160)

Let us not forget that the wavering of the judgement of reality was the cornerstone of his renunciation of the *Neurotica*. It is through this path that psychoanalysis mastered the understanding of the function of fantasy and grasped the essential role in psychic life of hallucinatory wish-fulfillment – including in normal daily life, that which drives our dreams and our reveries, our parapraxes and our "accidental" deliberate acts. However, fantasy is the "weak spot in our psychical organization" wrote Freud, because it always "can be employed to bring back under the dominance of the pleasure principle thought-processes which had already become rational" (Freud, 1911, p. 223). After this, Freud constantly redefines the gap between *Wirklichkeit* and *Realität*. If *Reales,* typically associated with *Welt* or *Außenwelt,* designates the reality of the world and its happenings, *Wirkliches* refers to the effects of intrapsychic action. Thus, to the patient who suffers from a feeling of guilt as if he had committed a serious crime, it does not work to appeal to his undeniable innocence:

> If a patient of ours is suffering from a sense of guilt, as though he had committed a serious crime, we do not recommend him to disregard his qualms of conscience and do not emphasize his undoubted innocence; he himself has often tried to do so without success. What we do is remind him that such a strong and persistent feeling must after all be based on something real (*in etwas Wirklichem*), which it may perhaps be possible to discover.
>
> (Freud, 1926, p. 190)

In this example, the real is assimilated into the product of an action of a *Wirkung*; the reality of the self-accusation stems from the efficiency of a punitive authority that does not stop from overwhelming the innocent. In contrast, it is the real existence (*reale*) of the Acropolis that was called into doubt in the "disturbance of memory".

Without doubt, this is what guides Freud's arguments in *An Outline of Psychoanalysis* (Freud, 1940) when he attributes to the ego, dominated by a concern about safety, the mission of working with the goal of self-preservation – which the id and its instinctual demands totally disregard. This is a daunting task, even if the ego has at its disposal alarms of anxiety, because the mnemic traces of hallucinatory wish-fulfillment associated with verbal elements can become completely conscious as perceptions. From this comes the necessity of establishing reality testing in order to protect oneself from such a danger. Thus, reality testing appears first as a defensive activity of the ego, an activity which free association and free-floating listening are supposed to lift like the dream. In contrast, in life, the action of inhibition exercised by the ego is essential: This is what "makes it weigh the consequences of its line of conduct" (Freud, 1940) and which leads it to quash the irruption of the drives which endanger its survival. This is an essential battle which is performed constantly on two fronts: One directed towards external dangers, when it is a question of measuring effects in real life of individual transgressions; the other directed towards internal dangers, when for example it is a question of resisting the dominance of "alternative facts" which, in the service of the satisfaction of desire, rely on the degradation of the systems of correspondence between reality and the representation that one has of it.

From this, we understand the inquiry of Anna Ornstein. It does not touch upon the ensemble of post-Freudian theories, but rather the border of those that are strongly inspired by the hermeneutic turn, by literary criticism, and by historical epistemology, and which in their wake consider that all truth is not only partial, but also determined by social and cultural schemas of thought, by systems of intelligibility that impose on us their strategies of interpretation (cf., Elliot & Spezzano, 1996; Goldberg, 2001, 2002; Spence, 1982; Stern, 1985). For example, according to Stanley Fish, one of the inspirers of this relativistic turn, the interpreting subject cannot be conceived of as an independent entity. The conventional sense imposed by these institutions makes each person the constructed product of mental configurations subordinated to the ways of understanding of the "interpretive community" in which he is integrated (Fish, 1980, pp. 320, 332, 335).

This position for the most part joins the Constructivism of Richard Rorty, for whom also every reader "constructs" the object according to the schemas of the group to which he belongs (Engel & Rorty, 2005, p. 73). In so far as there exists no possible extension of thought over its object, the theory of a truth-correspondence between reality and knowledge is de facto condemned. In place of this is imposed a consensual theory of the truth, freed of the demands of "objectivity" but tied to an "ethic" of conversation and understanding. The abandonment of the referential straitjacket permits the painless sacrificing of notions of reality, of reason, and of nature for the profit of a "better future" (Rorty, 1999, pp. 32–34, 37, 54, 81–82), the *socius*[9] determining the criteria of that which is true from the unique point of view of that which is "useful" to him. Likewise in psychoanalysis: The analyst is not omniscient; he knows little about the configuration of his own unconscious, and still less about the way it interferes with what he communicates to the patient. It is therefore illegitimate to affirm the "truth" of an interpretation concerning the unconscious psychic life of the patient, when the analyst's own listening is itself governed by his psychic mechanisms and his cultural environment. It is thus that subjective relativism and contextualization in the "here and now" gain their letters of nobility, at the same time as the inescapable mutuality of the lived affective experiences.

We clearly see the critique here taken against the ideals of objectivity such as advocated by an "absolute" realism, a critique that many analysts make their own. The desires and the needs of man are the measure of everything – the variability of the history and of the "facts" generated in treatment are commensurate with the variability of the perspective of the speakers. Not only would the belief accorded to the correspondence between a "something distorted" by the unconscious and a "something not distorted" (which would be the true reality) only express the authoritarian position of the analyst (of which the mark is the narcissistic constraint that he wields over his patient when he pushes him to straighten out his erroneous vision of the world) but also and above all, we live from mythic inventions: "Mind-made realities constitute for human beings their sole realms of existence, and ... it is only about these realms that anything at all can be known. No other knowable realities exist" (Geha, 1993, p. 209).

Starting with this isolated remark, one can grasp how Rorty invited himself into the debate where it is a question of emancipating oneself once and for all from the tyranny of the truth. If one grants, with Rorty, that "truth is as, in William James's phrase, what is good for *us* to believe" (Rorty, 1991, p. 22), how do we conceive the resistance to a community pressure mobilized by subjugation by a leader? If the desire of the pragmatist is to "expand the reference of 'us' as broadly as one can", how does one think of the force of a Winston Smith resisting the consensus of a perfectly homogeneous group which knows exactly what is useful for itself and which proclaims it regularly during the "Two Minutes Hate" in *1984*? How can he maintain, against the community of thought of "Ingsoc", that

> they were wrong and he was right. The obvious, the silly, and the true had got to be defended. Truisms are true, hold on to that! The solid world exists, its laws do not change. Stones are hard, water is wet, objects unsupported fall towards the earth's centre?
>
> (Orwell, 1997, p. 84)

One measures here the risk incurred if one believes in the notion of a truth relative to the words and phrases as Rorty defends it "since truth is a property of sentences, since sentences are dependent for their existence upon vocabularies, and since vocabularies are made by human beings, so are truths" (Rorty, 1995, p. 21). Moreover, as Robert Paxton stresses, one must remember with Orwell that surely the décor depends on the local culture:

> An authentically popular American fascism would be pious, antiblack, and, since September 11, 2001, anti-Islamic as well; in western Europe, secular and, these days, more likely anti-Islamic than anti-Semitic; in Russia and eastern Europe, religious, anti-Semitic, Slavophile, and anti-Western. New fascisms would probably prefer the mainstream patriotic dress of their own place and time to alien swastikas or *fasces*.
>
> (Paxton, 2004, p. 174)

But beyond the surface rhetoric, the problem is really to know what the power of these speeches, of these sentences and of these words, makes the very notion of reality suffer. Did not Orwell permit himself to intimate, starting in 1936, that the small marginal English groups that wore the Nazi swastika were less to fear than a movement skillfully dressed in the patriotic emblems of the country? That the risk of an English fascism would be a "slimy Anglicized form of Fascism, with cultured policemen instead of Nazi gorillas and the lion and the unicorn instead of the swastika"? (Orwell, 1958, p. 212).

This same Orwell did not hesitate to attest that "objective truth" is something that exists outside of us (Van Inwagen, 2008, pp. 161–185) something precisely that escapes the machinations of control and resists tirades. In *Looking Back on the Spanish War*, Orwell wrote:

> Against that shifting phantasmagoric world in which black may be white, tomorrow and yesterday's weather can be changed by decree, there are in reality only two safeguards. One is that however much you deny the truth, the truth goes on existing, as it were, behind your back. [...] The other is that so long as some parts of the earth remain unconquered, the liberal tradition can be kept alive.
>
> (Orwell, 1968, p. 259)

But the conquest of the occidental world by dictatorships able to control what is "true", that is to say, freedom of thought, was going quite well in 1942. Orwell wrote, "This kind of thing is frightening to me, because it often gives me the feeling that the very concept of objective truth is fading out of the world" (Orwell, 1968, p. 258). And in what way is it in the process of disappearing? In being fragmented without the power to refer to some common law, thus shattering the concreteness of the world and the sharing of it. According to Orwell, this is very precisely the instrument of destruction used by totalitarianism. Already, Nazi theories deny the existence of a thing such as "truth":

> There is, for instance, no such thing as "Science". There is only "German Science", "Jewish Science", etc. The implied objective of this line of thought is a nightmare world in which the Leader, or some ruling clique, controls not only the future but the past. If the Leader says of such and such an event, "It never happened" – well, it never happened. If he says that two and two are five – well, two and two are five.
>
> (Orwell, 1968, p. 260)

One can recognize the challenge of arm wrestling between O'Brian and Winston Smith which figures seven years later in one of the central scenes of *1984*. To free oneself from reality,[10] that which exists outside the power of the leader, seems indeed to be the necessary condition for procuring the enslavement of individuals: "Freedom is the freedom to say two plus two make four", Winston repeats to himself (Orwell, 1983, p. 790).

Is it a part of the relativistic horizon that Rorty considers O'Brian the torturer to be the essential character of *1984*? Whereby the stakes of the novel would not be the problem of truth at all, but rather the use of sadism destined to explode the ego of

Winston? (Rorty, 1989, pp. 169–188). Thus, according to Rorty, cruelty is the red thread of a personal reflection of Orwell on the way to demolish a subject by smashing his beliefs, among which is "two and two make four" – this in order to destroy the coherence of the subject's self (Rorty, 1989, pp. 178–179). Therefore, what Orwell achieves is not describing a fight to maintain contact with reality, but "a redescription of what may happen or has been happening – to be compared, not with reality, but with alternative descriptions of the same events" (Rorty, 1989, p. 173). Alternative descriptions which offset other descriptions : According to Rorty, Orwell made use of the same language tricks as any Stalinist leader. It is a matter of "playing off scenarios against contrasting scenarios, projects against alternative projects, descriptions against redescriptions" (Rorty, 1989, p. 174).

From "alternative description" to "alternative facts" isn't there only one step? One measures in this case the wandering which we watch out for in matters of interpretation of material givens. As Winston said so exactly, "The Ministry of Peace concerns itself with war, the Ministry of Truth with lies, the Ministry of Love with torture and the Ministry of Plenty with starvation" (Orwell, 1997, p. 225).

We can understand why *1984* was the bestselling book after the election of Donald Trump.

Notes

1 Edward Kenny: Training & Supervising Analyst, The Columbia University Center for Psychoanalytic Training and Research. Etk2@cumc.columbia.edu
2 *Négationnisme* in French. The prime example is denial of the genocide of the Holocaust, aka, Holocaust Denial.
3 *Instances interdictrices* in French.
4 *Psychologiquement laminées* and *sexuellement laminées*, literally "beaten into a thin plate", metaphorically "flattened", "wiped out", or "obliterated".
5 *Leur couper les vivres* – literally, to cut off things that keep them alive (essentially, food and water).
6 *Tout son attirail de pute* in French.
7 *Quel phénomène!*
8 *Verliebtsein ist die Normalpsychose* in German.
9 *Socius* here in the sense of the person who is considered the basic unit of society.
10 *S'affranchir de la réalité*, the French title of this paper and the same phrase at the beginning of this sentence, can be translated as "freeing oneself from reality" or as "ridding oneself of reality". In this English translation, both options have been employed.

Bibliography

Adorno, T.W., Frenkel-Brunswik, E., Levinson, D., & Sanford, N. (1950) *The Authoritarian Personality, Studies in Prejudice Series, Volume 1*. New York: Harper & Row. Retrieved from URL https://archive.org/details/THEAUTHORITARIANPERSONALITY.Adorno/page/n3/mode/Body2up.

Adorno, T.W. (1994) Anti-semitism and Facist Propaganda, *The Stars Down to Earth and Other Essays on the Irrational in Culture*. London/New-York: Routledge, pp. 162–171.

Adorno, T.W. & Bernstein, J.M. (2001) The Freudian Theory and the Pattern of Fascist Propaganda, in *The Culture Industry: Selected Essays on Mass Culture*. London and New York: Routledge.

Anglin, A. (2017) Macron Campaign Office Vandalized by Anti-Semitic Truth Bombs, Daily Stormer, Retrieved from URL https://stormer-daily.rw/macron-campaign-office-vandalized-with-anti-semitic-truth-bombs/.

Arendt, H. (1956) Authority in the Twentieth Century. *The Review of Politics*, 18(4):403–417.

De Freytas-Tamura, K. (2017) George Orwell's '1984' Is Suddenly a Best-Seller, *The New York Times*, January 25, 2017.

Elliott, A. & Spezzano, C. (1996). Psychoanalysis At Its Limits: Navigating the Postmodern Turn. *Psychoanalytic Quarterly*, 65:52–83.

Engel, P. & Rorty, R. (2005) *À quoi bon la vérité*. Paris: Grasset.

Fish, S. (1980) Is There a Text in This Class? *The Authority of Interpretive Communities*. Cambridge/Massachussetts, London/England: Harvard University Press.

Freud, S. (1911) Formulations on the Two Principles of Mental Functioning. SE XII.

Freud, S. (1915) Instincts and their Vicissitudes. SE XIV.

Freud, S. (1921) Group Psychology and the Analysis of the Ego. SE XVIII.

Freud, S. (1926) The Question of Lay Analysis. SE XX.

Freud, S. (1930) Civilization and Its Discontents. SE XXI.

Freud, S. (1933) New Introductory Lectures on Psycho-Analysis. SE XXII.

Freud, S. (1940) An Outline of Psycho-Analysis. SE XXIII.

Geha, R.E. (1993) Transferred Fictions, *Dialogues*, 3(2):209–243.

Glover, W. & Sulkowicz, K. (2021) Threat to Democracy. IPA online, Retrieved from URL https://www.ipa.world/IPA/en/News/_Message_on_Threat_to_Democracy.aspx.

Goldberg, A. (2001). Postmodern Psychoanalysis. *International Journal* of *Psychoanalysis*, 82(1):123–128.

Goldberg, A. (2002). American Pragmatism and American Psychoanalysis. *Psychoanalytic Quarterly*, 71(2):235–250.

Grubrich-Simitis, I. (1993) Verliebtsein ist die Normalpsychose, in *Zurück zur Freud texten, Stume Dokumente sprechen machen*, Frankfurt: Fischerverlag.

Hirsch-Geffner, A. (2004) In a round table: Is politics the last taboo in psychoanalysis? *Psychoanalytic Perspectives*, 2(1):5–36.

Ornstein, A. (2020) The Relativity of Morality in the Contemporary World. *Psychoanalytic Inquiry*, 40(4):223–233.

Orwell, G. (1958) *The Road to Wigan Pier*. New York: Harcourt Brace.

Orwell, G. (1968) '*Looking Back on the Spanish War*', *The Collected Essays, Journalism, and Letters of George Orwell: My country right or left, 1940–1943*. Harcourt, Brace & World.

Orwell, G. (1983) *1984, The Penguin Complete Novels of George Orwell*. Harmondsworth: Penguin.

Orwell, G. (1997) *The Complete Works of George Orwell: Nineteen eighty-four*. London: Secker & Warburg.

Paxton, R.O. (2004) *The Anatomy of Fascism*. New York: Alfred A. Knopf.

Rescan, M. & Lemarié, A. (2017) Les Républicains répresentent Macron avec des codes d'iconographie antisémite, Le Monde, Retrieved from URL https://www.lemonde.fr/election-presidentielle-2017/article/2017/03/10/dans-un-tweet-les-republicains-representent-emmanuel-macron-avec-des-codes-de-l-iconographie-antisemite_5092794_4854003.html.

Rorty, R. (1989) The last intellectual in Europe: Orwell on cruelty, in *Contingency, Irony, and Solidarity*. Cambridge: Cambridge University Press.

Rorty, R. (1991) *Objectivity, Relativism, and Truth: Philosophical Papers*. Cambridge: Cambridge University Press.

Rorty, R. (1995) *Contingency, Irony, and Solidarity*. Cambridge University Press.

Rorty, R. (1999) *Philosophy and Social Hope*. Penguin Books.

Roudinesco, E. (2020) Beware of the word "Macronovirus", *European Journal of Psychoanalysis*, Retrieved from URL https://www.journal-psychoanalysis.eu/articles/beware-of-the-word-macronovirus/

Spence, D. (1982) *Narrative Truth and Historical Truth: Meaning and Interpretation in Psychoanalysis*. New York: Norton.

Stern, D.B. (1985) Psychoanalysis and Truth: Current Issues – Introduction. Some Controversies Regarding Constructivism and Psychoanalysis. *Contemporary Psychoanalysis*, 21(2):201–208.

Van Inwagen, P. (2008) Was George Orwell a Metaphysical Realist? *Philosophia Scientiæ*, 12(1).

Chapter 9

On the Roots of Addictive Behavior in Narcissist Vulnerability and Lack of Transitional Area

Christine Anzieu-Premmereur

Addiction is a deadly disorder that killed 93,000 people in the US from overdose in 2020, a tragic number that has continued rising to record-breaking levels in 2022. We also know how younger generations are now addicted to screens and social media to stabilize their emotions. A compulsive behavior results from a heavy dependence on pleasurable or painful action, such as drinking alcohol and the ingestion (or injection) of medication and drugs. There are many forms of dependence: to food, sex, gambling, online shopping, physical exercise, work, video games, and to some groups or cults. In all cases, the other become the addictive object.

Dependance and repetition are parts of human self-preservation needs, too. We breathe, drink, eat, sleep on a regular and repetitive basis, from the time we are born. Addiction is a special form of repetition, however, and it is compulsive insofar as it is a repetitive urge, an impulse, and a constraint to behave in a certain way, even if it doesn't seem rational or goes against an individual's will and health. It's all consuming. Those repetitive constraints interfere with the capacity for transformational and diverse uses of libidinal energy (Freud, 1914). Of significance here is that Freud's libido theory was first developed from the instincts of self-preservation. As Laplanche and Pontalis (1967, p. 660) to in their dictionary:

> The role of libido as a *quantitative* concept is increasingly emphasized by Freud: it serves 'as a measure of processes and transformations occurring in the field of sexual excitation'. Its production, increase or diminution, distribution and displacement should afford us possibilities for explaining the psychosexual phenomena observed.

In psychoanalytic theory, the economic view underscores the importance of the quantity of emotions and affects. The daily life of a baby can involve experiences of excess and lack from the maternal object, which have psychosomatic consequences. We also see in adult patients how complains of excess and lack figure in regulating internal life; a common lament is a lack of intimacy with their partner yet an inability to tolerate rapprochement, leading to a preference for self-soothing and addiction. The process of opening to the external world, and the libidinal fantasy makes it desirable, has failed. The transitional object is fetishized in a continuing disavowal of

DOI: 10.4324/9781003384618-15

depressive anxiety. There is a failure to integrate self-soothing functions while staying in a stage of full dependency towards an object.

We can observe in babies' dependence upon self-soothing objects and adults' compulsive use of technology (streaming TV, video games, online porn), and even a new usage of adult size 'dolls' for comfort without a partner, the lack of mutuality in relationship. This invites an increasing need for therapeutic interventions aimed at creating transitional space. Addiction gives neither a long-term satisfaction nor a structure for the psyche. Mastering the object is the only way to avoid feeling the pain.

We can develop this theme further and apply the concept of the transitional object to contemporary psychosocial trends while looking at some relevant aspects of parent-infant relations. The capability for creating a new space between self and maternal object depends on the quality of attunement in the parent-infant dyad; this, in turn, has implications for analytic process. Namely, this serves the development of true transitional objects, which can be distinguished from the compulsive use of concrete objects or of repetitive body actions for decreasing anxieties and tensions. Just as caregivers can support transitional capability in the child, analysts can help patients develop creativity and free association. This can be contrasted with babies' excessive dependence on self-soothing objects and older children and young adults' compulsive use of technology as means of comfort without a partner, reflecting a lack of mutuality in their internal relationships. In such cases, therapeutic interventions centered on the creation of a transitional space are increasingly important.

Michel Fain (1971) has described forms of infantile insomnia that seem to be related to difficulties in the infant's use of the mother as environment. Some of the infants studied by Fain seem to have become addicted to the actual physical presence of the mother and could not sleep unless they were being held. These infants were unable to provide themselves an internal environment for sleep. Fain has observed that the mothers of many of these infants interfered with the attempts of their infants to provide themselves substitutes for her physical presence (e.g., in auto-erotic activities such as thumb sucking), thus rendering the infant fully dependent upon the actual mother as object. We observe here addiction to the mother as object.

On the opposite side, when we often talk about the danger of children's over-exposure to digital screens, we neglect the problem of the hyperconnection of parents to technology, which can leave isolated toddlers to deal with compulsive self-soothing activities. The overexposure of young children to digital screens is considered by pediatricians to be a public health problem. But what about children's experience of their hyperconnected parents? The pleasure shared with the parents contributes to the vitality of the toddler, the libidinal energy, and to the dynamics of his thought. The energy that circulates in the baby-adult exchanges functions like an instinctual fuel that irrigates all the investments of the child, promotes his creative aptitudes, enriches his relational capacities, builds his language, and increases his intellectual skills. The omnipresence of digital tools in the hands of adults can damage the relationship with the child. The parent hyperconnected to his laptop risks becoming a parent disconnected from his child, impoverishing the toddler's appetite for contact. It is a propelling force for his psychic growth—precious, vital.

Parents already addicted to certain behaviors are unaware of what they transmit to their baby: the need for contact with a concrete object while experiencing a diffuse anxiety at not getting the narcissistic support of the other's attention.

The object of addiction is invested with beneficial qualities, even love: object of pleasure to be seized at any time to attenuate affective states otherwise experienced as intolerable. As such, this object is perceived as good; to the extreme, as what gives meaning to life.

The psychic economy of addiction aims for the rapid discharge of all psychic tension, whether its source is external or internal. Moreover, this tension is not only a function of painful affective states; they can also be exciting or pleasant states. In the mind of the addict, a psychic call is translated as a somatic need, and this is the moment when the addictive solution becomes a somatopsychic solution to mental stress.

The psychic economy of addiction precipitates the loss of psychosomatic balance and its pathology as described by the French School: essential depression, lack of fantasy life, concrete thinking.

As J. McDougall (2004) reminded us, we should underline the extent of addictive flight behavior in everyone. When internal or external events exceed our usual capacity to contain and work out the conflicts, we all tend to eat, drink, smoke, more than usual; we take medicine, seek a state of temporary oblivion, or throw ourselves into relationships, sexual or otherwise, with the same aim. Thus, this psychic economy of addiction becomes a problem in the case where it is the only solution available to the subject to bear the psychic pain.

The Infantile Part of Addiction

Discontinuity in early relationships, experiences of neglect, and absence during infancy lead to defects in the psychic functioning that will eventually make internal conflicts unbearable. The infantile is at the origins of the drives. It is the source of a complex system of forces that Freud described in his metapsychology as a process of regulation of quantities and qualities of experiences. Infantile sexuality therefore starts as psychosomatic organization. The concept of the drives was Freud's discovery of a constant push that is never exhausted by satisfaction. At the beginning of life, pleasure is associated with its own economic balance, and its objects, sources, and goals are the source either of essential creative systems or of addictive repetition (McDougall, 1982). Autoerotic capacities develop in an intermediate space that gives room for all the creativity that makes us feel ourselves. In contrast, compulsive, self-soothing behavior can lead to fetishistic and addictive behaviors.

For the past ten years, and even more so during the pandemic, we are seeing patients taken over by repetitive addictive behaviors. We can observe how difficult it is to have them free associate and play with representations, and how poor is their libidinal capacity to develop pleasurable activities. It is in the transference that we can help the patient to recover in between sessions a capability for a hallucinatory representation of the presence of the analyst.

Let's think of the tiny baby buried in her unorganized body, overcome with sensations, touching her skin and the openings of her body, staring into a face that contains her with a smile. She is immersed in a sensory universe, where the mother's face, her skin, her eyes, her mouth, her smell, her warmth, and her breast whose nipples fit perfectly with her lips, where everything is felt as Me, without differentiation between internal and external sensations, in a primary identification.

When this maternal part of the self is absent after having satisfied needs and pleasures, caressing her own skin offers the child hallucinating the breast's stimulating presence. The empty mouth follows the experience of a full mouth. The sucking is associated with the fantasy of incorporating the breast. The fantasy of plenitude during the mother's absence is linked in the child by her sucking on the fingers that follows suckling on the breast, forming symbolic equivalences and associative games. The autoerotic oral incorporation of the breast leads to a narcissistic identification, passing from a relationship of being—*I am the breast*—to that of having it.

Autoeroticism is central in Freud's theory of human sexuality. Limiting satisfaction to a specific area of the body, autoeroticism has as its goal satisfaction without the presence of an object; it can be achieved by self-induced sensorial activity, either as masturbation with no mental representation, or as an autoerotism inhabited with representations of libidinally invested internal objects. Like in sexual intercourse with a partner, internal objects may or may not be called upon. The search for satisfaction can be under the imperious need for the presence of another person when there is a defect in the interiorization of love objects. The vicissitudes in constructing such an internal object and the insufficient psychic activity associated with it are the cause of sexual activity empty of representation, without what psychoanalysis means by the quality of 'sexuality'. Autoeroticism requires that an internal psychic object be established. This is the regressive path of the drive, cut off from the psychomotor activity and from adaptation to reality; it is a formal regression toward hallucination for a substitute satisfaction. The dream is the model of this transformation.

Any deficiency in the autoerotic capability will lead to self-soothing activities associated with the need for strict mastery over a concrete object. Since this does not create any internal object of satisfaction, it must be repeated compulsively.

Look at the intense pacifier-sucking repeated over and over, associated with insomnia in infancy, the endless swaying, or the pulling of the hair which tries to compensate for the emptiness of the mother's absent body (Anzieu-Premmereur, 2017).

Faced with the lack of representations associated with erotic satisfaction, adolescents use their own body, or alcohol and drugs, to master an invisible object. Tausk (1951) wrote that only autoeroticism can allow for the Ego's appropriation of sexual erotic areas in the body. Infantile sexuality and its immense variety of erotic activities is an important part of the integration of the self and then of the Ego organization.

Autoeroticism is also the source of differentiation, internal and external, and, as Winnicott discovered, of intermediate spaces. The capacity for transfer to 'not-me' objects of sensuality and erotic sexuality leads to sublimation, with the pleasure experienced by playing, by being aware of one's own mental activity. What's more, using the body, experiencing pleasure while maintaining satisfaction in self-preservation, and, most importantly, hallucinating the object of pleasure are all contributions autoeroticism makes to psychic health. This is where psychoanalysis, in sustaining the reestablishment of an efficient autoerotic object that is the guarantor of independent satisfaction, takes up a crucial role for the patient.

There is a strong association between the lack of transitional space in parents and the inability to be alone in a young child. We can observe the development of self-soothing activities, as detailed earlier, which try to recreate the experience of a bodily and psychic envelope when the child experiences being left alone without a sense of continuity provided by maternal anticipation or the capability to play at recreating her presence.

Especially during the pandemic, a time of confinement and remote sessions, the patient's inability to play and the compulsive need for action can make a therapy challenging and increases the analyst's urge to maintain an emotional link with the child and the parents while working at creating symbolic capacities.

Observing infants after the feeding process, the psychoanalyst Willy Hoffer (1949) noted the way babies were using their fingers to maintain the oral pleasure, some playing at introducing one finger into their mouth, others touching or caressing their skin. Winnicott was grateful to have those observations in order to screen the babies who were able to replay the oral pleasure with calm and to differentiate them from those who were still in need of intense arousal as if continually frustrated.

A Toddler with a Hair Pulling Compulsion

This clinical vignette illustrates how the lack of intermediate space in infancy that has left the patient regulating her affects concretely and compulsively.

A one-year-old girl never smiled and had a stern, unemotional face. Her hair was very poor. She started pulling her hair dramatically when the family moved to a new apartment, and she had to start facing separation in a day care. Her head was nearly hairless, and her skin was damaged. The parents reported that she was pulling her hair compulsively each time she was frustrated. They were satisfied to have an independent baby who didn't ask for rapprochement, since the girl was having her bottle alone on an armchair while her mother could be on a screen talking to friends. The mother was herself too depressed and needy to feel the presence of the baby as fulfilling her intense need for a concrete object. After intense work alone with the mother and many dyadic sessions in which I engaged the child in playful activities where her aggression could be discharged, she became interested at creating transitions between presence and absence, and the hair-pulling compulsion decreased. But every new discovery had to be made compulsive, and there were only very few developments in creativity after months of therapy. The concreteness in the parents, who had poor representative capacity, made them insensitive to their child's pain and relieved when the little girl found ways to sooth herself.

Trichotillomania is not only aggression against oneself but also the result of feeling deserted and unloved; the child attempted to hold onto the self when others failed to provide emotional support, and then bodily feelings were disturbed. The child learned to 'lean on herself' through self-injurious hair pulling and, in this way, satisfied her aggression as her need for contact. Thus, disturbed bodily feelings, detachment from the mother, and suppressed impulses had led to the development of trichotillomania and were followed by many compulsive activities.

The maternal function of containing plays its fundamental role here, as it is for seducing and exciting pleasure and desire. It is a dynamic containment made of a contact barrier, maintaining a sustainable level of excitement that is not painful, and made also of a screen for representations: A 'blank screen' where emotions can be projected and experienced as affects, inside a body Ego that is inhabited. The mother's responsiveness to the infant's needs and impulses involves her own libidinal cathexis of her child. So, the baby's needs are received by a benevolent mother, or by a seducer, or by a disgusted defensive one. Babies can be overstimulated, as they can be neglected. Early sensorial body-to-body contacts as early maladjustments in the primitive communication convey specific messages about the maternal representation. Satisfaction comes not only from discharge of the drives, but there is a relational component that infants integrate. Pleasure and desire start from there. The first disappointments, misfits and inadequacy will imprint a narcissistic wound that lasts. The girl with the hair pulling compulsion became a very stubborn, obsessive, rigid person, easily wounded by others.

The hungry baby can experience satisfaction through hallucination only after receiving real satisfaction of the need and a real experience of pleasure. Then the illusion of self-sufficiency depends upon the mother's capacity to provide, joined with the infant's capacity to receive. For Freud, hallucinatory possession of the breast amounts to investing the memory of prior satisfaction so that it becomes hallucinatorily vivid.

There is no escape from the pain of frustration and premature imposition of the reality principle. In keeping with Freud's view, however, we know about the impossibility of good hallucinatory solutions in the case of severe privation.

Autoeroticism Is Not Self-Soothing Compulsion

At the beginning of life, the body envelope is still fragile, and the baby's ability to maintain the sensations and experiences of being alive through movements, through the action of her own body, is essential. Restoring bodily dialogue is urgent. It is the economic aspect of maternal psychic functioning that is communicated to the child in the dance of preverbal games. Prosody, the rhythm of the utterance as well as of the delivery, the intensity of the gaze, the resonance of the voice are all essential signals to which the baby responds with her own register of primitive drive.

Autoerotism, with its infinite potential for playing out the recreation of memories, helps to associate sensations and representations and to develop further displacements. It is for the subject a background on which the imago is represented. Infantile sexuality starts out from there.

The affect associated with this process can change perception, since the psyche can transform, deny, or neglect external reality. The roots of the representational capacity are fully linked with affect. In cases of early trauma, violent affects will be discharged and destabilize the psyche and its ability for representation and symbolization. Affects associate emotions nascent in the body with energetic allotment from the hallucinatory experience. The lack of autoerotic capability and the risk for dependency upon addictive systems makes more and more important the analyst's work at giving meaning that instigates remembrance in the patient, recreating an opportunity for hallucinatory fantasy, and pushing for an associative process that could recreate libidinal and representative capacities.

The primary autoerotic bodily investment builds a network of 'nuclear representations', the source of the first object presentations, which in their turn will contain and modify them. These nuclear representations nourish the basic material of every psychic activity. The body, in its sensory experience, both object of cathexis and drive source, is the necessary open window to external reality, the indispensable go-between of the encounter of the drive with otherness. The mother's skin and her psychic attunement to her child offer a 'psychic envelope' that wraps the body and mind of the baby and allows for more self-discovery of what the body ego can provide as sources of pleasures.

That combination of stimulation, containment, attunement, mirroring, and reciprocal pleasures depends upon the mother's unconscious infantile sexuality, as well as narcissistic and oedipal cathexis of the baby. She arouses, filters, offers new experiences, adjusts to the baby's capacity and development, shares the experience, repeats it with different modalities, and plays with rhythm and intensity. As Julia Kristeva (2014) wrote, the mother is the source of 'psychisation' of the biological body. All the sensorial sensations associated with the body and her holding create a pleasure that will be forever a source of desire. Eros can never be fully appeased but allows for transformation from autoerotic touching of one's own body to hallucination, fantasy, dreaming, and all the creativity associated with more symbolic activities.

The capability for autoeroticism also coincides with the maternal counter-investment of a third party, the temporary disinvestment of her bond with her child. The mother becomes a lover, as Michel Fain and Denise Braunschweig (1977) wrote, and the fantasy of the primal scene originates from there. The mother's capacity for investing in a partner and introducing a third in the dyadic relationship opens the field for the whole process of representation and symbolization. Autoerotic activities are associated with playing with fantasies.

Pain and pleasure are both sources of addiction. As in the toddler case, the search for any sensation, especially for painful ones, is a powerful source of compulsion. We can observe this tendency now in our societies where the lack of meaning seems to aggravate masochistic, painful behaviors. The work of pain is associated to trauma and depression and is a signal of a physical fixation on an object psychically not representable. Like in self-harming adolescents, there is no capacity for symbolization of psychic suffering. The perception of the pain is then the only sign of mental suffering. For addicts, the failure of symbolization, of linking, leads to actions to overcome trauma. Freud, in 'Civilization and Its Discontents', makes a very strong link between happiness for individuals and happiness for populations, detailing the function that narcotics play in keeping misery and suffering at a distance, serving as a gain of immediate pleasure but also of independence from the outside world (Freud, 1930, p. 21). Addictions are protections against narcissistic flaws.

The death drive reminds us of a biological reality: the body is not solely a fantasy; it possesses its own limits, impassable, that escape the mental grasp. Most individuals do not need to verify it through repetition, but some must always trace the outline of their body (Zaltzman, 1984). Addicts live within the register of radical narcissistic substitution: 'They testify of failure, insufficiency of God, of the Father: one cannot rest upon him. One must unceasingly substitute failure for a symbolic instance' (Le Poulichet, 1987, p. 105).

Body pleasure is one of the best sources of representation in childhood, since through infantile sexuality and autoeroticism the child can develop figurative power. Later in life, when genital adult sexuality has been organized, the fantasy world is again supported by the quality of object relations. When differed action (Après-Coup) gives a sexual meaning to the childhood events, the narcissistic issues that the child faced will make the adult feel again the sense of emptiness of life. The primacy of addictions in modern society seems to be associated with those early troubles in the process of representation.

Often in the consulting room we hear of patients' frenetic need to use pictures or videos on the Internet to stimulate sexual fantasies, with the attendant intensive masturbation practices that replace a relationship with a partner, which we can understand as an equivalent to the lack of psychic representation. Early narcissistic failures can, later in life, be replayed in a sexualized way and become fixed. The protection against the void of the negative, if not in the figuration process, is being searched for in these arousing pictures and videos. If the capacity for representation has not developed or is poor in the child, the whole psychic functioning could be damaged long into adulthood, and the role of the psychoanalyst is to provide the child with a structure and containment for his own creativity and capacity for figuration. This process will also interfere with the primitive defenses and must be done as early as possible: the stakes are nothing less than the development of infantile sexuality, the vitality of the child, and his capacity for language and symbolization.

The Question of Representation

In classical theory, symbolization and representational activity in general are directed toward the question of the absent object. Following Freud, Bion (1959) takes the absence of the breast as the origin of thinking activity, and French psychoanalysis also roots the work of representation in the encounter with the absent object. The absence of the object, its 'perceptive' absence, compels the subject to widen the distinction between the object perceived in the present and the internal trace of previous perceptions of the object, from which construction of the internal object representation is made possible. When the object is present, the internal object representation is superimposed upon the perception of the object. Thus, it does not appear as a representation, it is not 'reflected' like a representation, except of course if the subject perceives a gap between his or her object representation and what he or she perceives of it. The presence of the object and the link with a present object do not pose any problem, for they are deemed 'givens' through perception. Only absence, separation, differentiation, and loss appear as potentially problematic (Anzieu-Premmereur, 2013).

The treatment of narcissistic pathologies has broadened the scope of psychoanalytic metapsychology: the construction of links and the investment of linking processes are at the center of the subject's suffering. This calls for a more complete conception of earlier or more archaic aspects of the symbolization process (Roussillon, 2011).

Modern patients show that the construction of the primitive link between the object absent in perception and its trace in psychic representation is not a given. They demonstrate that a process which, if it encounters too many difficulties, may present issues rendering such a construction vulnerable to the vicissitudes of social encounters. They display 'autistic', 'melancholic', 'antisocial' traits, or even de-subjectivation more akin to the splitting of subjectivity than the repression of a part of psychic life. It therefore seems necessary to refer to the action of forms of destructivity which requires us to reframe our theory of construction of early links.

When we consider the construction of the primitive link and the work of specialists in very early childhood, we must then address the broader question of the emergence of early forms of symbol representation and to consider that these are produced within the mode of encounter and mode of presence of the object. The failures of these early encounters produce a 'primary narcissistic disappointment', and mobilize primitive defense mechanisms in which, at one end we see the early forms of retreat in an autistic line and, at the other, the attempts at healing by an intensified primary masochism. Between the two, the forms of psychotic, borderline, perverse, or anti social processes are situated (Roussillon, 2011).

Winnicott's (1953) notion of transitional space offers the possibility for changes in the analytic work with difficult narcissistic patients and with young children. Winnicott pointed out the conditions required for a subjective appropriation of mental life: the relationship to reality, as to 13 the internal world, needs to be 'transitionalized' within an intersubjective space. The mother, as the first mirror, through her looking at the child and her way to hold and handle it, can provide this ability to reflect.

The alpha function of the mother in Bion's (1959) notion, and as the Skin Ego and the psychic envelope described by Didier Anzieu (1985), supply a theoretical foundation for the early experience of being felt, seen, understood. The introjection of this capacity to feel oneself is followed by the one to represent. Through the libidinal cathexis of the object, the intrapsychic binding is in process, and the reflexivity is then integrated, associated with shared experiences of pleasure. Rene Roussillon's (2011) work on reflexivity demonstrates that our ability to form the idea that we can think and represent is dependent on the development of the ability to represent oneself. The roots of this process are in the experience of being held, understood, and seen by the mirroring mother. There is pleasure in it, even when it's about sharing the experience of displeasure when a maternal containment transforms the experience.

Transitional Space

Certain aspects of the contemporary world—social media, mobile phones, 24-hour news—make solitude and being alone difficult and the reality of isolation much more threatening. The hazards of libidinal development play an immense role in addictive behavior. There are no specific morbid entities in addictive behaviors. The singularity of the status of drug-addiction depends primarily and fundamentally on a failure of the 'state of being'. A 'slave of quantity', the drug addict is in an interminable pursuit of drugs or repetitive actions, a process whose libidinal consequences have been detailed above.

For the child analyst, the transitional object is the only visible part of a more general transformational process that structure the psyche. Winnicott (1953) observed children's behavior and discovered the creation of a new space between mother and child. The transitional object manifests the existence of that space, between internal and external, object and self.

There is also a transition between the first state of undifferentiation to the internalization of the maternal object, so the transitional object is first an object of addiction just as the mother was, then 14 moves to another stage, when this new space in between is created and owned by the child. Then the child will move again to another stage, leaving the transitional object that is not needed anymore, to experience the existence of himself in a state of aliveness. The transitional space has been created and will last (Winnicott, 1954).

An adopted child is silent for weeks in her analytic sessions. Finally, she says, 'When I am silent with you, I am fully there'. It is in this moment that she has located the self. It is in daydreaming and in the fluidity of associations that links unconscious fantasies to present representations, not only protecting the body from emotional discharge, as we have seen, but partakes in the pleasure of arts and culture. An object that is used in an addictive way plays a different role, however, since it cannot replace the mother's presence, and is used as a denial of the lack of her presence and the need for her when she is absent.

What is remarkable in addictive solutions with concrete objects is the total lack of playfulness, in contrast with the fluidity of the use of any transitional object or function. Infants use caressing the skin or singing while using a teddy bear or a pacifier, young children create scenarios with the doll or a favorite truck that helps when they are sad or angry. The addictive solution is rigid and compulsive, not allowing for any associativity and imagination.

We can therfore differentiate the transitional object, which will be a prerequisite for the internalization of the object, from a neo-need or a fetish object which hinders it and replaces it. A 'fetish object' is an object allowing the child to maintain the denial of the lack of the mother. Winnicott specifies that it is not the object, which is transitional, it is the use that the child makes of it. Among the different characteristics of the transitional object, in addition to the essential notion of the created-found object, is that it 'disengages the child from the need of the mother herself', becoming 'more important than her'. It must also be indestructible, allowing the child to act on his instinctual movements without risk.

Within the model of need satisfaction, creating a false need is an adaptive solution and allows for a generally immediate response, thus replacing the elaboration of desire and its hallucinatory realization and, ultimately, short-circuiting autoeroticism.

A precious object in the intermediate space shows the beginning of a new capacity, generating states of being, as described by Ogden (1997). Psychic health for the child involves not only the ability to live in the absence of the mother; it is about discovering the feeling of being oneself. The transitional quality of the object frees the child from the need of the mother herself without denying her absence. It would be the evolution and the deployment or not of the transitional area that would then make it possible to identify its quality as a created-found object and then to distinguish it from a fetish object and a neo-need. The use that the child makes of the fetish object would allow him, on the contrary, to deny the lack and the absence, and thus would hinder the processes of introjection. In the case of neo-needs, according to McDougall (1982), the question of lack and absence would be diverted because they are disguised by false needs, allowing an immediate response on the model of satisfaction.

Fetishistic Objects

Some mothers experience any movement of individuation as loss. Their own separation anxieties are then obviously very active and must be avoided with their infant; and the responses proposed to deal with them engage their own mode of defense. Freud wrote about the satisfaction of the little child's needs in the Project for a Scientific Psychology:

> Excitement can only be suppressed by an intervention capable of momentarily arresting the release of quantities inside the body. This kind of intervention requires some modification to take place outside, a modification which, as a 'specific action', can only be done by certain means. The human organism in its early stages is incapable of bringing about this specific action which can only be achieved with outside help and at the time when the attention of a well-informed person turns to the state of the organism.
>
> (1895, p. 317)

He then insists on 'the extreme importance of the secondary function acquired by the path of discharge—namely, that of mutual understanding' (ibid).

It would then be necessary for the satisfaction of the need to leave traces sufficiently charged with pleasure so that the hallucinatory process can reinvest them. The necessary creative illusion from the child's point of view would require on the part of the mother an identification which would allow creativity and establish the bases of mutual understanding. Otherwise, incapable of having recourse to hallucinatory processes in the absence of its mother, the infant would contribute to the establishment of a relationship of reciprocal control and would organize a type of relationship with objects (fetish or neo-need) to deny the absence for lack of being able to elaborate it. In this hypothesis, it is not the excessive presence of the mother that would hinder the development of the hallucinatory realization of the wish, which allows the baby to bear her absence, but the lack of maternal reverie from the moment of satisfaction.

This comes from the illusion of 'creating the breast', in an 'invisible oneness' of mother and child. The space is intersubjective, since the mother has provided the child with the experience of omnipotence when she was the one feeding him. This is a personal space, containing emotions allowing for total relaxation. An addictive behavior that tries to recreate the mother as an object for the needs, not as an environment. The infant therefore stays fully dependent upon the actual mother as an object.

The essential feature is the acceptance of the following paradox: the baby creates the object, but the object was there waiting to be created. This is not only need satisfaction but also shared pleasure. The appearance of a relationship with a transitional object is not simply a milestone in the process of separation-individuation. The relationship with the transitional object is significantly a reflection of the development of the capacity to maintain a psychological dialectical process. The consequences of this achievement are momentous and include the capacity to generate personal meanings represented in symbols. Again, addiction cannot give a long-term satisfaction, nor can it provide a source for the structure of the psyche. Mastering the object is the only way to avoid feeling the pain of loss. This is important when doing psychoanalysis with vulnerable patients who need an analytic frame into which the quality of the intermediate space can be developed, but their 17 addictive neediness to real relationship interferes for a long time with this creative capacity.

The paradox is that when the child is ready to face the loss of the breast, and of its omnipotence, he doesn't experience losing forever the object but plays with its representation and its equivalences. Illusion-disillusionment is a new process into which the mother is absent, but she still does exist somewhere else. The true self is made with her past presence and her non-intruding into the self. The transitional space is created-owned by the child as the reminiscence of the interplay between omnipotent possession of the object and making it disappear. The destruction—negative hallucination—of the object that can survive is at the core of the space. As we observe in analysis with patient who need to make the analyst absent to play or to associate.

In *Playing and Reality*, Winnicott (1968) has made us aware of a neutral space between the internal reality and the external reality. This third area, labeled as the area of Illusion, is vital for maintaining a sense of being. Winnicott wasn't so much interested in describing the transitional object. He focused on transitional phenomena, which constitute a space overcoming the splitting between internal and external and into which there is no question about me and not me. This is a space into which the playful activity can be discovered. There is no compliance toward the environment, a new field of experience is now open. The analytic setting is the means for the actualization of this area of illusion. Transference offers this illusion that will eventually help for a better adjustment to reality.

Like in dream interpretation, the back and forth between the patient reporting the dream and associating, and the analyst choosing details to point out a new construction, like in the squiggle game, will be produced. Winnicott's psychoanalysis is about providing in the analytic set up a facilitating environment that permits the emergence of the patient's creative potential. Winnicott's concept of the maternal environment (1945) made little room for the role of the father in the Oedipal constellation. And it should also be noted that in much of the clinical research that has been carried out on addiction, the father, if he is not dead, is frequently absent or, if he is there, is often presented as inconsistent, guilty, or incestuous, and even, in some cases, himself addicted (often alcoholic). In my clinical experience, the father was repeatedly described to me as overloaded professionally and absent. But the point on which Joyce McDougall (2004) insists is the hidden role of the father in addictive behavior—where the addictive object shows itself as an unconscious protection against the dangerous aspects of the maternal imago. Addiction tries to recreate the mother as an object for the needs, not as an environment. The infant stays fully dependent upon the actual mother as an object.

In analysis, there are different kind of spaces, from a narrow space where the analyst is stuck and the patient feels him/her as intrusive, while maintaining a need for symbiosis, to a more comfortable space where imaginative free-floating associations are shared in a creative stance. In this situation, the uncanny is opposed to the sense of familiarity.

A six-year-old girl, in a rage against her constantly working parents during the lockdown, stuck in compulsive self-soothing balancing and sucking, wanted to show me all the different spaces she was using, moving her iPad to bring me inside her secrets, under the bed where she was reading alone, or in the large room where her mother was working and required her to be silent. By moving the iPad, she made me feel dizzy, and I interpreted her lacking a closed space that was silent and familiar. Then we spoke about places, some comfortable, pleasant, well contained, some dark and frightening. During the next session, she had prepared for me the description of all her transitional objects since birth, and the box into which she was keeping her intimate treasures like jewelry, memories, and writings. Reporting then about her dreams, she created a world into which she could stay alive while her mother was working.

Freud (1920), in conceptualizing psychic space, wrote that 'the psyche is extended; it knows nothing about it'. The perception of space is a product of the extension of the psyche. From the common skin with the mother to the Skin Ego separated from the maternal skin, a continuous space of shared sensation leads to symbolic equivalences. Then this is the important question of the capability for autoerotic activities versus self-soothing or fetishist ones, sources of compulsive repetition. Here the drive activity interferes with a space into which the maternal object is absent, or benefits from the creativity of symbolic equivalence of her presence. It seems to me that Winnicott's theory is based on Freud's drive theory. The hallucination of the satisfaction is an illusion, essential for the fantasy to develop at the beginning of life and to reduce the pressure of the drives. Winnicott wrote about the self, but not so much about the Ego. This was about the sense of being, of feeling alive in a continuity. Between moments of integration and periods of nonorganization, infants experience more and more that they can be reassembled and unified around bodily activities, inside the maternal preoccupation. Then the pleasure principle can be maintained without helplessness.

Narcissistic patients are wounded in their infantile omnipotence. The transference therefore faces the tough move of thinking about the other. The analytic couple is in a space that can make the patient feel Being while coexisting with the analyst. What Andre Green (1993) has called the desire for the One is about erasing traces of desire for the other. An Ego can become a unity in the awareness of a spatial separation that created a delay for getting satisfaction. The reality principle and the fundamental taboos interfere with the omnipotent wishes. In Green's view of the space, there is an active part from the subject: the negative hallucination of the mother. This is a primitive process giving form to an internal space while the mother is present and negated. A representation of the mother can be built. In her absence, the space is still in common with her representation. Autoeroticism starts from there, opposed to all the addictive systems.

Prevention of Addictive Compulsion

Winnicott's (1954) differentiation between the transitional object as the source of being independent and the fetishistic way to use it is associated with the lack of representation of the maternal object. This leads to intolerance towards absence and provokes the need for dependence on real objects like food, drugs, sexuality, or denying dependence by not eating, as in anorexia.

Early therapeutic intervention in childhood could be a prevention of addiction later in life. Being perpetually at the breast, at the bottle or with the pacifier made the child in a constant state of neediness, with no possibility to differentiate between pain and fear, sensations, and emotions. Any difficult feeling was associated with a physical need. The drive for love became the need for a short-term oral satisfaction. The pacifier was an object of addiction, associated with a kind of neo-need: eating and sucking as the only way to calm down, whatever the cause of the distress.

Mothers tend to reproduce their own calming system, and when they deal with an issue like introducing the father and separateness, they tend to promote for the child a quick solution, more mechanical and behavioral, rather than creating a dual system with the baby. As we have seen, the ubiquity of smart phones, videos, social media are easy ways for parents to be distracted from anxiety or not knowing what to do. Technology has invaded our intimate lives. The universal need for connection and the ability to humanize anything that can become the object of our fantasies and desires has now the form of adult dolls, sex robots, concrete toys with artificial intelligence, and computer-assisted technology, which are not functioning as transitional objects inside a transitional space, but concrete bodies that maintain the need for an always available and present maternal figure. Sherry Turkle claimed that one of the differences between Winnicott's transitional objects and the technological objects to which we develop attachments is that the latter are not meant to be abandoned.

Excessive dependence can never be interrupted, it can become an acute support necessary to get through a crisis (of which adolescence is the prototype). But the encounter with the object of dependence can respond too immediately, too adequately to the need to appease the suffering linked to a developmental flaw in the psychoneurosis. Dependence, by proposing a short circuit, first seems to magically liberate the subject from the need to think, to suffer external reality and its internal reality to eventually transform itself or transform the external reality by the action adapted according to possibilities and prohibitions. But the object of dependency creates a sort of progressively dehumanizing shunt because it is compulsive, repetitive, and non-conflictual. We are then in the opposite process to that of an original capacity for mourning.

The appeasement provided by the object of dependency makes it possible, in favorable cases, to avoid disorganization and authorizes a resumption of proceedings. But when the subject experiences an intolerance to lack, to absence, the dependence will tend to become fixed, selfsustaining in the compulsion of sterile and repetitive behaviors, and it will proceed to a progressive destruction of the capacities of self-organization.

A flaw in the organization of the primary relationship will have prevented sufficient harmony between mother and child—excess frustration of absence, gratifications, and dysrhythmia of exchanges. The encounter is not fruitful, and, during the maternal absence, the child cannot easily appeal to the development of his auto-eroticisms in connection with the representation of the absent object. He will have to use other means: self-calming processes and neo-needs, which provide the release of tension, but which are not linked to a processual or libidinal activity.

The difficulties of investing the paternal third party are already induced by the mother-child bond, but a father who is not very present fleeing conflicts, falsely egalitarian or on the contrary violent, arbitrary, will be perceived at the same time as weak, not penetrating the narcissistic dyad and yet too violent, disturbing, reinforcing with elements of reality a disorganized and disorganizing oedipal fantasizing. The father cannot then be the representative of the law. It is difficult to give meaning to the oedipal desire. It does not constitute enough of an identifying pole. The child then lacks a negative operator, a symbolic third. The work of mourning regarding omnipotent illusions is hampered and the child remains attached to the mother, to the reassurance that she brings concretely by her presence. Difficulty in grieving hampers drive transposition and object change. The ideal ego remains prevalent.

Addiction is thus an attempt at self-healing, soothing the identificatory conflict, the existential distress; it can provide a containing and transient anxiolytic supplement. But when addiction interrupts the emotional experience, degrades it, or even generates it falsely, it is the food for processual development that will be lacking. To the poverty of the representation is added an affect itself degraded on the sensory and bodily side. The same object of dependency (whether it be a guru or a psychotropic substance) can enrich the imagination of a subject whose perception of reality is dull due to a lack of fantasy capacity. It can restore affective experience, reduce anxiety, but also has the power to increase oblivion, dementalization, disinvestment from the body, the psyche, the object. There is no play as it could have existed in childhood, allowing the projection of fantasy.

The advantage of such a system is to procure a pseudo-representation, a limited libidinal satisfaction, a mastery. The television or the computer, through their screen function, replace the internal screen formed by the negative hallucination of the mother's face. The use of gambling, similarly, distracts from a depressing life of agonizing failures with the illusory promise of instant narcissistic redress. When this screen fails, it can be replaced by the pornographic video, a prosthetic substitute for sexual fantasizing. Associated with masturbation, this consumption becomes a source of dependence: the excitement is thus relieved, controlled, without calling on another. Addictive sexuality uses the eroticization of a tension stemming from an unthought infantile distress. The object is disqualified, substitutable. It serves as the short-circuit discharge of potentially disorganizing experiences. Sexuality, then, has an anti-processual goal, without real fantasy, without remembering. Chemical intoxication makes it possible to magically reconnect with the ideal Ego and the omnipotent unity abolishing conflicts. Finally, the guilt, and the superego are dissolved (by alcohol, for example).

The imagination, stimulated by drugs, provides a pseudo-reality in hallucinated revival, potentiates a pleasurable sensory experience at the expense of reflective and representative activity. It is a transformation by hallucinosis as Bion (1959) described it, attacking the links, providing the illusion of a self-generated world in a lying omniscience. The addict can only fear rediscovering a depressing or brutal external and internal reality. Here again, the quantitative takes precedence over the qualitative and causes regression and fixation on abandoned infantile positions, tyrannical, terrifying relationships with loved ones, subjection to the dealer, to lack, to the body. The attack on body and psyche reveals a hatred of reality and genitality; it allows by dementalization to find, in the zero degree of excitation by exhaustion, a new desperate conformity between body and psyche.

By triggering the secretion of endorphins, self-calming processes provide euphoria and anesthesia. According to Bion (1959), the psyche can then function like a muscle, becoming evacuative. It is about getting rid of unwanted tensions in the absence of an auto-erotic restraint linked to a fantasy activity. Exhaustion in work can also serve the need for discharge. The pseudo-thoughts of a demanding intellectual work paralyze the conflicting object investments, block, and empty the fantasy activity.

New needs, thanks to the use of rather pleasant or painful bodily sensations provoked repetitively (smoking, eating, scratching, tearing of the skin, etc.), restore psychic composure but can also replace psychic activity itself. The repetition of painful physical traumas then has a containing aim. The de-objectalization at the end of the evolution of addictions evokes the logistics of autistic defenses. The borderline pathology, the depressiveness of future addicts recalls the protective, enveloping strategies of the autistic as well as his desolate internal world (Tustin, 1981).

Resistance and Negativity

Addiction can be a source of negative movements that interfere with the analytic process in the form of resistance to change, leading to decathexis of psychic development, with aggressive reactions when facing repetition of the pain. This gathers significance eventually, in the aprèscoup, with the analyst's work of interpretation. But a more negative and destructive move can freeze the process when negativity invades transference and countertransference.

Like in Winnicott's (1954) conception of regression to dependency, the threat to the Ego's integrity requires technical adjustments to the setting and the analyst's position. That's why the evaluation of the patient regarding his access to the depressive position as it pertains to oedipal features is essential to anticipate which kind of anxieties will play a role in the negative transference. Interpreting the negative transference seems to be the motor of the process. Some negative manifestations reveal the patient's displacement of the investments associated with different qualities of affects that can be transformed and symbolized. Some, however, are a negation of the process by the destruction of the investment in the analysis and a fight against emotions. Due to envious destructiveness, fear of passivity, or vengeance toward a painfully frustrating object, massive regression makes the analysis chaotic and difficult to tolerate for the analyst. Equally important, then, is to try at first to evaluate in the patient the narcissistic foundation of the primary link to the object, the ways in which the patient invests an object as the quality of identifications.

Winnicott, in a prophetic article, 'The Metapsychological and Clinical Aspects of the Regression within the Psychoanalytic Situation' (1955), proceeds to an overall reassessment. The psychoanalytic process is the creation of a 'second reality' born from the sessions, in perpetual reworking, of what can be known and of what would make an interpretation susceptible to triggering disruptive effects which must be avoided.

This has the effect of placing the analytical couple in an attitude of expectation, interested in but still potentially worried about what might happen (Ogden, 1997). At the end of Freud's work, a process is identified in the negative conjunction between the repudiation of the feminine and the deployment of destructive impulses. In fact, since 1920, the center of gravity of analysis has gradually shifted to repetition compulsion and negative therapeutic reaction, renouncing the removal of infantile amnesia when trauma had prevented fixation and construction (Freud, 1920). The focus now is linked to the Ego's vulnerability to psychosis, which makes it an ally on which one cannot rely, either because of its duplicity or because of its insufficiency in the face of determinisms.

When the Ego is like a hostage, renouncing its own activity of knowledge, watching the movements of an object, the patient's communication shows a confusion between the instinctual source and the object experienced as omniscient and omnipotent. Its goal is seen as preventing the development of the subject's personal autonomy. In those structures, it is the activity of representation that suffered in the integration of the experience. What will appear is not just a lack of insight, but the 'abrasion of interpretive capacity' (Green, 1975) limited to the moments when projective activity is set in motion to signal a manifestation of hostility from the object. The function of the analyst in these situations remains fundamentally the same: avoid reinforcing defenses and wait until the transference gives sufficient clues by punctuating it, less to interpret it than to mark it that this has been heard (Winnicott, 1969).

Some negative transference cannot be interpreted, due to the level of destructiveness, while a clearly hostile transference seems to access the symbolic value of the interpretation. This is about the importance of destructiveness, the tendency to evacuate, and the absence of psychic space, as the manifestations of destructive narcissism. The indication of analysis nowadays is based on the compatibility between the mental functioning of the patient and the conditions of the frame. To benefit from the construction of a personal space, the patient must adjust to the setting, the way the analyst maintains the analytic frame and offers it concretely, with rules, containers and safety. If this is a good enough environment, then the generative function of the Ego would be able to move from denial and splitting to better resources associated with repression. The analytic attention has shifted from the contents of the psyche to the psychic activity itself (Ogden, 1994).

Working with identity issues or narcissistic disorders put at risk the analyst's capacity for symbolization. Laplanche (1997) observed that the analyst as an object is not only containing but also mostly seducing, while unconscious sexuality stays in the background like the maternal sexuality that has shaped the origins of the psyche.

It is classical to say that we should listen to a session like a dream: the characters in the narrative are seen as representing different parts of the patient. But with narcissistic vulnerabilities, we can observe that this is the Ego that takes center stage instead of those other characters that inhabit the session. Narcissistic identifications are a source of confusion and in the transference, there is only the 'shadow' of the object. The analyst has here a new function, that of being a 'malleable medium' (Roussillon, 2011), by the 'tuning of the affects'. This will promote the analyst's reverie and its transformative quality.

References

Anzieu, D. 1985 *The Skin Ego*. Translation N. Segal. London UK: Karnac, 2016

Anzieu-Premmereur, C. 2013 The process of representation in early childhood, in The Work of Figurability. From *Unrepresented to Represented Mental States*, H. Levine, G. Reed, & D. Scarfone, eds. Routledge. pp. 240–254.

Anzieu-Premmereur, C. 2017 Perspectives on the Body Ego and Mother-Infant Interactions. I've Got You Under My Skin, in A *Psychoanalytic Exploration of the Body in Today's World: On the Body*, V. Tsolas & C. Anzieu-Premmereur, eds. Routledge, Chap. 6, pp. 89–99.

Bion, W. R. 1959 Attacks on Linking, *International Journal of Psychoanalysis* 40:308–315

Braunschweig, D. & Fain, M. 1977 Des Mécanismes Communs a L'auto-Érotisme et a L'interprétation, *Revue française de psychanalyse* 41:993–1002

Fain, M. 1971 The Prelude to Fantasmatic Life, in Dana Birksted-Breen, *Sara Flanders and Alain Gibeault Reading French Psychoanalysis*, 2010, Routledge.

Freud, S 1914 Remembering, Repeating and Working Through, *S.E.* 12:1913–1914.

Freud, S. 1920 Beyond the Pleasure Principle, *S.E.* 18:14–17.

Freud 1930 Civilization and Its Discontents, *S.E.* 21:57–146.

Green, A. 1993 *The Work of the Negative.* London: Free Association Books, 1999.

Green, A. 1975 The Analyst, Symbolization and Absence in the Analytic Setting (On Changes in Analytic Practice and Analytic Experience)—In Memo, *International Journal of Psychoanalysis* 56:1–22.

Hoffer, W. 1949 Mouth, Hand and Ego-Integration, *Psychoanalytic Study of the Child* 3:49–56

Kristeva, J. 2014 Reliance, or Maternal Eroticism, *Journal of the American Psychoanalytic Association* 62:69–85

Laplanche, J. 1997 The Theory of Seduction and the Problem of the Other, *International Journal of Psychoanalysis* 78:653–666.

Laplanche, J. & Pontalis, J. B. 1967 *Vocabulary of Psychoanalysis.* Paris: PUF.

Le Poulichet, S. 1987 *Toxicomanies et psychanalyse. Les narcoses du désir.* Paris: PUF.

McDougall, J. 1982 The Narcissistic Economy and Its Relation to Primitive Sexuality, *Contemporary Psychoanalysis* 18:373–396.

McDougall, J. 2004 L'économie psychique de l'addiction, *Revue française de psychanalyse* 68(2):511–527.

Ogden, T. H. 1994 The Analytic Third: Working with Intersubjective Clinical Facts, *International Journal of Psychoanalysis* 75:3–19.

Ogden, T. H. 1997 Reverie and Interpretation. *Psychoanalytic Quarterly.* 66:567–595

Roussillon, R. 2011 *Primitive Agony and Its Symbolization.* IPA Karnac.

Tustin, F. 1981 *Autistic States in Children.* London: Routledge and Kegan Paul.

Tausk, V. 1951 On Masturbation, *Psychoanalytic Study of the Child* 6:61–79

Winnicott, D. W. 1945 Primitive Emotional Development, in *Trough Paediatrics to Psychoanalysis.* Basic Books. 1975. pp. 145–156

Winnicott, D. W. 1953 Transitional Objects and Transitional Phenomena- A Study of the First Not- Me Possession, *International Journal of Psychoanalysis* 34:89–97

Winnicott, D. W. 1954 Withdrawal and Regression. *Through Paediatrics to Psychoanalysis* 1992:255–261.

Winnicott, D. W. 1955 Metapsychological and Clinical Aspects of Regression within the Psycho-analytical Set-up. *International Journal of Psychoanalysis* 36:16–26.

Winnicott, D. W. 1968 Playing: Its Theoretical Status in the Clinical Situation, *International Journal of Psychoanalysis* 49:591–599.

Winnicott, D. W. 1969 The Use of an Object, *International Journal of Psychoanalysis.* 50:711–716.

Zaltzman, N. 1984 On Melancholic Sexuality: Baiser La Mort, *Psychoanalytic Inquiry* 4:243–268

Chapter 10

Reaching for the Impossible Jouissance

The Contemporary Addictive Female

Vaia Tsolas

The individual of any epoch struggles with two trends, "one towards personal happiness and the other towards unity with the rest of humanity, must contend with each other … So must the two processes of individual and of cultural development oppose each other and dispute the ground against each other" (Freud, 1930, Kindle edition p. 97).

Recent events of the last decades (COVID, political and climate misfortunes, economic devastation and war, etc.) have brought the contemporary subject into a constant, unavoidable state of overwhelm and despair. In the US, we see an astronomic increase of depression, addictions, abuse of painkillers, drugs and suicide. Depression has been the number one illness in the world with 264 million people affected worldwide. Close to 800,000 people commit suicide every year, the second leading cause of death in 15–29-year-olds (WHO, 2020).

In a *New York Times* article, "There's a Name for the Blah You're Feeling. It's Called Languishing" (April 19, 2021), Adam Grant writes about languishing as a sense of stagnation and emptiness. He compares it to looking at your life through a foggy windshield, suggesting that languishing might be the dominant contemporary emotion, with many people struggling with the emotional consequences of the pandemic. Grant places languishing as the "middle child of mental health," the void between depression and flourishing, attributing the term to the sociologist, Corey Keyes, who argued that languishing is and will be the new mental health pandemic of the next decade, replacing depression and anxiety.

Where do addictions stand?

In June 2022, a *New York Times* article reported that more people are dying of drug overdoses in the US than at any point in modern history with annual overdose fatalities in 2021 surpassing 100,000 for the first time ever (*NYTimes*, June 2022). According to the same source, in the middle of 2022, the rate appears to be rising even further, 300 people dying from overdose per day, or more than 12 people every hour, on average. In the reaching out for the cessation of unbearable overwhelmedness, death is not far off.

DOI: 10.4324/9781003384618-16

Addictions and Jouissance

Freud made few remarks about addictions and maintained a skeptical stance toward the treating them. He writes:

> The insight has dawned on me that masturbation is the one major habit, the "primary addiction," and it is only as a substitute and replacement for it that the other addictions—to alcohol, morphine, tobacco, and the like—come into existence … And here, of course, doubt arises about whether an addiction of this kind is curable, or whether analysis and therapy must come to a halt at this point.
>
> (Freud 1897, p. 272)

Similarly to Freud, Lacan's references to addiction have been minimal. However, Lacan directly links addictions to the administration of the drive satisfaction (jouissance), which the subject creates for himself bypassing others and castration. Braunstein (2020) writes that addiction relates to behavior and not to a structure as it may appear in neurosis, perversion and psychosis; one "supposes that his addiction allows him a privileged, direct, and short-circuited access to jouissance … a renunciation of jouissance … a radical difference between the object of the drug addiction and the object of the drive."

The ambivalent stance toward addiction in psychoanalytic literature continued after Freud and Lacan, resulting in limited psychoanalytic writings on the topic. So, it is not a surprise that the treatment of addiction has been associated mainly to other than psychoanalytic means (medications like buprenorphine, Cognitive Behavioral Therapy (CBT), family therapy, motivational interviewing). It is important and vital, however, for our new world of disaffection and addictions to correct this omission and to use psychoanalytic Inquiry and listening to address the deeper layers of the psyche.

My focus in this chapter is on addiction to medication, both in the acceleration of the drives (stimulants) and the calming of excess (sedatives), as it applies to a female case whom I name Hippolyta. In the pandemic, her use of medication turned quickly into abuse of stimulants/sedatives, posing challenges to our analytic work. Performing as a superhuman, detaching herself from others and from the traumatic reality of the pandemic, Hippolyta aimed for complete control over her overwhelming drives with medication serving as her singular trustworthy object. My attempts to seduce her out of her narcissistic enclosure seemed more futile during the crisis of COVID-19 and the altering of the analytic frame by the virtual.

The Soma, the Body, the Skin Ego and Addictions

Addiction is a symptom that highlights the intricacies of the body and psyche.

Anzieu's contributions to psychoanalysis return the body to center stage in psychoanalytic theorizing; his notion of the skin ego specifically highlights the psychic envelopes between the body ego and the soma.

Anzieu's skin ego (2016), as the primary representation of the corporeal Ego, in its two functions of protective shield and psychical container, is supported by the sensoriority in the exchanges of care from the primary object. It has a structure of wrapping, holding together psychic contents, and stands as the prerequisite of identity. Directly at the border between soma and psyche, the skin ego forms the foundation for the experience of oneself as I, distinguishing inside and outside, protecting and preventing excess of stimulation and states of overwhelmedness. The skin ego has two faces: internal and external with a space in between for free play (Anzieu, 2016). It is incomplete; it does not cover the whole psyche. Both the incomplete covering and the space in between allow for exchanges with the object.

I propose that it is the skin ego's capacity to perform its function, to wrap/protect the ego, that is at stake during crises and trauma. Equally important, I suggest it is the skin ego's elasticity and capacity for penetrability without being riddled with holes that allows for psychic growth by the libidinal nourishment of the ego from both poles, drive excitation and external stimuli, simultaneously preventing states of overwhelmedness.

"My life is a shitshow. I just feel I can't keep it together. Anger is leaking out constantly. I am fighting with everybody. I feel safe when I lock myself in front of a screen. This weekend, I binged watched one TV episode after another nonstop and ate so much shit. I am out of control," Hippolyta announced emphatically.

The daughter of a highly decorated military officer, Hippolyta moved from one location to another every few years. Born in the South, her journey as a child took her from her birthplace to Europe and back to the US multiple times. Hippolyta had very few early childhood memories other than a vivid memory of sitting on her mother's lap dressed in white but feeling stiff like a doll, repulsed by the smell of a heavy cologne and to this day she avoids all scents. Her mother, a highly attractive, infantile and dependent woman used Hippolyta for her own preservation as the special baby and bond to the father. Neglected by her husband, a narcissistic, emotionally volatile and charismatic man who carried on multiple affairs, she "had an unbelievable capacity to deny what was in front of her eyes." "She was delusionally invested in her idea of the perfect family," Hippolyta told me. A heavy drinker, smoker and philanderer, her father had a heart attack while with a prostitute and died "in the saddle" when Hippolyta was 11. She reported the loss of her father coming as a relief as the family relocated near her maternal grandmother who had been a stable figure in her life. Her mother however, fell into a deeper depression from which she was never able fully to recover. Hippolyta, her mother's replacement partner and confidant ever since, cut on her arms and between her thighs in early teens to get relief from the overbearing maternal presence and of her terror of becoming a woman like her mother. In an unavoidable journey to relocate her father psychically and to make her mother whole again, Hippolyta eventually found the path of addiction during late adolescence and early twenties, ending up abusing drugs, drinking, smoking and being sexually pro-miscuous with either men or women without distinction.

Hippolyta was in her late thirties, a strikingly attractive woman when I met her. She was in her last year of training to become a nurse and was living with a woman.

She had been in and out rehab centers and therapists throughout her adult life. She spoke favorably of her last male therapist who had been also her psychiatrist. Supportive and sweet on one hand, but also somewhat neglectful on the other, she was able to manipulate him to obtain extra prescriptions of meds, which she abused.

She immediately speaks to me of her difficult life, the multitude traumas as she tracks my facial expressions. Disaffected but seductive, she assigns sole credit for her survival to her physical beauty and seductiveness, even though her resilience is apparent. "I know how to cut off emotion and function like a robot," she almost brags. She speaks with no apparent guilt or shame about luring others into helping her and abandoning them shortly after.

I feel drawn in almost instantly, mesmerized by her presence even with a heavy feeling in the pit of my stomach. Her narcissistic and perverse presentation almost fades into the background, as the lost little girl desperate for shelter appears every time she breaks down into tears. She speaks of her darkness and how it surprises her that she draws people in. I feel her under my skin, fascinated by her, yet burdened with a heavy, parasitic presence that extends far beyond the session's end. Her tattoos, a sword held by a female with the female body fading into the background and wings extending on both sides, cover her arms where cuts used to be.

The Myth of Hippolyta

What I saw on Hippolyta's tattooed skin was the image of an Amazon. Amazons mated, but then killed their mates right after copulation. The daughter of the god of war, Ares, and the queen of the Amazons, Otrera, Hippolyta is the female heir to the throne, being the bravest Greek Amazon of mythology. Her name means "horse let loose." Her father gave her a magic girdle as an emblem of her invulnerability in both aggression and sexuality. This girdle became the object of Hercules ninth labour. Hippolyta's girdle is perhaps performing the function of a wall of the narcissist inclosure. Interesting enough, Hippolyta offered Hercules the girdle willingly without a fight. This made Hera jealous and, transforming herself into an Amazon, spread rumors that their queen was abducted by Hercules. The Amazons furiously attacked Hercules and his crew and in the fray that followed, Hippolyta, now without her protective girdle was killed by Hercules.

Hippolyta, having submitted to becoming a sexual being, rendered herself vulnerable. In addition, the etymology of the name Amazon may be traced to "a" (without) and "mazon" (breast) naming them for the act of cutting off one breast in order to have better bow control. One breast cut off and the other one exposed, the image of Amazons may easily be interpreted as androgyny, another way of delineating narcissistic invulnerability and impenetrability.

Our Hippolyta speaks of her androgyny when she elaborates on her sexual encounters. She often goes to sexual parties and there seduces a man by kissing a woman. She enjoys having them both, arousing the man watching her while she is penetrating a woman with a dildo. "I am just on. I know what they want," she says as if sexual difference is an irrelevant fact. "I get off when I fuck them hard." Hippolyta calls her partner a copy of her mother; dependent and needy. "My skin crawls inside out when she attempts to touch me" she says. She assigns her partner, however, the maternal ego role of regulating her drives, giving her the extra meds when she feels at risk of relapsing and overdosing.

The Double Wall of the Addictive Girdle Begging for the Paternal "NO"

Interestingly, the Greek word for medication is *Pharmakon*, meaning both *poison* and *cure*, and attesting to the dual potential of re-establishing the lost state of equilibrium and of its toxic character. Stimulants and sedatives, however, seem also to have this dual potential by fogging and curing the pain of intrapsychic and intersubjective intrusions and in bypassing the other. They foreclose the possibility of the quantity of excitation to be psychically shared and elaborated, throwing the subject into the toxic loop of the demonic nature of the death drive. Michel De M'Uzan's notion (2013) that certain individuals are Slaves of Quantity, "condemned to a destiny dominated by the quantity of excitation that cannot be psychically elaborated," speaks to the case of Hippolyta. In a state of constant unbearable tension, Hippolyta's abuse of medication aims to relieve her from the pain of overflow of drive excitation and by inducing mania to maximize control of her ego performance. The oral indulgence is the fogging of the boundaries between herself and the outside world as well as between the erogenous body and the soma. This results in a robotic existence, detached and floating without any anchor.

Anzieu (2016) elaborates further on the specificities of the topographical perspective of the skin ego as it applies to narcissistic cases. The focus is on having their own psychic wrapping suffice and not to depend on the common skin with another. However, since this is impossible to achieve, given that as the skin ego is just forming it is still too fragile to function independently, two operations must take place. One is to get rid and seal off the space between the two faces of the skin ego, the external and internal, which turns it into a double center; "for both the person themselves and for others, it tends to envelop the whole of the psyche" (p. 135). This double center creates certainty but lacks flexibility, which creates easy tearing and narcissistic wounding. The other operation aims to transform the personal Skin-ego into a cement barrier against the outside by appropriating the maternal skin that is not shared, but rather stripped off from the mother and worn triumphantly in order to endure a heroic destiny and achieve great things.

Anzieu calls this double wrapping, "the double wall."

> The double wrapping—its own plus that of its mother—is gleaming and ideal; it provides the narcissistic personality with the delusion of being invulnerable and immortal.
>
> (Anzieu, 2016, p. 135)

Extreme states of anxiety due to unbearable intrusions of persecutory objects could lead to an even further sealed off state. Anzieu points to drug addiction as "a solution by building an additional barrier of smoke or fog between the Ego and stimuli" (p. 111).

It is several years into analysis when we abruptly depart due to COVID. We decide to use virtual sessions instead of phone sessions as Hippolyta enters into a constantly overwhelmed state. Working around the clock as a nurse attending to sick and dying COVID patients superimposes a fresh layer of trauma. Hippolyta finds crisis undeniably addictive. "I am good in crisis" she tells me. "It gives me focus, purpose … I feel alive." Returning to her partner, however, feels like her mother's return to her hometown after the death of the father. They often engage in irruptive quarrels. "She is useless in my life. I wish I could come home and be alone. She asks so much of me … I don't have much left to give." Interestingly, I feel like the same useless partner in the countertransference. I am a burden, another thing she must go through, longing to be done with and to go to bed. I bring this up but she denies it. Her sessions feel exceptionally detached, filling me with the unbearable heaviness and dread of a motionless clock. I witness her eyes fixated on the painting behind my head. Her complaining and outpouring of resentment of people with privilege, people who fled the city versus the ones who stayed behind, vibrate in her associations. I become aware that she can see the reflection of the trees in the glass of the painting behind me, which clearly suggest that I am in the country away from the dangers of the city; the dangers she is battling with on an hourly basis. Guilt overtakes me. Hippolyta's destructive envy feels like arrows shot silently at me from a powerful bow.

She tells me then that she is engaging in a slippery slope with her stimulants. "I am definitely taking more. I found some at work. My addiction is gaining strength. I was really late to work this morning." My futility and alarm keep me on edge as Hippolyta remains unreachable. The lack of real, physical presence accentuates my sense of helplessness as she feels even further away. I try hard to keep myself from enacting and burdening her with my own castration anxiety. I wish to be able to give her something of continuity to hold onto between sessions, but it feels futile as if I am stripped of my analytic role.

Following the session, I have a dream of our sitting in a bar together. She talks to me and I turn to bartender to ask what he thinks. I long for a third to come and help, to offer an insight. However, I am mortified by my asking the bartender. I stand up abruptly and ask Hippolyta to meet me in the courtyard to have lunch. It feels good to walk away from the scene of the bar. I am worrying about the analytic frame being transgressed to a degree that it will be too late to repair. The courtyard is the courtyard of the analytic institute I belong to and that feels comforting. However, the guilt of having transgressed the analytic frame continues to haunt me. My countertransferential futility and need for the intervention of the third is captured by my analytic institute attempting to repair the devalued bartender.

She brings a dream:

I went to visit my old therapist. I really needed a refill. He said "well, let's have another drink first." He took me in his car, but instead he drove me to his home. Once we got there, he took me to his bedroom. "We are hinting about this for a very long time," he said. "It is about time; let's do it." There was no feeling.

We had to do what we had to do. It was like a payment for all the refills. It was matter of fact; just have sex. It was not like he was raping me or seducing me. It was simply a payment for all those years of service. He did not seem happy, but he felt relieved. "Let's stop the games," he said. "Let's do it and it will be done." That is all I remember. It feels odd now, but in the dream it felt just straightforward.

"Once an addict, always an addict," Hippolyta continues reporting it matter-of-factly as the prophesy of her fate. "It is the truth I have to face," she adds. "You would like me to say, it is time to stop the games," I say, thinking of her need for a paternal presence. She agrees, but her eyes bypass me and fix on the reflection. "But instead I bring you in my room," I say, "and expose you to a peek at my life." She recalls sleeping with her mother when the father was away and to being traumatically exposed to the primal scene when the father returned home, often drunk.

She appears averse to exploring her dream further. Words seem to be devoid of their magic; the affective resonance and my ability to penetrate Hippolyta's girdle psychically seem severely handicapped. Perhaps, I was telling myself in my dream that a bartender might be more useful. In the competition with her stimulants, I will always lose the battle, I thought with a feeling of frustrated surrender.

She continues to tell me that her masturbation helps her relax before sleep. Otherwise, she always feels on the edge, ready to erupt into panic. Her stimulants help her function. She continues to speak with hatred of her friends who are posting pictures on social media about their country homes. Her envy of others' homes reminds her of her mother's envy and dependence on others and how much she hates herself in that resemblance. She finds herself trapped in the paternal identification, seeking relief with deadening masturbatory orgasms at night while her worst fear of a heart attack like her father's stands as a punishment for the addictions.

Hippolyta's girdle as the double wall seems to solidify even more during this phase. My exposing her to the primal scene of my home provokes the oral envy of the pregenital omnipotent mother who spreads further fear of castration and paranoia, foreclosing sexual difference and ultimately destruction of coupling in sessions. Her disaffection and mine symbolize the nirvana principle of the addictive process. The image of the cut off breast in order to draw her bow better and to survive psychically help me to survive similarly the narcissistic sealing off and to wait patiently for the other nourishing breast to appear. However, the question of whether we need to suspend sessions until we return to the office continues to gnaw. The clicking on and off her doxy sessions make them seem almost as another addictive clicking away of her time. Is maintaining the virtual sessions while I witness the increase of her addictive behaviors an addictive collusion similar to the mother's turning of a blind eye, begging for a paternal "no"? How can I voice the "no" when Hippolyta lives through the most traumatic moments of our lived history and tries her best to survive? My standing up abruptly and asking her to meet me at the courtyard of my analytic community pointed me in the right direction, away from the suffocating death drive of narcissistic seduction. I suggested that we suspend sessions for now and meet again when we can begin our psychodynamic work in person. I realized afterward that I said "begin" and not "resume." Reckoning with my castration anxiety, I aimed perhaps to open the possibility of analytic work if Hippolyta ever asked for it. "Castration means that jouissance must be refused so that it can be reached on the inverted ladder of the Law of desire" (Lacan, Ecrits, p. 827) guided my unusual intervention. Hippolyta agreed eagerly.

Further Considerations: The Addictive Contemporary Subject of the Instinct and the Decrease of Eros

Could we say perhaps that Hippolyta represents the lonely, lost, overwhelmed contemporary subject of our days? As that lost subject, is she left unsupported by the "social" skin ego[1] and, unmediated by the Other, resorts to the more immediate ways of discharge of excess that only addictions can offer? Is this the contemporary subject of self-preservation where Eros is an unwanted and unnecessary Xenos?

Just as Michel de M'Uzan (2013) points to "Slaves of Quantity" being condemned to a destiny dominated by the quantity of excitation that cannot be psychically elaborated, the subject of the self-preservative instincts is condemned to the destiny of discharge of primal angst at all costs. The pleasure principle of the death drive reigns the destiny toward discharge and elimination of tension to which Eros is an unnecessary Xenos.

In "The Psychoanalytic View of Psychogenic Disturbances of Vision," Freud (1910) writes:

> From the point of view of our attempted explanation, a quite specially important part is played by the undeniable opposition between the instincts which subserve sexuality, the attainment of sexual pleasure, and those other instincts which have as their aim the self-preservation of the individual—the ego-instincts. As the poet has said, all the organic instincts that operate in our mind may be classified as "hunger" or "love."

In this duality and irresolvable tension between "hunger," the pulse to satisfy the ego instincts, and "love" or "Eros," the push to satisfy the object instincts, Freud had initially reserved the concept of libido for the libidinal object instincts. However, his advancement of the concept of primary and secondary narcissism made him revise this distinction. Object libido and narcissistic libido became intertwiningly bound to each other.

The conservative character of instinctual life, however, apparent in the compulsion to repeat, led Freud to his pessimistic stance against the stubbornness of the instinct and resistance against change as well as to his introduction of the death drive (Thanatos) alongside the life (Eros). "Beside the instinct preserving the organic substance and binding it into ever larger units, there must exist another in antithesis to this, which would seek to dissolve these units and reinstate their antecedent inorganic state" (Freud, p. 71).

The death drive "worked silently within the organism towards its disintegration" (p. 71) with the capacity to direct outward some of its energy, manifesting itself as aggressivity toward others. This silent, "mute" drive of death, however, directed inward to fuel the unconscious sense of guilt and need for punishment gave the superego the same instinctual intensity and character. The superego's directive to happiness and enjoyment contained the directive for the organism to follow the path of its own destruction and to return to the inorganic zero tension. Therefore, the preservative/ego drives from the first topography expand to death drives of the second, operating in a continuity with the preservation of the individual, but paradoxically aiming to return the individual into the inorganic life. The sexual drives, which later expand to object drives and Eros of the later topography, stand in opposition and serve for further unities and evolution of the species into new forms of culture and civilization.

An interesting cultural example that gives a hint into the contemporary addictive subject of discharge is the Cuddle parties. The Cuddle parties were founded in New York on February 29, 2004, by a pair of self-described coaches but in order to meet the astronomical demand, the founders began a training and certification program in January 2005, and have since trained a large number of people. Cuddle activities events closed permanently due to COVID-19, but following relaxation of restrictions in the region, the cuddle community "Hugz & Cuddlez," offers free group-cuddle events on a weekly basis, with an average of 30 guests in attendance at many different locations.

A recent article *New York Times* (Gettleman, 2022), "Kyiv Nightlife Comes Back Amid Urge for Contact. 'This Is the Cure,'" describes cuddle parties as part of the cure for battling the death drive of war.

"Cuddle parties started before the war, but the people who came two Sundays ago—a mix of men and women from their early 20 s to mid-60s—said they really needed them now," the article describes.

"The cuddlers gathered in a large, tent-like structure near the river, and as new age music played, they lay on floor cushions in a big warm heap. Some stroked their neighbor's hair. Others clutched each other tightly, eyes closed, like it was the last embrace they'd ever share with anyone."

The cuddlers, the article continues, after 15–20 minutes opened their eyes, untangled themselves, stood up and smoothed out their pants. Seeking bodily comfort to combat the alienation of death is not a foreign idea. But curling up with a stranger is perhaps a new phenomenon of our days. "They found new cuddling partners and new positions" the article describes. Moreover, the instructor was clear that none of this was supposed to be sexual or romantic.

How do we understand these cultural manifestations? At a first glance, these could be interpreted as a wish for bodily touch and human contact. However, undeniably these cuddle parties share the non-committal component of the social media. Their members hug strangers whom they might not see again. Is this another form of the addictive virtual but as the incarnation virtual? Can we even say that the human contact here falls under the domain of the preservative narcissistic ego drives that seek to alleviate death anxieties and to null, existential pain? Is here anything libidinal toward others or does it stay solery within the masturbatory/narcissistic jouissance that any addictions share? And more importantly, what can we learn from these cultural manifestations about our contemporary patients in the rise of the addictive jouissance of elimination of tension that bypasses castration and the Other?

Discussion and Conclusion

Hippolyta, as many other patients, informs us that when it comes to an instinctual discharge of psychic excitation that cannot be elaborated, survival (Ananke) takes the upper hand to Eros (desire), aiming at reduction but reaching paradoxically toward the jouissance of the addictive death drive. The addictive character bypasses others and the laws of castration. "The drugs that intoxicate and offer a shortcut to jouissance (although not through desire) reach the brain from outside the diaphragm of speech, making the compromises that link the body to culture come apart" (Braunstein, 2020, p. 286).

If we take the cuddle parties as a representation of the contemporary subject in the social group, the discharge of tension in the cuddle has the aim of the contact bypassing the peculiarities of the other and the limitations and pitfalls of a sexual relationship. This lowering of stress with a touch and the bonus of pleasure of the pleasure principle of discharge requires a "single use" stranger as a partner, a partner to whom you have no responsibility to respond and where vulnerability and castration are negated as with Hippolyta. It is a short-circuited access to jouissance with the predictability of masturbatory behavior where the others with their "whims" are bypassed. "Drugs are not substitute sexual objects because they lack phallic value. On the contrary, they are a substitute for sexuality itself, a way of distancing oneself from the relational constraints imposed by the phallus" (Braunstein, 2020, p. 283).

This chapter has forwarded the hypothesis that today the discharge of unbearable tension has overtaken desire resulting to new pandemics of disaffections and addictions operating under the death drive. This overtaking has served to decrease the works of Eros not only at an individual but also more in collective manifestations.

> Drugs are related to the auto-eroticism of original prohibition: the subject administers himself a substance that connects him directly to a jouissance that does not pass through the filter of acquiescence or the forcing of the other's body. The destitution of sexuality is thus achieved.
>
> (Braunstein, 2020, p. 283)

The internet advances this death culture of the jouissance of addictions that bypasses the Other; the consequences for the psyche appear undeniably severe. And if this be so, we are creating a different texture of subjectivity over time to which Hyppolita bring testimony. This new subjectivity places real challenges for psychoanalytic technique, a technique which is solely based on transference. Moreover, there is an imperative for the evolution, indeed for the future, of psychoanalysis to augment its scope to include the needs of the contemporary addictive subject, this subject who pulls for a paternal "no" but tries relentlessly to bypass the problematics of eros, desire, castration and the other.

Note

1   I am applying here the Anzieu's concept of the skin ego to designate a parallel structure of wrapping, holding together a social group that has functional ideals which provides its members with a sense of containment, belonging and growth.

References

Anzieu, D. (2016) *The Skin-Ego: A New Translation by Naomi Segal*. Karnac Books. Kindle Edition. http://a.co/499hRI8

Braunstein, N. (2020) *Jouissance: A Lacanian Concept*. SUNY Press. Kindle Edition. http://a.co./9kB0ucN

De M'Uzan, M. (2013) *Death and Identity: Being and the Psycho-Sexual Drama*. Routledge. London and New York. Kindle edition. http://amzn.to/1r0LubW

Freud, S. (1910) The Psycho-Analytic View of Psychogenic Disturbance of Vision. *The Standard Edition of the Complete Psychological Works of Sigmund Freud* 11:209–218

Freud, S. (1897) Extracts from Flies paper. *S.E.*, 1:177–281 London: Hogarth

Freud, S. (1930) *Civilization and Its Discontents*. General Press. Kindle Edition. http://amzn.to/1r0LubW

Gettleman, J. (2022) In *New York Times*. Kyiv Nightlife Comes Back Amid Urge for Contact. 'This Is the Cure.' https://www.nytimes.com/2022/07/26/world/asia/kyiv-ukraine-war-nightlife.html?referringSource=articleShare

Grant, A. (2021) In *New York Times*. https://www.nytimes.com/2021/04/19/well/mind/covid-mental-health-languishing.html?referringSource=articleShare. There's a Name for the Blah You're Feeling: It's Called Languishing

Interlandi, J. (2022) In New York Times. https://www.nytimes.com/2022/06/24/opinion/addiction-overdose-mental-health.html?referringSource=articleShare. Experts Say We Have the Tools to Fight Addiction. So Why Are More Americans Overdosing Than Ever?

Lacan, J. (2007) *Ecrits*, (B. Fink, Trans.) WW Norton.

WHO, (January 30, 2020) https://www.samhsa.gov/data/sites/default/files/reports/rpt35325/NSDUHFFRPDFWHTMLFiles2020/2020NSDUHFFR1PDFW102121.pdf

Chapter 11

The Risk of Loss
Anxiety and Depression in Women

Jacqueline Schaeffer

Translated by M. Civin

Daily practice and epidemiological studies reveal twice the frequency of depression in women. It is appropriate to ask about the specifics of this statistical difference.

First of all, let us note that since the dawn of time, scientists, researchers, philosophers and other thinkers have studied the phenomena of the human being, of thought and of the social world without taking into account the difference between the sexes. This observation, for example, has never been a principal object of philosophy. Up to and including in psychoanalysis, we observe that, theoretically, many structural or psychopathological entities have not been examined with respect to this difference, even if from a clinical point of view, one could take it into account. Nonetheless, in the case of hysteria or obsessional neurosis, for example, we know it influences both presentation and degree of severity.

Even more, when we talk about borderline, narcissistic, delusional or psychotic personalities, we rarely invoke sexual difference. However, even when it is closer to the neurotic organization tied to an oedipal conflict, this does not exclude the fact that these so-called non-neurotic configurations, in which the neurotic structure is weak, do not present in the same way for a boy as for a girl, a man as for a woman.

Depression, which is primarily a narcissistic suffering, is an example in which most of the literature does not point out this difference. We speak of depression in babies, children, adolescents, the elderly, and post-partum. Rarely do we talk about depression in women as distinct from depression in men.

And yet, one does not enter into depression, nor does one come out of it in the same way depending on whether one is a boy or a girl, a man or a woman. We could understand this as a prevalence rather than a radical difference, because it is possible to find feminine forms of depression with many men, when their phallic defense is in danger or put at risk. Regardless of the sex, the collapse of this bulwark, this rock that is the "refusal of the feminine" can make humans run aground on the same shore.

What might be the reasons for this?

It is useful to differentiate a depressive state, the kind we call "the blues", from the pathological form of depression. The depressive state seems to be less and less tolerated

DOI: 10.4324/9781003384618-17

by today's society, which pushes for an ideal of happiness, of individual accomplishment, and accentuates narcissism, the cult of the body, and the ego ideal to the detriment of the superego and of the oedipal object relations. Feelings of shame prevail over those of guilt. Intolerance to depressive states can lead to an overconsumption of antidepressants, which only deprive the subjects of the use of their own psychic resources.

The depressive state leads us to talk about loss and dependence.

We can observe that the form of dependence, the sense of loss, the loss of object, the object of the loss, damage to the object or damage to self, the expression of pain or suffering often have different manifestations from one sex to the other and have an influence on the causes and the forms of depression.

The Situation of Dependence

One can say, dependence is constitutionally inscribed, in the "neoteny" of the small human being, that is to say the state of prematurity of its birth, where the primary experiences of distress and satisfaction are rooted.

A situation of dependence cannot really be completely non-existent, but if it continues excessively and becomes fixed, it exposes every human being to the risk of either hatred or depression.

All psychic development, like all psychoanalytical treatment, tends to free a subject, as far as possible, from alienating bonds of dependency.

What are the internal resources and the substitutive satisfactions which allow this?

In the early stages, they are ensured, when the rhythm of presence-absence of the mother is modulated well, by the first psychic activities of the baby, which are the hallucination of satisfaction and autoeroticism.

Freud (1905) specifies that the breast object, that of the sexual drive, is lost at the moment when "it became possible for the child to form the whole representation of the person to whom the organ that provided satisfaction belonged ... The sexual drive then becomes autoerotic" (pp. 164–165).

So the object can only exist as a lost object.

This is essentially the moment that Melanie Klein designates as the advent of the "depressive position". The object in its totality risks being damaged by the projective attacks of the subject. If this phase, in its numerous evolutions, is well-elaborated and well-framed by a reassuring environment, it protects against later depressive states.

Later, the construction of the internal object will be reinforced by the representational activity and the reality testing.

It is the organization of anality that promotes the true experience of independence from the maternal body at the level of the corporeal and phantasmatic functioning. It is the sphincter function that psychically provides the capacity to open and close the ego to the drive and to the object.

Many women, when their structure is prevalently hysterical, do not achieve a solid organization of their anality, which makes their independence precarious.

But it is the phallic logic, the castration anxiety and the Oedipus complex that will reorganize and resymbolize afterward this first development in the sense of sexual identity and sexuality in that of the difference of the sexes and the generations. It is this organization that ensures a stronger release from the dependence on the maternal body, by the triangulation, by the crossed identifications and by the creation of a super-ego, which in women is described by Freud as insufficiently "impersonalized".

The Maternal Investment: The Messenger of Expectation

From the very beginning, a mother does not invest narcissistically or erotically in the same way in a boy or a girl.

The son can satisfy better his narcissism known as "phallic". He can thus receive simultaneously a phallic investment on the side of the paternal identification and by the projection of the maternal phallic narcissism.

Whereas the daughter – of the same sex as her own mother – can send back the mother either to the rivalry, or to the anguish of a representation of feminine "castration", but also to the substitutive representation that this conceals: namely the anguish of the feminine jouissance and that of the incest. Mother and daughter incest could be considered as the fundamental homosexual fantasy.

The mother, when she finds her erotic life, by inciting her child to sleep, exerts a censure, the "censure of the lover", by silencing the erogeneity of the sex of the small girl, establishing a "primary repression of the vagina". It is more a question of sheltering the girl, not from the desire of the father, but from the maternal enjoyment, and thus of preparing her for the awakening of her own sex with the lover. It then submits the girl, most often, to the phallic, symbolic logic, to the father's law. Because of this primary repression of the vagina, the whole body of the girl is going to develop and diffuse erotic capacities in the expectation of its awakening. The tale of Sleeping Beauty offers an age-old illustration.

For Beauty to fall asleep peacefully, protected by this primary repression, she must be able to cathect the waiting.

If the mother, messenger of castration, says to the little boy who rushes forward, penis right in front: "Be very careful, otherwise trouble will befall you!", to the girl she will say: "Wait, you will see, one day your Prince will come!" Thus, she is a messenger of expectation.

The boy, the man, destined in principle to a sexuality of conquest, that is to say to penetration, organizes himself more, well-supported in his anality and his anxiety of castration, in the activity and the mastery of waiting and loss.

The girl, the woman, on the other hand, is dedicated to waiting: she waits first for a penis, then for her breasts, for her "period", the first time, then every month, she waits for the penetration, then a child, then childbirth, then weaning, and so forth. She never stops waiting.

But all waiting is a painful excitement. And as all these expectations of the woman are for the most part linked to non-controllable experiences of real losses of parts of herself or of her objects – which she cannot symbolize, like the boy, in anguish of loss of an organ, never lost in reality – as well as to upheavals of her narcissistic economy, she needs the anchoring of a solid primary erogenous masochism. This allows her to cathect erotically the painful tension, to support the dissatisfaction of a drive by nature impossible to satisfy, the gap of the hallucinatory satisfaction of desire compared to the expectation of real satisfaction, and later, to support the pleasure-pain of sexual enjoyment. It serves as a point of fixation and as a stop to the mortifying disorganization. It is thus a powerful antidepressant factor.

Indeed, the depressive state can be linked to a disappointed expectation, whether it is conscious or unconscious. Winnicott states that the worst thing that can happen to a little man is not so much the deficiency of the environment as the hope raised and always disappointed.

There is a very likely link between disappointed expectations and depression in women.

The dependence of the girl on the archaic preoedipal mother, the so-called Mino-Mycenaean period, has a duration that Freud acknowledges having underestimated for a long time: "a certain number of female beings remain attached to their original link with the mother and never manage to divert it truly onto the man". Her primary object, of the same sex as her, is necessary for the identificatory support, and forges her autonomy much later. How, for the girl, can she tear herself away from the maternal imago, when her body begins to approach and resemble the body of the mother?

The paradox of the feminine destiny lies in the difficulty of freeing itself from a maternal primary object, because of a necessary identification and of an equally necessary disidentification. The separation carries the risk of losing a part of oneself and thus the advent of a depressive state.

Narcissistic Loss Anxieties

In 1926, Freud described the path of the elaboration of the anxieties of loss according to the situations of danger. He went from the distress of the infant, and the danger of the loss of object bound to the dependence of the first years, to castration anxiety in the oedipal conflict, until the latency period's anxiety facing the superego. So a pathway from the anguishes of total loss to symbolic partial losses would allow the whole object to be rescued.

The Oedipus complex allows the child to renounce his incestuous vows. Oedipus is antagonistic to incest. The constitution of the superego, heir of the Oedipus complex, moral instance, and agent of guilt makes it the vigilant guardian of any incestuous transgression or murderous vows.

This oedipal operator, whose heir is both prohibitor and protector, serves as an anchor and allows the reorganization of a number of previous archaic anxieties, oral as much as anal anxieties, as nameless anxieties, those that certain psychotic manifestations allow us to qualify as annihilation, liquefaction, or re-envelopment in the maternal body, such as M. Klein or Winnicott, for example, have to described them.

A good oedipal organization, if the family environment is sufficiently reliable and framing, can thus also protect from any plunge into depressive.

Anxieties of loss and the defenses against these anxieties differ according to gender, which will orient the fate of the Oedipus complex and the depressive state differently.

In the boy, the loss will be symbolized more on castration anxiety, which can serve as a limit, as a limit to the depressive plunge. In the girl, the loss will be more that of the whole, hence the prevalence of a depressive risk.

At the moment of the perception of the anatomical difference of the sexes, which Freud qualifies as a trauma, how can the girl make herself recognized as a sexual being in the absence of this penis that she perceives as carrying all the narcissistic valorization? Depression, suffering with narcissistic power, threatens her.

Her unconscious ruse will be to eliminate this difference which creates problems, and to adopt phallic logic. The "desire of the penis" is a narcissistic phallic desire, not an erotic one. Because on the erotic level, the girl knows very well that the absence of penis does not prevent her from feeling all kinds of voluptuous sensations. She also feels intensely that its autoeroticism is the object of a conflict, a conflict which has a bond with the parental objects.

The phallic organization is an obligatory passage, for the girl as for the boy, because the narcissistic overinvestment of the penis allows the release of the pregenital imago of the all-powerful mother and of the maternal hold.

The boy, in principle, is favored by the fact that he possesses a penis that the mother does not have, from the moment when the denial of the mother's penis is lifted, and because he can manage, thanks to his castration anxiety, to symbolize the part for the whole by supporting himself on his paternal identification. He renounces his incestuous vows in a violent way, to save his penis. The threat of castration anxiety makes him leave the oedipal conflict. The phallic organization saves him from any depressive threat.

With the girls, the women, the impulse remains very close to the body, to the source. It is the belly, the interior of the body that can be the object of anxiety, or threatened with destruction, as Melanie Klein theorizes. It is more by invasion and intrusion than by what can be torn off, cut.

What is it then about an erotic feminine? The negotiation of the part for the whole being hardly possible, how to symbolize an interior, which is a whole, and how to separate her own from that of her mother? Is a symbolization, a "psychization" of the female sex, possible?

The girl is thus deprived of a castration anxiety that is very useful for symbolization since, says Freud, this castration "is already accomplished", but it is her castration complex that will make her enter the oedipal conflict.

Since the mother did not give her a penis, which renders the mother worthy of the most hateful reproaches, says Freud, the girl is going to turn to her father.

But is it only a question of expecting a baby from the father, in reparation for the prejudice of not having received a penis from the mother, in order to complete herself narcissistically, or is it not more a question of expecting to be loved erotically? The desire for a child, for Freud, precedes the erotic desire. The female erotic desires for the father are not evoked.

However, Freud notes the oedipal erotic character of the masochistic desire of the daughter in his article "A child is beaten" which he elaborates at length. It is the guilt of this oedipal desire that leads the daughter to express it, in a regressive mode, in the second highly repressed part of the fantasy: "Daddy, beat me! Daddy, rape me!". But Freud quickly returns to his phallic theory. In 1926, it is her clitoris that the little girl beats. Having his daughter Anna on his couch, with her fantasies of fustigation (being beaten with a club), did not make things easier!

If the phallic organization is necessary, supported by a theory of infantile sexuality, that of a unique sex, the phallic penis – to the point that Freud constructs a phallocentric theory of psychosexual development from it, and that Lacan makes the central signifier of sexuation, desire and jouissance – it is because this organization has played the role of a major defense against the eruption of the discovery of the difference of the sexes in the oedipal period, and that this phallic organization tends to maintain it.

The phallic organization is a solution that aims at cancelling the source of the problem: the feminine. It is also a strong defensive construction against the anxieties of the oedipal phase. Castration anxiety will be doubled by "anxieties of the feminine", those of the opening of the female body and of penetration, for both sexes, but in an asymmetry which signifies the difference of the sexes.

The awakening of the puberty arises well before the capacity to assume a sexual relation is elaborated. As Winnicott suggests, sexual activity intervenes rather as a way of getting rid of sexuality than of trying to live it.

It is at the time of cathecting sexual penetration and the erotic vagina that deficiencies of internalization can reappear in the adolescent girl and threats of narcissistic invasion, anxieties of the feminine. Puberty then has a traumatic effect. The depressive state can manifest itself, as well as all the phobic or character defenses.

The predominantly feminine pathologies in adolescence, such as anorexia and bulimia, concern feminine anxieties, those of the opening and closing of the body, and testify to the failure of their elaboration. The bulimic responds by the act of filling, the anorexic by that of closing all the exits, the orifices. Becoming pregnant can also be a way to fill and close all the exits. The prohibition of the law arrives to punctuate this mode of controlling the anxieties of opening up the body of the women.

The Object of the Narcissistic Loss

If the narcissism of men is above all phallic, because of the castration anxiety about their penis, in the women, it is their whole body which is cathected, but this body is subjected to the reassurance of the gaze of the other which makes the women dependent on this gaze, on the desire and the love of the object.

In men, the phallic narcissism of the boy, gaining support from the identification with the father, is prolonged in the ego-ideal, which can prove to be crueler than the superego, and even more so if it is supported by a precocious superego or an ideal-ego.

The phallic narcissistic attack, the collapse of the ideal, seems more frequent in men, in the sense of a depression of inferiority, of impotence, of insufficiency. The loss of a state of power, the victory of a rival, the breakdown of sexual power, retirement, the decline of age expose men to the risk of a depression of inferiority, devaluation, feelings of uselessness. This depressive risk can also occur when too much success results in the feeling of being unworthy of it.

Female narcissism is above all corporeal, even if it can also be invested in a phallic manner. This is how "femininity" is differentiated from "feminine". Femininity is based on superficiality and seduction, on the lure and the masquerade, on the accessories of seduction and which harmonizes well with the phallic and assuages the castration anxiety of the men. The feminine remains completely internal, invisible and wary, the carrier of all the dangerous fantasies and the anxieties of the feminine. Femininity is the body; feminine is the flesh.

In women, the narcissistic wound touches their whole body, that of the erotic feminine deprived of reassurance by the gaze or the desire, that of the wounded maternal, and depression takes on more of the tone of a vacuum. The damage to bodily narcissism goes hand in hand with somatic fragility and more marked depressive tendencies.

Mid-life crises will exacerbate these anxieties as well as the risk of depression.

Objectal Loss Anxieties

Freud contrasts castration anxiety in men with separation anxiety, loss of object and love in women. He thus maintains that the absence of castration anxiety in girls exposes them to anxieties of loss of the whole, an all that is more one of being than one of having. The loss of object and the loss of love threaten them with depression.

The oedipal girl turned to her father awaiting a substitute for the penis in the form of a child. The woman will have to wait for a man, for a lover of enjoyment, the revelation and the awakening of her feminine sex. I have theorized a feminine erotic masochism. The one that reveals the oedipal little girl: "Daddy, beat me!" The one that the woman in love offers to her lover, that is to say a capacity of opening and abandonment to strong quantities of libidinal excitations and to the possession by the sexual object. In the unbinding, it assures the necessary link to the cohesion of the ego so that this masochism can be undone, and it requires a reliable object.

A woman cannot give herself fully without love. It is what poses her dependence and her submission to the domination of the man in the sexual relation. Her dependence on love makes her more threatened by the loss of the sexual object than by the loss of a sexual organ, an anguish around which the oedipal sexuality of the boy and the "compromised" sexuality of the adult man are more easily structured.

This is why she is more exposed, as Freud says, to the loss of love, to disappointment, and is so threatened by depression in case of loss of a love object.

If the mother did not give a penis to the girl, which, according to Freud, makes her turn into an object of hatred, it is not she either who gives her a vagina. It is by awakening, by exposing and overcoming his feminine sex that the man will be able to tear off the woman from her autoeroticism and from her pregenital mother. The change of object is a change of submission: the anal submission to the mother, from which the girl tried to escape by the desire for the penis, becomes then libidinal submission to the lover. Since the night of time, men must apprear to wrest women from the night of the mothers, from the queens of the night.

The other sex, whether one is man or woman, is always the female sex. Because the phallic is the same for everyone. To assimilate the phallic in the masculine is a necessity from the first investment of the boy for his penis, but at the hour of the adult sexual encounter, phallic and masculine become antagonistic. Otherwise, how not to turn toward the devaluation, the contempt, the fear or the hatred of the feminine?

Beyond the phallic, the feminine.

The male-female couple is built in a co-creation, in the discovery of the female sex. In this same movement, the masculine of the man is built, by the relinquishing of its own anal and phallic defenses.

The Object of the Objectal Loss

The Opera has highlighted well the asymmetry of the feminine and masculine position in facing abandonment.

"If you leave me, I will kill you", Don José shouts to Carmen.

And Madame Butterfly: "If you leave me, I'll kill myself".

The abandoned man kills the object, in general phantasmatically, the abandoned woman becomes a lost object.

The loss of the investment in love and the feeling of failure that accompanies it awaken the traces of the oedipal failure, and the mourning of the oedipal desire must be resumed. The devaluation by loss of object love, experienced as a narcissistic trauma, can disorganize the feminine system of valorization, and in the man, it can re-actualize the entire problematic of castration.

The mode of defense against separation, radical and symbolic, implemented by the boy to escape the oedipal conflict, remains an exemplary tactic for the man against all the anxieties of subsequent objectal loss, a loss in love for example. The object of the male loss can be negotiated by his castration anxiety, which serves as a limit to the depressive affliction, and limits the damage.

"If you leave me, I will kill you ... or I will replace you".

We know the adage: "One lost, ten found". The phallic quest takes over. In the heart of every man, a Don Juan slumbers. There are three types of restraints to the polygamous temptation of men: the love of a woman, the fear of women or ... the super-ego.

For a woman, often, the loss of a love can mean losing everything, being sent back to nothingness, being nothing.

A patient was abandoned by her younger lover. She is possessed, obsessed. She has lost 15 kg and has a constant pain in her lower abdomen. She thinks of dying. When she sees this man, her insides sink into the ground, she says, she empties herself, she is nothing. It's like a drug, but it's sweet inside, she says, and you can sense that she doesn't want to get rid of it. She cannot feel hatred, because to cut herself off from him is to cut herself off from a part of herself, to amputate herself. She does not understand. How did she not feel anything, not see anything coming, how did she not perceive that there was another woman? "I want to know", she says, "but I don't want to hear it".

The lover tore himself away from her, probably like a child who emancipates himself, but taking a part of his body with him. She was discovered to have uterine cancer.

Do we dare to think that it was necessary to fill the void and suffer at the same time? And that this fusional relation, making the emptiness of any otherness, would have given way to a melancholic incorporation in the form of somatization? This would be at odds with proven theories that deny a primary sense of somatization. It would be more relevant to think that a more "essential" depression, therefore "not felt" and impossible to "see coming", preceded such somatization.

One can say that female depression is linked to the disappointment of the expectation, to the difficulty of symbolization of her female sex. When her primary erogenous masochism is not well anchored, when it does not serve as a limit, the fall can be deep and turn to melancholy. The disappointed expectation of the desire of a man, the disappointed expectation of a child confronts her with a feeling of emptiness: emptiness of a body that is not inhabited any more by a body narcissism, which is not enlightened any more by the glance of desire of a man, or by the tenderness of a child.

The dependence, which could be dissimulated in the presence, is revealed and discovered brutally when the lack is actualized, when the confirmation by the object and by its glance disappears.

Then, in the woman an objectal loss, confused with a total narcissistic loss, is revealed. "If you leave me, I will kill myself, I will ruin myself, … or else I will remain alone".

The solitude of women is a fact of society, whether it is chosen or suffered. Men rarely stay alone: the female object was first of all maternal … and it remains so.

The disappearance, the erasure or the wearing off of the love felt for an object constitute a test. The disinvestment leaves a void, and a support; an occasion is lost, that of expectation, of phantasmatization, of exaltation, of excitation, of auto-excitement.

The suffering is an interior object which can sometimes be precious, exciting, and the feminine lament can also be a jouissance. This reveals a link with female erotic masochism.

"Ah I wish I had never seen you!" writes the Portuguese Nun, who immediately exclaims: "I would rather be unhappy in loving you than never to have seen you" (Letter Three).

Castration Anxiety in the Feminine

The experience of the "the mirror stage", according to Lacan, seems appropriate to shed light on the constitution of narcissism, masculine as well as feminine. The child looks at the look of his mother looking at him, confirming what he sees in the mirror. It is a time of recognition by the object of the specular image. The mirror of the mother's eyes, according to Winnicott, joins this confirmation.

The recognition by the real father of the femininity of the girl is essential. It is this paternal gaze, different from the "mirror" glance of the mother, which will mark the destiny of the femininity of the woman in the direction of the desire to be looked at and desired by a man. The glance of a father who can say "You are a pretty little girl", but also, in an oedipal register anti-incestuous, "One day your Prince will come!"

This paternal investment is what can prevent the depressive risk of the feeling of absence of sex, or of castrated sex.

The woman, whose narcissism cannot be supported by phallic confirmation, remains more dependent on the object that confirmed her being in the narcissistic image, and she builds her libidinal object in accordance with this desire to be desired.

But if the woman is only dependent on her image in the mirror, if she has not constituted sufficiently valorizing internal objects, and if a loving object does not give her another mirror with the brilliance of its gaze, she risks a depressive collapse at the time of any separation. At the time of a break-up in love, of a betrayal, of a mourning, what she misses brutally is this glance; and then at the same time, the woman can then lose her symbolic points of reference, as if she were nothing anymore.

Current women, those who have experienced the liberation of their body and the mastery over procreation, know and can feel that their anxieties of femininity cannot be appeased nor resolved in a satisfactory way by a "phallic" type of realization. And, significantly, they experience that the fact of not being desired, or of no longer being desired, by a man sends them back to a painful experience of absence of sex, or of denied feminine sex, and revives their wound of the little girl forced to organize herself in a phallic mode when facing the test of the perception of the difference of the sexes. It is there that their "castration anxiety" is situated.

The Depressions of the Middle of Life

In the crises of the middle of life, the representations move unrelentingly toward the destiny of sexuality and toward the inexorable of death. This requires a re-elaboration of the castration complex and the depressive position of the previous crisis moments.

In women, middle age is often marked by a depression, either temporary or definitive, sometimes accompanied by anguish, a hostile devaluation of one's own image and a loss of self-esteem. The possessed is lost, the hoped for has not arrived.

At menopause, in connection with real losses to be suffered, many renunciations must be achieved by the woman: they concern childbirth, youth, the archaic mother and the oedipal mother, the childhood of children who have grown up, parents who have disappeared or are close to death, etc.

The cessation of the function of the organs of procreation can be experienced, in the period of crisis, as a castration that has actually occurred.

A woman also relives her female castration anxiety, which is that of no longer being desirable and desired. She relives her adolescent anguish: her body image and her ability to seduce become once again a central factor in her self-esteem, which previously depended on the gaze of others.

Patients tell of their catastrophic feeling of having become transparent, suddenly invisible in the street, of having lost the anonymous look of passers-by.

"Often, I stop in amazement in front of this incredible thing that serves as my face … writes Simone de Beauvoir. Perhaps the people who cross me see simply a fifty-year-old woman who is neither good nor bad, she is the age she is. But I see my old head where a pox has set in that I will not heal".

This narcissistic wound can return the woman, not only to the time of the puberty, but to that of the disappointment of the small girl of the phallic phase, who lives herself as not having sex. At that point she does not feel capable to be either a mother or to be a woman, and she is not a man either.

Envious affects are aimed at men for whom it is possible to remake their life with a young woman and children.

They also target young women, who have all these possibilities in front of them. The shadow of a young and beautiful woman falls on the ego, which can lead to hostile feelings toward a girl. "Mirror, my beautiful mirror, tell me". We know the answer. The object of rivalry is no longer the mother, but the daughter.

The feeling of emptiness can become haunting, emptiness for women for whom motherhood had been the center of their identity and who had projected all their phallic narcissism on their children, emptiness especially for women who have not had children.

The departure of the children risks reactivating this experience of emptiness. This is the "empty nest syndrome".

They often take refuge in disease, in physical sufferings and in somatizations. Injured narcissism replaces, degrades or diverts the libido.

The depressive affects and the psychic pain can be denied, often by an act, an overactivity, or a hysterical exacerbation.

How to Try to Conclude?

The total commitment of a woman in the love relationship, body and soul, which can be found just as much in some men, is very similar to that of the first days of life with the primary object. And the depressive state can refer to the mourning that accompanies any experience of otherness. The other is the one who is born in hatred, the one who comes to break the fusion, it is as well the father, the baby brother or sister or … the oedipal mother.

Why are we suddenly invaded by a feeling of sadness or despair when nothing serious has happened, only an allusion to a painful or overly happy past that evokes nostalgia?

When "we have everything to be happy for", as the saying goes, why does the feeling suddenly arise that nothing is going right anymore, that the joy of living has vanished, that the meaning of life has fled, that the engine of the libido has broken down, that the belief in illusion is no longer possible, that the future is no longer of interest?

It is impossible not to evoke an after-effect of this primary relationship. The impossible mourning of the maternal object.

The anguish and the depressive state are constitutive experiences of the being, linked to the internalization and the maturation of the human being, an attempt to master the conflicts, the disappointment or the loss.

The depressive feeling (the great sadness according to Dante) is not born from a particular circumstance but from existence itself. It is due to the inevitable confrontation of the human with the life, to the separations, the uprootings, the losses, to the feeling of our insufficiencies, to the presence of the evil, to the ineluctability of death and ageing, to the experience of the nonsense, and to the reaching of the limits. It has the value of a "signal", that of the advent of an insurmountable difficulty in facing these challenges.

This situation of existential crisis can lead in the direction of a depressive collapse, or it can be the occasion of a narcissistic and objectal reorganization.

It constitutes, as it is known, the test met and overcome by outstanding personalities: heroes, mystics, artists, great philosophers, "creative geniuses", in the ways that some women have distinguished themselves.

Didier Anzieu notes that Freud's great discoveries and most important books were accompanied by moments of depression (memory problems at the Acropolis, death of his father, stopping smoking).

Falling in love is often the customary way to escape a depressive state. It is the functioning of love that is especially invested. Christian David has qualified it as "affective perversion". For women it is often the mode of entry into and exit out of depression.

But it can be more beneficial, in terms of psychic economy, to call upon the virtues of sublimatory activities to compensate for objectal or narcissistic losses, and to collect the scent of nostalgia that is in their wake; a freedom found or rediscovered to enjoy the pleasures of life, to reinvest sensoriality and autoeroticism; an impulse that can be addressed to objects of nature, to landscapes, to works of art, but also to new bonds of tenderness, those of a grandmother, for example, a literary or artistic practice.

The engagement in a psychoanalytical approach also allows a new objectal and narcissistic investment directing toward consolation, the acceptance of the limitations, and the renunciation of the illusions. The expected narcissistic benefit is that of the discovery of psychic work, of interiority, and of a new capacity to bear all that happens in life and to take pleasure from life.

Can we say that it is thanks to such capacities to overcome trials, anxieties and depressive risks, that a majority of women would have, as established, a life expectancy superior to that of men?

Reference

Freud, S. (1905), *Trois essais sur la théorie de la sexualité*, Paris: Gallimard, 1987, pp. 164–165.

Chapter 12

Enemies of Unpleasure

Panos Aloupis

Introduction

The human being, impotent about his birth and his death, endures life and gives sense to it throughout with the presence of pleasure. Philosophy, questioning the essence of human life, approached pleasure and quiescence as fundamental qualities for the construction and the continuation of a good enough mental and somatic state. Freud mentioned several times his debt to Fechner (1848), (1873) for the notion of the pleasure principle. Fechner defined a principle of stability and outlined the action according to a pleasure or unpleasure principle. For his part, Freud described the principle of pleasure in "The Interpretation of Dreams" (Freud, 1900a, chapter VII) surprisingly based on the unpleasure principle. His notes let us think that both states are intimately bound one to another. We may suggest that this way of binding forced its way through into the proposition, many years later, of the simultaneous existence of eros and death drive from the very beginning of life.

Reading chapter VII (Freud, 1900a), and especially the parts concerning the mechanism of repression and the role of reality, we have at our disposal enough elements to make sense of Freud's construction of the psychic apparatus. The latter needs energy and constancy to pursue its existence. The notions of pleasure, libido, cathexis, and sexuality are necessary for the description of life movements that take form in the frame of the object relationship. However, in this system, the unconscious is built as a direct effect of unpleasure, while pleasure enforces the mnemic traces and orients the hallucinatory cathecting of the memory of satisfaction. The primary processes of the unconscious prefer discharge and apply repression, if possible. Reality makes things evolve over time and the preconscious through the secondary processes uses inhibition for its development. The basic aim remains the psychic transformation of the excitation. Freud notes: "The unpleasure principle clearly regulates the course of excitation in both systems" (1900a, p. 600). Therefore, he added the principle of constancy, indispensable for the expansion of the preconscious and of the ego. In the first topography, the ego is driven between two antagonistic masters, the weight of self-preservation and the attraction of the sexual object. It seems logical that the mental apparatus needs quiescence for its own transformation and for the transformation of perception into representations. Through this trajectory, fantasying and

DOI: 10.4324/9781003384618-18

thinking constitute the building blocks of the psychic inner world, condensed, and progressively symbolized into language.

Freud covertly remarks on something important: "Our thinking always remains exposed to falsification by interference from the unpleasure principle" (1900a, p. 602). This note may be heard both as a statement and an intuition, for it reveals the defence strategy towards the perception of the attack of unpleasure. The work of negative, carefully studied by A. Green (1993), organizes specifically the vicissitudes of the unpleasure principle. The falsification concerns the object's perception producing repression, suppression, denial, rejection, splitting, foreclosure, and negation, and these effects may influence the affects' expressivity, the representations' interactions and thinking. The violence of unpleasure leaves its first traces on the body, however throughout life it is visible and experienced in thinking and speaking.

Even if Freud, after the traumatic experiences due either to his personal life's events (family losses, conflicts, difficult cases) or to the collective trauma of the war and its social consequences, introduced a new topography, the pleasure / unpleasure principle remained central and present in his theoretical works. "Beyond the Pleasure Principle" sums up this important shift and offers the essential material for the notions of masochism and death drive. In the following note, we find the same elements Freud had formulated in his first works and at the same time it summarizes the way masochism is built:

> Under the influence of the ego's instincts of self-preservation, the pleasure principle is replaced by the *reality principle*. This latter principle does not abandon the intention of ultimately obtaining pleasure, but it nevertheless demands and carries into effect the postponement of satisfaction, the abandonment of a number of possibilities of gaining satisfaction and the temporary toleration of unpleasure as a step on the long indirect road to pleasure.
>
> (1920g, p. 9)

Effectively, masochism, as drive binding of Eros and Thanatos, aims for the pleasure, but mostly it targets the appeasement of the effects of unpleasure in the circuit of the death drive. Some paragraphs further, Freud outlines:

> Most of the unpleasure that we experience is *perceptual* unpleasure. It may be perception of pressure by unsatisfied instincts; or it may be external perception which is either distressing in itself or which excites unpleasurable expectations in the mental apparatus—that is, which is recognized by it as a "danger."
>
> (1920g, p.10)

Indeed, if a subject, especially a child during his primary years, is confronted with a traumatic situation without a solution of constancy, the unpleasure becomes an absolute danger to the pursuit of psychic life and constitutes the major enemy of it.

In "The Ego and the Id," Freud returns to this idea by means of the second drive theory:

> If it is true that Fechner's principle of constancy governs life, which thus consists of a continuous descent towards death, it is the claims of Eros, of the sexual instincts, which, in the form of instinctual needs, hold up the falling level and introduce fresh tensions. The id, guided by the pleasure principle—that is, by the perception of unpleasure—fends off these tensions in various ways.
>
> (1923b, p. 46)

In neurosis, the secondary processes maintain these tensions insofar as the quest of pleasure is associated with guilt. In perversion, constancy presupposes the extinction of tension using the sexual object for its own needs, while "psychosis is a conjuration of the object" (Green, 1980, 179-181), which means that peace is found when the object as sexual other is rejected or disregarded.

The principle of constancy reinforces the need of the mental apparatus to metabolize the quantities of excitation of perceptive origin. The constancy is like the latency period for the child, necessary for the progressive integration of the Oedipus adventure. The transformation of both perception into object representation and excitation into drive progress through the same path. The transformation of quantity into psychical quality needs a certain time and personal rhythm in relation to the subject's history and the experience of the primary relationships. The first transformations concern the self-preservation that gets cathected by the libido, signalling the construction of auto-erotisms; they highlight the sexual cathexis of the body and establish the foundations of a sexuality that has already started identifying its enemies.

According to the first drive theory, pleasure establishes sexual destiny, while displeasure founds the unconscious. Constancy, as mentalization progresses, appears like a compromise that balances the conflicts between the principle of pleasure and the principle of reality. However, in the second drive theory, the principle of nirvana indicates the presence of the death drive and brings back the principle of inertia which Freud had proposed in his first works. The notion of drive presupposes the permanent existence of an energy source and motion, but the question of the excitation and its destinies forced Freud to formulate some responses in relation to its appeasement and extinction. The principle of constancy is, in fact, a principle of self-regulation located at the extremes of both pleasure and unpleasure.

Before a further discussion on the state of "enemy of unpleasure," I would like to present a case of a man who constructed his life since his childhood avoiding, as much as possible, "the feeling of unpleasure." Even recently, after the apparent decrease of his somatic pains and suffering, he reminded me that "all his life had been built on the feeling of comfort," "Uneasiness is my enemy!"

Clinical Vignette

Albert is a man of 35 years old I saw for the first time in 2019. He had been suffering from functional colonopathy since 2017, followed by a significant loss of weight and a loss of taste and of "emotions." He had consulted several doctors and had been administrated several treatments. Despite some short remission periods, the disorders had not ceased to worsen and become chronic.

When he arrived for the first session, I found myself in front of a "young man of nearly 20," a strange impression that disappeared when he started talking. He talked straight away of the colonopathy and particularly of the painful gastric pains that forced him to spend almost one hour every morning trying to stand up before being physically able to have his breakfast. However, along with his somatic disorders, he suffered especially from a progressive lowering of his desires and of his vitality; "I feel nothing, I have no joy." This state started in 2015, just before his moving into his new apartment. He moved out of the apartment he had lived in with his parents to a new one where he could live with his girlfriend and work. He is a leading dancer of contemporary dance. He stressed that all this happened during a happy period of his life and could not understand why his gastric disorders appeared and progressively deteriorated, associated with the erasing of his desires.

He is the only son of a couple of civil servants and spent his childhood in a seaside town. He had started dancing at a dance school at the age of five, but being a dancer became a strong commitment at the very beginning of the high school; "I felt a sort of existential malaise, because everything had changed." He felt he was not well enough prepared for this kind of diversity, "many teachers, many pupils and many exams" and dancing became his refuge.

He described himself as a quiet child, sometimes bad-tempered and temperamental when he wanted to obtain something. When he was 14, his parents decided to move to Paris to give him the chance to enter a famous dance school. Some years later, before the age of 18, he placed first in a competition, and his career expanded. He let me know that these years had been also difficult and punishing, but it did not prevent him from pursuing his goals without giving up on his way of understanding and practicing contemporary dance.

He added, without further details, that he had felt the same gastric ailments at the age of 20, and some minutes later, with no apparent link, he reported that his parents had divorced the same year. "The same year?" He answered that his parents' divorce had not affected him! After his father's departure, he kept living with his mother.

I asked him if he still lived with his girlfriend, and he began talking about "girls." He had not felt interested in girls before the age of 25. Why? They were not on his mind! Having sex was not often satisfactory, but it never bothered him. Did it bother the girls? He did not think about that either!

Since the manifestations of colonopathy, he consulted many specialists, took many pills, had some treatments and above all he lost his feelings. Even when he dances, he feels nothing and only through the reactions of the public does he realize the dimensions of his emotions. There are some situations in which he cries without knowing the reason and without feeling. In addition, he has lost his appetite and a lot of weight. "Food for me before was a real pleasure of life, now it's only a task."

Just before the end of this first session, he asked me what I was thinking about his situation; he was feeling desperate. I told him that listening to his life story I imagined that his life, his evolution from the childhood to the adolescence, from the adolescence to the adult life demanded of him, consciously and unconsciously, responses he was not ready to give and perhaps this had led to obviously intractable conflicts. He said he did not perceive the conflicts; however, he was impacted by their effects. He had been at the top of his life, had learnt how to avoid conflicts and could not realize how he got there! I told him perhaps he contained two parts in himself which were in conflict. He seemed both surprised and sceptical about my proposition; he wanted to pursue our conversation and we arranged a new appointment. He added that he wanted to rediscover the zest for life; besides, he broke up with his girlfriend because he could offer her nothing more.

A week later, he brought a dream.

He is with a friend, and they go to a restaurant of a famous chef who suggests to them that they taste his dishes. He does not like the chef whom he finds to be violent. (The chef's name begins with the same letters as my name!). They leave the restaurant and his friend transforms himself progressively into his ex-girlfriend. She proposes to him that they take a bath together and he wakes up rather perplexed.

I listened to his ambivalence towards myself condensed in the chef's name; he is violent, but he suggests tasteful dishes to him. In his dream, his friend became a woman who suggested to him to share moments of pleasure. I asked myself if our first session had been perceived as a violent encounter because of the contact with a stranger-object and of my concluding suggestion. However, the transformation of his friend into a woman made me think that maybe the presence of a man could allow him to meet a woman. Keeping all these elements in mind, I made only the remark: "Fortunately in your dreams we find your desires."

In fact, during this session, he seemed more alive and talked about his impasse. His life was deteriorating, and he described me his somatic ailments. I realized that his painful life had transformed into a permanent struggle for surviving. Talking about his own body, several times he used the word "attacking." He was feeling continuously attacked and impotent, in a state of destructive passivation where he is the spectator of his own extinction. He remembered a film titled *Limitless*, and pointed out that his body's limits are unbearable for him; before the "attacks" he was living in a limitless world! His skin was also inflamed all over with patches that get bigger and make wearing clothes unpleasant and difficult. Every morning he had to devote a lot of time to applying a special ointment on his body. Actually, he was disturbed most by his ingrown nails for they made dancing extremely painful. Despite of medical care, the symptom reappeared incessantly.

At the end of this encounter, we agreed on a psychotherapy with regular sessions. Before leaving the office, he said: "I need help and I hang on everything people suggest to me!"

During the first period of the treatment, our sessions seemed to go well. He seemed invested in our sessions and a series of short dreams, like flashes, implied a homosexual transference, with male figures either older than him, often dance professors, or fraternal ones, like friends or colleagues. These dreams lacked fiction; they looked like moving pictures with enigmatic questions or brief dialogues. He seemed astonished, because usually he had no trace of dreaming. He understood through my own interest that something had shifted in him in complete contrast to his deserted and painful daytime world.

Reanimated by our encounters, he started telling me his life story slowly and cautiously, as if he was approaching an obscure field, despite of the apparent brilliance of a phenomenally successful childhood. He let me know that at the age of five, his mother decided to register him in music, but as there were no more places available, he was registered at the dance school. This activity seemed to him easy and pleasant. He talked also of moments of intense excitation in relation to some female classmates at the age of seven or eight and of wrath, which appeared to me like manifestations of a premature ego. I had the impression of a boy who had to respond in his mind and towards his drives without having adequate means at his disposal because of his age.

In talking about his parents, a certain ambivalence appeared and over time his story telling was reinforced by some other details that darkened their portraits. Undoubtedly, they were loving parents and radically modified their life by moving to Paris to offer to their son a better life and a good career. His mother was described as anxious, rigid, as a person who needs to control everything, without a capacity to express her feelings and tenderness; she was functional and present. The father seemed more complex; Albert was more intrigued by him and his way of being, maybe because of their distance, which he linked to his father's solitary life. He transmitted to Albert his love for food.

After a dispute with his mother, he displayed his own view of the parents, how it had been consolidated during his childhood. He perceived them as feeble, disappointing persons and the de-idealization was a hard moment for him. They existed to help him, to protect him; he depended on them from a practical point of view, but he could neither admire nor love them. For music and dance, idealized narcissistic objects, his parents became a disaffected operational support.

He also let me know, in a fragmentary way, that after every school and life stage (primary school, high school, moving to Paris, dance school) he felt disturbed and distressed, because he had to confront the changes and the exams without having the possibility of avoiding them. Progressively, dancing became his best ally, as an external object incorporated in himself, embodied in a fusional and inseparable life for two as one. Listening to Albert, I realized how castration was his enemy, while sublimation occupied intensely a defensive space, sculpted on a smooth, brilliant, and extremely fragile piece of marble. In a sense, he tried to explain me that he oriented his choice for dancing, because it was pleasant, easy, satisfactory for his environment and allowed him to avoid unpleasure.

Some months after the setting up of our therapy, the COVID-19 lockdown arrived! He accepted to continue the sessions via telephone. His narrative, always rich and fluid in associations, became gloomier and more anxious. My physical absence, the absence of our exchanges and contact, the brutal stoppage of his life activities, and the context of a threatening world reinforced his impression of being the victim of privations and external attacks. His life became much more monotonous and above all he could dance no more, neither for himself nor for the public. He felt hypersensitive, flayed alive like his skin, and tried desperately to feel better, multiplying his contacts through social media with known and unknown persons, just to have the sense of appearing alive. During this period, two signifiers appeared frequently in our telephone sessions. The signifier "neutral" came from him and the signifier "beast" was introduced by me.

When they appeared, I gained some more elements about his intimate life and his trajectory, which looked like a dangerous slope leading to the precipice. When he started his career, released from the examinations and the competitions, a kind of manic reaction pushed him to build the life of a miraculous child, in the role of a fascinating dancer, feeling omnipotent, almost of divine grace. He confessed to me that he hated dancing with other dancers because either their presence disturbed him or his own coherence could not accord with the coherence of the ensemble. He preferred dancing solos or working with some colleagues or choreographers he appreciated and admired.

During a session, whilst seeking the reasons of his unhappiness, he remembered a fact which had shaken and terrorized him. After a brutal movement, he had felt his foot to be wounded and realized it was bleeding; the x-rays diagnosed a fracture of a small bone. For him, this event registered as an irreversible break in his life. He tried to get over it through dancing, restaurants and "girls," like a headlong rush to avoid his seeing the unseeable.

A month later, he brought a dream. He was dancing "freely" with some friends, one of them told him his toes were bleeding, there were traces of blood on the ground. He felt no pain, poured some water to clean the blood and captured a gaze of terror in his friends' eyes. I reminded him of the event of the wounded foot and he said: "When I was a kid, my mother repaired my wounds; she can do nothing now, she cannot repair my wounds ... my life looks like a deep divide."

Hearing his unsuccessful and harrowing attempts to overcome his "body attacks" I had the impression of hearing the screams of a wild trapped beast he was trying to tame in the interior of Albert. As he was talking of his sleep problems and his morning pains, I told him: "You make me think of a wild beast you try to exhaust, expecting it will fall asleep." He said he found the image right. In the next session, he told he had dreamt of pleasant things, and that it had occurred for the first time after many years. "I was playing ping pong and my father was there; I started jumping like Matrix, I got outside and flew in the air. My father was looking at me and said it was nice." I told him that it was nice he brought me pleasant dreams. He compared his pains to the beast, "Either it comes over or it lets go." He feels exterior to all this, and at the same time, he suffers the consequences. "My mind searches for the relaxation that I find perhaps in my dreams. The other day I released myself during the performance and I felt neutral, as exterior to it ... there is a duality, but my aim is to feel neutral no more." He added, some minutes later, that he got to know and live with the beast, and he realized his toes had recently been less attacked by the nails. Some days later, he brought the following transference dream: "I am with one of my dance professors; he is bandaging my toe which hurts, but the nail gets better. I ask him if he has the same thing and he says, 'No, you do have it!'"

Discussion

Freud clearly noted the dependent state of the infant and the need of the ego's development for good enough primary cares:

> The biological factor is the long period of time during which the young of the human species is in a condition of helplessness and dependence. (…) As a result, the influence of the real external world upon it is intensified and an early differentiation between the ego and the id is promoted. Moreover, the dangers of the external world have a greater importance for it, so that the value of the object which can alone protect it against them and take the place of its former intra-uterine life is enormously enhanced. The biological factor, then, establishes the earliest situations of danger and creates the need to be loved which will accompany the child through the rest of its life.
>
> (Freud, 1926d, 154-5)

If the environment fails in this task, the ego for surviving must develop mechanisms it is not ready for. It looks like a premature baby who meets the external world without the efficient equipment.

Albert, despite his suffering, had an appearance of a man in eternal youth; he was proud of the absence of the time traces on his body and on his face and confessed me recently, after a remark on the neutral state, he got separated from his girlfriend because she looked no younger! During the first period of our encounters, the signs of the essential depressioni and of the operational life, as his last defence of surviving, were palpable and visible: diffuse anxiety, absence of feelings, concrete thinking. He tried to take himself in charge as a desperate mother with her slowly dying child. His life and his body disintegrated, and he became the spectator of his own extinction.

The first transference dream proved the existence and mobility of his libido. He was able to invest my own investment of his story telling, of his person, of his affects and thoughts and our sessions facilitated the recovery of his bleeding narcissism. During our sessions, I imagined the construction of a narcissistic world, living with pleasure and comfort, in a sort of sensorial fortified castle, protected from the castration threats and attacks. He related me how, after the rejection from a girl he had idolized at the age of nine, he had felt totally humiliated, and in his memory after this event, the dance became his faithful companion and the girls stopped existing for years! Suppression of the affects and denial of the object loss accompanied him loyally despite the transformations in his body and in his life, but probably they were not enough sufficient to protect him from his mental and somatic decline.

The fracture of the small bone and the painful wound of his foot acted like a reification of the castration, which psychically and bodily was not evident for him to hide and to overcome. It functioned as a trace of a traumatic attack, never healed and never more fully negative. The monster was born and grew up feeding upon his master's food. Albert had reached the top of his life and fell face to face with the monster. Could this be seen as a figure of the unbound death drive?

As the latency period of his childhood had proved unable to undertake the conditions of the oedipal world, his adult responsibilities and pleasures turned out to be fatal for his anti-castration narcissistic equilibrium. He tried in vain to re-establish a certain neutral constancy, but the pains and somatizations reminded him violently the miserable reality. He became poorly functional for his ill body and his unpleasant life exactly in the same way he had placed his dis-idealized parents towards him.

We could suggest that the hubris of a life without unpleasure, as a metaphor of the unbound eros drive, liberated the death drive against the invasion of the castration. However, in Albert's psychic world, the death drive in this context did not act in the frame of a masochistic drive fusion, but it was put into action for calming, for neutralizing an overwhelming traumatic excitation. His premature ego did not have the efficient tools to protect itself from the perceptive excitations of a reality animated by the castration rules.

For Michel Fain, failure of the primary environment leads to the creation of a defensively premature ego: "The premature ego formation could be the result of a situation of excitation, as a reaction to the inefficiency of the anaclitic objects, supposed to provide this function" (2010, 181). If the ego does not grow according and in respect to its possibilities, the excitation cannot be transformed in psychic drive work and the reality perception (either internal or external) becomes traumatic. In these cases, parts of reality are not cathected, but they are counter-cathected; this means they build psychic sectors of splitting and denial in which the death drive is demanded for calming the traumatic excitation. In cases when psychic defences of this kind, self-calming processes or acting out do not prove efficient, somatizations may appear as the last witnesses of the death drive process.

When constancy and satisfaction are missing either in primary childhood or in traumatic circumstances, masochism is unable to sustain its binding drive work and passivity becomes an enemy face to the unforeseeable. Psyche needs regression and passivity for receiving and transforming perceptions; in this way, affects and representations can be bound and registered in one of the psychic agencies. If pleasure nourishes the psychic energy, unpleasure organizes the psychic architecture. The enemies of unpleasure, like Albert, have enormous difficulties to develop rich object relations, insofar as every human relation, because of the otherness and despite of the satisfaction, comprises inexorably conflicts and suffering. Often, their solution is taking refuge in an idealized narcissistic world, covered by hyperactivity, concrete thinking and ideal ego demands.

Before concluding, I would like to outline that society cohesion and civilization promote inhibition and patience whilst the quest of pleasure must not threaten their rules and limits. The pleasure and unpleasure principles are integrated in ideal processes framed by the superego requirements. Both subjectively and socially, the avoidance of conflicts and pains may result in a life struggling against passivity and thought. In our contemporary world, we have been witnesses of social phenomena in which hyperactivity, denial in community, and destruction of thinking are emphasized and privileged. At the same time, the non-tolerance of unpleasure provokes violent actions and movements of denying submission.

Most of the times, collective conflicts, even with sacrifices, set out to transform society and often it is an incident of unpleasure that serves as the fuse of the firework. However, war, divide, and destructivity are often the consequences of personalities whose narcissism was built against the unpleasant intrusion of the primary object. The immaturity and helplessness of the human being needs time and satisfaction to construct its own maturity. Albert did not experience the latency, the adolescence, and the adulthood as processes of progressive psychic maturation; his masochism without the solid foundations of the castration patience and vision freed the forces of destruction, which had been enmeshed in the hatred of the unpleasure. His tragical figure made me imagine mythological heroes, artists, and societies who, on behalf of enemies of unpleasure, turned their intolerance and rejection against the unpleasant reality or ruined themselves, victims of their own destructivity.

References

Fain M. (2010) À propos de l'hypocondrie, *Revue française de psychosomatique*, 2010, pp. 177–184.

Fechner G. T. (1848) *Über das Lustprinzip des Handelns*, in Zeitschrift für Philosophie und Philosophische Kritik, Halle.

Fechner G. T. (1873) *Einige Ideen zur Schöpfungs- und Entiwicklungsgeschichte des Organismen*, Leipzig, Breitkopf und Härtel.

Freud S. (1900a) The Interpretation of Dreams, *SE*, vol 5 (1953)

Freud S. (1920c) Beyond the pleasure principle, *SE*, vol 18 (1955), 7–64.

Freud S. (1923b) The Ego and the Id, *SE*, vol 19 (1961), 15–59.

Freud S. (1926d [1925]) Inhibitions, symptoms and anxiety, *SE*, vol 20 (1959), 87–172.

Green A. (1980) La conjuration de l'objet. Passions et destins des passions, in *La folie privée*, Paris, Gallimard, 1990

Green A. (1993) *Le travail du négatif*, Paris, Les Éditions de Minuit.

Marty P. (1966) La dépression essentielle, *Revue française de Psychosomatique*, vol 3, 1595–1598.

Chapter 13

Resistance to Psychoanalysis

Catherine Chabert

Sometimes the engagement with analysis does not impose itself from the outset, as if the uncovering of an internal scene were not safe enough for the classical treatment to be indicated. Other treatment modalities can be suggested in such cases, especially with young patients, all the more so when their tendency to act may colonize their symptoms, sometimes in compulsive forms. After much reflection, I have decided to present one of these particular experiences: one in which, after having taken part in a patient's psychodrama treatment in an institutional setting, I extended the analytic work in private practice. This experience – a relatively common one for some of us – comes with a surprising characteristic in this instance: the patient was seemingly not the same, as if the process undertaken in psychodrama and then in analysis involved two different individuals and, virtually, two different analysts too. Psychic productions do not pertain to the same associative channels and modalities of events to the point where the analytical work seems to unfold in contrasting ways. And yet, I remain convinced that the face-to-face analysis could not have taken place without the prior experience of psychodrama, as if psychodrama had provided the waiting time for the analysis. But this thought could only come to me in retrospect, *après-coup*.

Gabrielle I

The initial reason for consultation put forward by Gabrielle was twofold and not unusual: she experienced disordered eating – some overeating but no bouts of bulimia or induced vomiting – and battled against the risk of becoming overweight through the addictive practice of running. Gabrielle would run 40 km a day through Paris; her course was methodically organized every month. In addition, she was a model young girl, she completed her high school studies without any problems, rather brilliantly but not overly, and she carried on in law school with the same resolution and ease. However, she started to be bothered by the compulsive dimension of her symptom and by a sort of reversal in causality links: at first, she was running in order not to gain weight, but now she was running in order to carry on over-eating. During her interviews with the consultant, she was very resistant to the idea of psychotherapy, and she agreed to psychodrama with some reluctance.

DOI: 10.4324/9781003384618-19

Gabrielle was a beautiful young woman who, from the first session, presented as an elegant runner. She came running and left running. She told us from the outset that she started running when she was 10, that she was now 22, and that 12 was the age difference between her and her older brother, whom she never knew and to whom she believed she owed her birth: if he had not died, why would her parents have wanted a new child so long after the other two? What she carefully hid under her ample tracksuit was a body that made her ashamed, a body that was too heavy, too round, a body whose curves exasperated her, the body of a woman she could not tolerate. She had been a skinny little girl with short hair who ran around a lot and played soccer with the boys; the brutal and slightly premature emergence of puberty had immediately mortified her: it was evidence that time was passing, that she was past the age her brother was when he died; but it was also the blatant manifestation of her difference with him: her female body was indeed proof that she was not a boy and that she could definitely not replace him.

The 18 months of psychodrama thus focused on her dead brother, on the impossibility of taking his place, on the painful constraint to have to do so, unwillingly, even though she was a girl. She spoke very little during the play sessions, and silence was one of her preferred means of expression. I don't remember much from this period, but I have not forgotten one remarkable feature of this treatment: throughout all the psychodrama sessions, Gabrielle never once chose me to play; her gaze went from one participant to the other and she visibly did not see me, so to speak. Sometimes the analyst-playmaker would include me in a scene, often as a double for her – she spoke so little – and I remember the inner speech I would voice for her in those moments, especially in one scene fittingly pertaining to her silence. I had to say: "In any case, my brother hasn't spoken for a long time, and everyone adores him … I'm not going to speak for him on top of that."

When she stopped psychodrama, she was running much less, eating less, and had found an internship with a solicitor in the provinces. She left us without any effusive thanks, and always without looking at me.

Gabrielle II

I saw her again two years later. When I saw this tall young woman all dressed in black who looked very thin, very pale, and was obviously very anxious, I did not really recognize the girl from before – she used to be a little stout and always in a tracksuit. She cried incessantly, letting tears flow abundantly, without showing them, without hiding them either, as if they did not belong to her, as if they did not come from her.

What made her cry so much? At first sight, based on what I knew of her, of her history, of her lost brother, of what was the key focus of the psychodrama, the interpretation could impose itself at the outset. She cried like the unfortunates, like the mourners of the dead, like the grieving widows, like the murderous mothers. Of course, the initial meaning that imposed itself then as manifest content was not wrong in itself. There was undoubtedly a link between her brother's death and her tears but the path going from one to the other was not clearly drawn in a linear topography. It meandered across a complicated network of representations and affects, getting lost in fantasies and sinking into the depths of childhood.

From the first months onward, Gabrielle began to speak with unexpected ease, she was almost voluble, the words flowed like tears. Very quickly, she delivered – and it was the first time she spoke about it – an unspeakable secret: she was eight years old when a cousin approached her, too closely, regularly. For her, a first link was established between her passivity, her submission to her cousin's wishes and her mother's indifference to this situation. Nothing was seen, heard, nothing was undertaken to try to understand what was happening to the child. This was a mother who was permanently bereft and paradoxically "always in good shape," displaying all the external signs of success. She was a busy woman who was never there, always concerned with her professional investments, always looking outward, toward somewhere else that seemed to absorb her completely and made her a strange figure of success, because pleasure seemed to be lacking completely.

Après-coup, her older cousin's attention took on another meaning for Gabrielle: in truth, he was tender with her and she experienced pleasure in their erotic contacts. When these ended, she believed she was rid of a situation that was heavy for her to carry. However, she became very sad, started to eat a lot and to run compulsively, no doubt mobilized, internally, by the immense sorrow of having lost the young man's attention and of having to give up this tender love whose incestuous quality distressed her and escaped her at the same time.

Such is the double destiny of infantile love, condensing at once Oedipal guilt and the anxiety tied to the loss of the object's love. Gabrielle found herself desperately alone, having furthermore gone past the limit of her brother's lifespan, this eternal child who, unlike her, never had to disappoint his parents' ideal expectations because he never made it to genital sexuality. The estrangement from her older cousin fueled the idea that her woman's body could not be looked at, that it could not induce desire and, as such, had to be attacked by her.

In my opinion, two essential elements can be highlighted in this process. The first one evidently pertains to the attentiveness, in the dynamics of the transference, to internal perceptions that had hitherto never been recognized or even identified. While displaying the most eloquent and visible signs of despair, Gabrielle could not really put them into words. Identified with the avoidant attitude that she ascribed to her mother, she had wholly thrown herself into an active over-investment of exteriority, which tended to deny what she could feel inside: the sorrow, the pain, the despair admittedly, all tied to the certainty of having failed to console her mother on the loss of the son she loved so much. The investment of the erotic and love relation with her older cousin could then also take on a mad significance: that of returning the lost son to her mother. But this over-investment of exteriority also targeted the hate entailed by narcissistic disappointment, an ambivalence that could not be recognized and the associated fear of being abandoned. The paradox was acutely striking: while denouncing the bankruptcy of her family environment, while accusing her parents and especially her mother of indifference toward her, she could not resolve to separate from them because she upheld, split within her, the equally persistent certainty that she was indispensable to them, that their already precarious universe would collapse without her: therefore she did not have the right to engage in her own life, a life that belonged to her in her own right.

The new transferential intimacy that brought us both together– and both of us only – found, in my silent listening and in her words, an associative dynamic that was conducive to interpretation; but our common past, our family history, which psychodrama had somehow constructed, made this closeness bearable and productive. I could speak to Gabrielle; I could suggest constructions with interpretative potential to her and their hypothetical dimension inscribed meaning in modalities that were less direct than those involved in psychodrama. At the same time, the form of my interventions still carried the wealth of our prior experience, notably in the dramatization that supported them.

The question of sexual identification returned substantially: to be born a girl to replace a dead boy, to grow up as a girl, a living girl, in order to become a woman, this could all be radically denied. The passivity inherent in sexual transformations and in their effects – in terms of excitation and desire – could only become known with increasing intensity. What Gabrielle kept secret for a long time, perhaps via the powerful play of repression, was her intense attachment to her father: the analysis of the transference with the analyst-playmaker in psychodrama had led to the possible emergence of this love. For a long time, Gabrielle avoided the topic of the powerful bond she had retained with the playmaker: after all, if he had wanted to, she would have engaged in analysis with him. I was therefore a second choice, or a substitute object and she kept this transferential construction to herself at first: she could not let me see her attachment to the playmaker and she could not show her mother her attachment to her father because of the fear of the rivalry and hate that it might induce in her, in me. Such love could not be recognized as the propping and Oedipal foundation that cemented it, it could not be admitted because of a tyrannical and tormenting superego that prevented her, out of loyalty to the model set by her mother, from indulging in the least form of satisfaction, in the slightest sign of pleasure.

The same dynamic that led Gabrielle to engage with a female analyst – a displacement, a transference – elicited the uncovering of the essential place held by her father in the construction of her history. It was essential in the narcissistic identifications that welded them together: a father as silent and suffering as his daughter; it was also essential when she was able to discover, to accept, to build that the love of her father was hers in full. In other words, it did not only apply to the child – the boy child, the lost child, the neutral child in her bisexuality – but that it applied just as much, if not more, to the girl that she was, the little girl who, in her difference, supported the belief that she, at least, would remain alive.

Here is the first epilogue that I could have written after some time: the young woman is still pursuing her analysis with me, she is blossoming in her career; she left the dark and persecutory partner who was her first love; she met a young man whom she can't really think of herself as being in love with; she gets along with her family well enough to be less dependent on them. It recently occurred to her that, all going well, she would have to leave me and she then immediately informed me of the – temporary – return of her symptom – as if her symptom alone could justify my attention and my interest in her.

This cue and her wish to continue the analysis encouraged me to pursue the treatment. Despite the positive effects, I remained perplexed by two characteristics that persisted in the analytic process: the first one had to do with the transference whose stability and positivity never wavered; the second one had to do with the total lack of any dream memory in my patient. These two elements made me think that the interiority of the analytic scene remained fragile and precarious: she could not take the risk of any form of aggressive expression and she did not allow the emergence of wishes via the mediation of dreams. In this double hurdle, I saw the massive effects of a superego that remained as harsh and severe as ever, badly tolerated drive-related satisfaction and persisted in masochistic and persecutory torment.

One of the most striking psychic manifestations of the superego consists in the massive reversal of aggressiveness that becomes directed against the ego, a reversal likely to pave the way to self-sabotage, if not self-destruction. The mechanisms of melancholia can be distinctly identified in this context: the self-reproaches and the attacks that patients inflict upon themselves are originally intended for the beloved and disappointing object and they in fact target the latter and reach their goal thanks to narcissistic regression.

What accounts for the magnitude of the anguish and the attacks against the ego – via the violence imposed on body and psyche – is the fact that the superego fails to hold its protective function: the capacity for renunciation while avoiding destruction can be considered as an effect of this function. This vicissitude of guilt highlights the living part of the ego whose tie to the object is unbreakable; in the course taken by melancholia conversely, the living part of the ego is discarded and the subject gets mired in a narcissistic solution featuring the highjacking of an object that is intro jected but dead.

However, the strength of the superego can be gauged by the power of the drive-related energy and the wishes that it fuels: the more intense the wishes, the harsher the superego. Its deadly violence also tallies with the excess in desire. Arising in a barrage of love and hate impulses that are deficiently bound together and encroach on the ego's borders with sometimes barbaric magnitude, the tyrannical savagery of the melancholic superego is in some way consubstantial with the incestuous impact of the Oedipus complex, with the preservation of and the need for no-separation and with the permanence of a merger with the object which inevitably results in confusion. Via narcissistic regression, a despotic and cruel superego emerges in the confusion of roles – criminal and executioner. And the share of pleasure drawn from the masochistic scenario that is concurrently at play continues to fuel the fury of the superego, as long as this scenario remains operative. But when this share of pleasure dissipates, so does the only condition to remain alive.

Many psychoanalysts, and not only female analysts, have objected to Freud's view of the female superego: Freud states that its functioning is clearly defective in women. However, the superego loses its strength as a result of the deficiency, if not the failure of its protective function, while the critical function remains harsh and unyielding: the alleviation that tenderness and benevolence may bring does not apply and the girl's tendency to suppress her aggressiveness and turn it against herself grossly and relentlessly fuels the accusatory part. The possible relief entailed by this reversal can, in turn, sustain a punitive logic, sometimes in a compulsive form: the question of being loved by the superego remains open, like a tentative breach, waiting to be filled, in keeping with the sense of safety which remains just as precarious. Girls would therefore remain fixated on this "primal" way of expressing guilt and bound to the fear of losing parental love. This primal form of expression confirms the superego's lack of independence as underlined by Freud. Such lack of independence naturally reinforces the attachment to love objects, to their gaze and to their judgment.

If guilt refers to the superego, if it emerges because aggressiveness has been turned against the ego, if it translates into a dependency on "being ill," it seems hard to think that the feminine superego is in fact weak and deficient. When it is a major source of psychic suffering, such deficiency can rather be seen as a departure from a well-tempered ambivalence that ensures a good arrangement for the object as well as for the ego – this servant torn between competing masters. The feminine superego (and not only the superego of women) could thus consist in the tyrannical and harsh form of moral conscience – the least loving and the most powerful form. This may account for its occasional lack of tolerance as it bears the full mark of the absence of love, a dynamic obstructed by anxiety and its persecutory corollaries. Its devastating action affects the most precious objects, the most anticipated ones, and, among them, the body and the child, the representatives of fertility, creativity and therefore, of sexuality and life.

Slowly, surreptitiously, Gabrielle embarked on a transferential path that brought to light her way of attacking her objects: unknowingly, she undid the most essential aspect in her life, which the analysis had allowed her to construct, her love bond with a man she did not want to know she loved. When they settled down to live together, she inflicted on him all the constraints of her obsessionality, all her domestic preoccupations, combined with her feminist demands; she humiliated him by making him feel the gap between their two cultures. He resisted. To her, the decisive moment came about: the meeting with her boyfriend's family, and above all the meeting with his mother. In the weeks that preceded this confrontation, she questioned everything, she was convinced that she did not really love her partner, she became odious, he left her.

What appeared to me very quickly, in this instance, was the transferential dimension of her acting out: if the analysis had allowed the young woman to let go of her ghosts and to reconcile herself with her internal objects, she could not for all that tolerate this success, she could not recognize it as the outcome of her link with her analyst. We could, of course, bring up the negative therapeutic reaction – it resonates with what we have said about the compulsion to happiness, about the superego, about masochism and melancholia. Failing consisted in using acts to attack her links, the only possible way to implement a negative transference, via the repetition of her compulsive self-destruction and its ambivalent underpinning: she was attacking me by hurting herself, she was offering herself as a victim so that I would stay alive, so that the analysis would continue. Gabrielle set herself up as a shield to protect the object (mother) against the attacks that might destroy it (her). "I destroy myself so that you remain alive," here is a scenario that is relatively easy to construct, even though this somewhat simplistic formulation is but one aspect of a much more complex organization whose narcissistic foundation is obvious: "The protection I offer you is the one that I expected from you, you who abandoned me because I betrayed you or you believed I did." Doing for the other what we expect from them, out of the certainty of never having had our share, is this not the most frequent form of action when words are not enough?

Such is perhaps one of the most active elements of resistance: to remain ill to maintain the analysis, to prevent the separation, to block the death fantasies tied to the disappearance of the analyst. I return to that famous – and scandalous – section by Freud:

- When you have found the right interpretations, a new task presents itself to you. You have to wait for the right moment to communicate your interpretation to the patient …
- How do you know when the right moment is?
- It is a matter of tact […] the rule is to wait until he [the patient] is close enough that, under the guidance of the interpretation proposed by you, he has only a few steps to take …
- I don't think I'll ever learn that. And when, in the interpretation, I have obeyed these precautions, what then?
- Then it is reserved for you to make a discovery for which you are not prepared.
- Which would be?
- That you have misunderstood your patient, that you have absolutely no right to count on his help or his docility, that he is ready to obstruct the common work by all possible difficulties, in a word: he especially does not want to heal. (Freud, 1926, p.250)

Without resistance, there is no analysis: hysteria is a good testament to this, and, in the crucible of seduction, it shows the actualization of the forces of repulsion, at the service of repression "demonstrated by the undeniable fact of resistance." "This model offers a violent depiction of the analytic action between patient and analyst: one must "unearth" the infantile character of the patient," Freud writes to Fliess (1897), in order "to make him bend," to "throw the interpretation in his face" so that the resistance may become an objective and tangible thing. What follows is of interest to us: this initial confrontation, this clash of brute forces will later be abandoned in favor of infinite patience, of measured waiting and unfailing endurance – between speech and silence. But for the time being, the struggle against resistance looks like conquest.

This procedure, directly linked with the analytic treatment of hysteria, obviously contains a scene of suggestion, a scene of seduction between a father/analyst who is both exciting and constraining and a child/patient who resists and refuses to give in. Featured here, already, are the kernels from which, much later, the fantasy of "A child is being beaten" will crucially grow (Freud, 1919), unfolding the wish for love and its satisfaction via a scene involving blows and the priceless workings of a reversal into the opposite.

The next stage, that of the discovery and recognition of the transference, leads Freud even further: why is it, he asks, that, in the analysis, the transference opposes the strongest resistance when, in other situations, it can be considered a major healing agent? It is because resistance stamps any idea, any action likely to provide a compromise between the forces tending toward recovery and those that oppose it. The transference arises precisely at this point of convergence: "Each time an element of the infantile complex is transferred to the person of the doctor, the transference takes place, provides the next idea and manifests itself in the form of a resistance" (Freud, 1912, p.100). The personification inherent in the transference via the displacement of images and affects elicits, to some extent, the embodiment of the resistance through the fluctuating play of identifications.

One can be surprised and even object to the necessity of this embodiment: the resort to human representations and, among them, the choice of the most familiar ones – e.g. father and mother – might be an attempt to tame what induces fear in the unknown of the resistance, fiercely violent as it sometimes gets. But the resistance perhaps precisely summons these images to signal the power of these representations, or at least their force of attraction. Freud initially locates the resistances mainly on the side of the father, within the complex of which he is the center, a complex constituted by insurgence and challenge, a "no" to his power and to the threat he utters. But the mother, who is ever present in his shadow, could also inhibit any dynamics of investment and defeat any progress toward change.

Regardless of their identificatory inflections, the resistances are always featured in scenes that are both similar and different: similar in the sense that the two protagonists are, obviously, the patient and the analyst; different in the sense that the fantasy or the fantasies that orchestrate them emerge in a plurality of versions, in the variations of the drive-related dynamics and the representations that process them. Such variations developed during Gabrielle's treatment: the same scenes returned but took on a different meaning.

Due to its conflicted affects, transferential ambivalence inevitably entails an alternation between a positive representation of the analyst – a trustful representation, undoubtedly directed to and by self-preservation – and a negative representation – a troubling, alien representation borne by sexuality. Ambivalence must be interpreted but choosing the right moment is testing. How can one find the words to convey love as well as hate, the good and the bad analyst? Between the two, the fight is suspended because the victory of one or the other involves a risk of loss: the fear of losing the object's love becomes an actual threat if a self-preservative surge rises up against the erotic aspects; the fear of losing the containment of the ego becomes overwhelming if the spark of love escalates into transferential passion. On the one hand, narcissistic isolation harbors a major resistance, the hardened core of the struggle against the effects of the analysis; on the other hand, the shadow of dependence – however daunting the state of dependence may be – looms in the irrepressible attraction to the other, to the prospects of seduction on offer, the promise of a return to childhood, to its wishes, its pleasures, and its pain.

The superego is a force that is often blind, intolerant to difference, and crudely impervious, and we must take it on board when considering the development of girls and the question of "how one becomes a woman" (Freud, 1933). Featured centrally is the object choice whose extreme complexity is common knowledge, caught up as it is in the networks of identifications. For the girl – for Gabrielle – the change in object, the investment of the father, is justified by the early disappointment of the link with the mother and, in itself, it can already constitute a betrayal, exacerbated by the wish to take the mother's place in relation to the father. The risk incurred is very high: she might lose the love of the mother who is already suspected of deficiency for not having given everything; she might destroy the vital affection that ensures narcissistic investment and buttresses the initial formation of identifications, which crucially mobilizes the drive-related forces that sustain the feeling of existence and its libidinal continuity.

I mention these metapsychological developments because, in my view, they bolster the counter-transferential process that underlies the work of construction and inter-pretation, at the service of the discretion and the vital wait that are required to avoid undue hastiness. In the presentation of Gabrielle's analysis, it is difficult for me to recapture my own words and only a detour via theory and method allows me to explore the singularity of this treatment. In fact, I think that interpretation does not only pertain to an elucidation of the meaning arising solely from our listening to the pa-tient's words; in its unconscious resonance, the analyst's countertransference implies not only their own analytic experience but also their metapsychological investigations, which offer a substantial contribution to the analyst's anticipatory activity in its counter-transferential dimension. Obviously, it is not a matter of imposing dogmatic or systematic configurations in any way: the distortion inherent in the transference forces us to consider the singularity of these configurations within the psychic reality of each patient, in each therapeutic undertaking. As far as Gabrielle's treatment is concerned, if I had not looked for the father, I would not have been able to hear the strength of his psychic presence in his daughter: I had to reverse the Freudian adage – behind the father, the mother – into a singular dynamic: behind the mother, the father!

The violence of Gabrielle against her objects was determined by the overflow of an excited and disappointed ego, monopolized by the magnitude of its expectations, its wishes, and its claims, as well as by the power of its dependence. The repetition compulsion unfolded an alienating cycle on a loop: the lack of expected satisfaction weakened the ego's footing and condensed its attacks against the disappointing object, but the ego was equally hit. I was able to show her her twofold unconscious aim: to damage or destroy her mother (or me?) but also to damage or destroy herself.

During Gabrielle's analysis, this scenario was actualized in an almost caricatural way: I seemingly hastened to grant a positive value to her love encounter – I said nothing or almost nothing about it, just a question whose interpretative scope undoubtedly escaped me: "Why would you not have the right to fall in love?" I might have been better off keeping quiet because the interpretation and the analogical realization of desire that it could convey led to a worsening of Gabrielle's resistances. The increase in the repetition compulsion entailed intense discontent, displeasure, and pain: one can consider this traversal the denial or the impossibility to admit that a change bringing pleasure could ever occur. The resistance then consists, for the patient, in fighting bitterly against the emergence of any sign of change, and it manifests as psychic pain displayed with the relentlessness of despair.

In such extreme moments, the negative therapeutic reaction very specifically implies the refusal to heal, the rejection of the benefits of the treatment whose toxic, diabolical dimension it exposes in order to uphold the suffering stance of moral masochism against all odds: indeed, there is no way to go against the aims prescribed by the forces of destiny, behind which the tyrannical injunctions of the parental figures hide. With Gabrielle, the resistances were embodied not only in reference to a seductive father but also to a controlling and powerful mother who guarded her power jealously and could not bear to share, enslaving her child to her sole needs. In this abusive influence, Gabrielle drew a surplus of pleasure from the belief that she was indispensable to her mother (and her analyst) – perhaps a precarious belief but one she vehemently defended all the same.

In this negative persistence against her love bond, one must hear the refusal of passivity and therefore the refusal to be loved, if one accepts Freud's proposition that the passive position is most obviously put to the test in the fact of "being loved." "Being loved" constitutes the very essence of femininity and the fear of losing love is the equivalent of castration anxiety in men. Being loved *can* be intolerable; the pleasure inherent in this discovery or this recognition *can* generate extreme displeasure; renouncing pain *can* be inadmissible; the idea of a possible cure *can* prompt a perpetual fight against healing. Happiness and the pleasure of living *can* appear as an unbearable constraint in view of an active form of masochism that mobilizes a tyrannical and vengeful superego.

This scandalous assertion – the cruel constraint of happiness – is however commonly found in the current pathologies dedicated to compulsive self-destruction. In such situations, the superego loses its civilizing aims, its benevolent dimension is erased in favor of a barbarity that primarily victimizes the subject but equally targets the object – the mother.

Gabrielle sank into one of these inescapable melancholic moments (Chabert, 2003), which are sometimes crucial in the unfolding of a treatment: this melancholic period could however be transformed into true love despair with the paradox that it maintains: the loss of love and the certainty to find it again. This is exactly what happened once she was able to hear that her self-destructiveness was aimed at me too, since she was violently attacking the analytic work and its effects, even though, in this process, she was sacrificing her life as a young woman, her future, her happiness. By continuing to be unwell and by continuing her analysis with me for ever, she might have found a way of protecting me from an impossible separation, a devastating renunciation so as not to lose me as she had thought she had lost her mother by having a life of her own.

Epilogue

At the end of this melancholic period, Gabrielle decided to return to her lover: she was lucky, he was waiting for her! Her wedding preparations, somewhere between joy and anguish, made up the living matter of her sessions. I was the witness of all the vulnerabilities of her emotional states, her exhilarating joys and her disheartening doubts. I knew how fragile her choices could be and how they could turn against her. The date of the wedding arrived: the day before, Gabrielle spoke to me at length about her finally completed wedding dress. But I was not allowed to hear the story of the wedding party: Gabrielle did not come back, she stopped her analysis precisely at this moment in her life, without a word for her analyst.

References

Chabert, C. (2003) *Féminin mélancolique*, Paris, PUF.

Freud, S. (1897) Letter from Freud to Fliess, May 25, 1897. *The Complete Letters of Sigmund Freud to Wilhelm Fliess, 1887–1904* 42:245–246.

Freud, S. (1912) The Dynamics of Transference. *The Standard Edition of the Complete Psychological Works of Sigmund Freud* 12:97–108.

Freud, S. (1919) 'A Child is Being Beaten' A Contribution to the Study of the Origin of Sexual Perversions. *The Standard Edition of the Complete Psychological Works of Sigmund Freud* 17:175–204.

Freud, S. (1926) The Question of Lay Analysis. *The Standard Edition of the Complete Psychological Works of Sigmund Freud* 20:177–258.

Freud, S. (1933) New Introductory Lectures On Psycho-Analysis. *The Standard Edition of the Complete Psychological Works of Sigmund Freud* 22:1–182 Lecture XXXIII Femininity, p.111–135.

Chapter 14

"Unjoined Persons" [*]

Psychic Isolation and Bodily Symptoms in Adolescence

Mary T. Brady

Bodily changes and psychological separation from parents can lead to painful states of psychic isolation for some adolescents, when all that is new cannot be easily expressed or even thought. Although psychic isolation is possible at any age, it is particularly prevalent in adolescence for developmental reasons. I conceive of adolescent psychic isolation as an affective state with important developmental underpinnings. The affective elements are estrangement and loneliness, and sometimes a feeling of freakishness. The developmental underpinnings include shifting (conscious as well as unconscious, internal as well as external) object relations and senses of the self. While there could be limitless variations of the experience of psychic isolation in adolescence, there is a common developmental trend. I am not referring specifically to teens who are socially isolated, but to an internal state (see Barrett, 2008, who comments that the driven way some adolescents socialize can be misconstrued as if they are not lonely, rather than as a defense against loneliness).

I suggest adolescents are the group most affected by rapid cultural changes and that adolescents are more alone than ever before. It would seem that all adolescents suffer the strangeness of bodily changes somewhat alone. And yet some elements of adolescent loneliness are contemporary developments. Pressures on contemporary adolescents can leave them very little room for an inner, intimate space. Many adolescents I work with are highly scheduled and are in settings over-focused on external markers of success.

Transitory or lingering states of psychic isolation are common for adolescents, but also interact with other affective and developmentally related experiences such as rage, rebelliousness, depression, mourning, sexual confusion, spontaneity, individuating, and identity formation. I focus on psychic isolation in this first chapter for two reasons. First, I think it has not been sufficiently discussed in the psychoanalytic literature (psychic isolation is a frequent theme in literature written about

---

[*] From Brady, M.T. (2015). 'Unjoined persons': psychic isolation in adolescence and its relation to bodily symptoms. *Journal of Child Psychotherapy*, 41(2), 179–194. Reprinted with permission from Taylor & Francis.

DOI: 10.4324/9781003384618-20

adolescents, such as *The Member of the Wedding* (McCullers, 1946) or *Catcher in the Rye,* (Salinger, 1951)), as well as literature written for adolescents, such as the post-apocalyptic *City of Ember* series (DuPrau, 2003) (described to me at length by a pubescent boy). Second, psychic isolation can leave the adolescent cut off from others who can contain, relegating his body as the likely receptacle for troubles.

Mourning (Wolfenstein, 1966; Green, 2013) is a fundamental aspect of adolescence. The adolescent process requires withdrawal from childhood love objects (particularly in relation to authority and erotic attachment) in order for development to proceed (Katan, 1951). Unconscious mourning of parental love objects is one element that can contribute to psychic isolation, but so can a feeling of strangeness at one's body changing unbidden. One latency age girl told me that her early adolescent sister had sworn her to secrecy regarding having hair start to grow under one arm, but not yet the other. Of course, it is easy to imagine that the younger girl was previewing her own impending physical changes. Yet, what seemed closer at hand was a sense that it was mysterious to her why her older sister felt so much turmoil about her bodily developments. She knew that her sister felt shameful and bizarre, but she could not yet understand what it meant.

When an adolescent is cut off from internal and external containing objects or aspects of the self that could be fallen back on in latency, he or she can take drastic measures. Feeling cut off from one's own or others' minds can leave chaotic emotions to be played out on the body. I will propose here that psychic isolation can make adolescents particularly vulnerable to reliance on somatic symptoms (eating disorders, cutting, substance abuse, suicide attempts, etc.). Without an understanding of adolescent states of mind, bodily symptoms can be misunderstood as reflective of greater disturbance than sometimes is the case during the fluctuating mental states of adolescence.

Bodily changes and separation processes in adolescence create pressures on the mind that can lead to astonishing new ways of thinking and relating. Bion saw separation or lack as the pre-requisite for thinking. In Bion's (1967) "theory of thinking," he says the mind (mental container) is stimulated to think when it senses the "breast" is no longer available (p. 112). Bion's ideas are particularly relevant to the psychic separation processes of adolescence, which can cause a pressure or need to think and to develop. At the same time, the strains of separation that cannot be tolerated can also lead to projective identification, sometimes expressed somatically.

Although Bion did not himself treat adolescents, several of his conceptualizations are helpful in understanding adolescent states (Brady et al., 2012). As is well-known, Bion extends Klein's understanding of projective identification as a defense to seeing projective identification as a beginning form of thinking and communication. The infant expels unbearable anxiety into the mother's mental container, where "maternal reverie" (Bion, 1962, p. 36) can transform it into bearable elements that can be thought about. If mother receives her infant's fears, they are modified in such a way that when the infant re-introjects them, they become tolerable. Translating this into the language of adolescent development: unmetabolized states (for instance intense sexual feelings or separation fears) are sometimes expressed or evacuated in some chaotic action (for instance self-cutting or wrecking the family car). Thus, parents or analysts are confronted with new and sometimes life-threatening situations and are being asked to metabolize adolescents' intense states.

The physical symptoms of adolescence are like the desperate cries of a baby seeking a mind that can encompass them. When an unimaginable experience is shared with someone who has the capacity to comprehend it, beta elements are transformed by alpha function. An aspect of experience is digested. (Beta elements are experienced as things in themselves, not as something to observe or think about, propelling projective identification and acting out.) Bion (1962) distinguishes "the class of muscular action" from the realms of thought (p. 13). For instance, purging could be thought of as a somatic effort to rid the self of beta elements. Alpha function develops when an adolescent begins to wonder with their analyst about the motivations in their desire to purge.

Bion is clear that this process is not just a cognitive reconsideration, but also an emotional experience. Through repeated experiences of being understood (the translation of beta elements by alpha function through "maternal reverie"), he says, "there arises the apparatus for thinking the thoughts" (1962, p. 92). The child internalizes the experience of the containing function. Thus, not only might an adolescent feel understood, but is gradually internalizing a new containing structure[1] in relation to their emerging bodily experiences.

Adolescent states of mind are very much contents seeking a container. In the face of profound psychological shifts and identity development, the capacity of the adolescent's objects to be containing becomes more crucial. When intense adolescent experiences are not met by either internal or external processes of containment, they degenerate into "inanimate" (1962, p. 14) exchanges, where there is no reverie and no containment. This leaves some adolescents trapped in repetitive physical symptoms, which threaten chronicity. Bion suggests that learning depends on the capacity for the container to remain integrated, but not be rigid. This allows the individual to retain his knowledge and yet be receptive of a new idea. This is relevant in adolescence. Parents and children must somehow retain some sense of who they were to each other, while undergoing sometimes violent throes of a "new idea"—that the child is no longer a child. This is a profoundly interactive and experiential process.

In adolescence, previous containing structures of the mind can break down because they cannot sustain all that is new (e.g., new fantasies and experiences of the self related to menarche and first wet dreams). New structures and senses of the self must be created. Yet, adolescents are often not ready to enter the psychic spaces their bodies are propelling them into.

The term "break down" is not used here in the psychiatric sense, but with the broader meaning of breakdowns in psychological space, for instance, in desperate self-destructive acts, which convey a psychotic aspect of the personality. When a psychotic aspect of the personality is in ascendance, the capacity for development breaks down. Of course, there is a spectrum of the extent and persistence of the breakdown. The adolescent process in fact requires the re-organization of the personality, as the former organization cannot contain the meanings of new developments, such as menstruation or sexual penetration. Anderson and Dartington (1998) contend that the adolescent process requires the "experience of being out of balance" and suggest that those adolescents "who have the inner strength and resources to bear to continue the experience of being naturally out of balance, as well as an environment that can support this … can achieve the best adjustment in adult life" (p. 3).

When the adolescent mind is overwhelmed and a containing object is not available, the body can receive and express evacuative projective identifications or concretely express evocative forms of projective identification. Although a desperate measure, a physical symptom can stimulate the container/contained to growth by conveying that there is something urgent to be understood.

Anderson, influenced by Klein and Bion, describes that in latency, the non-psychotic or integrative parts of the personality may be in ascendance, "which try to make order, and in which paranoid-schizoid functioning moves toward depressive functioning toward a wholeness, whole objects and cooperating objects, like the two parents" (2005, p. 3). He sees latency as "an uneasy truce, a compromise between conflicting desires and priorities, which could hold, provided the tensions were not too great" (pp. 2–3).

The pressure of adolescence[2] and adolescent developmental crises can lead to psychotic or disintegrative aspects of the personality becoming prevalent, along with reliance on severe splitting, expelling, and disowning. "Children who had felt or appeared quite healthy, or at most a little nervous, can suffer quite serious break-downs as a result of even moderate extra strains," particularly at the onset of puberty (Klein, 1922, p. 55). Psychic issues can be expressed in somatic symptoms at any age (Burloux, 2005); however, the body has a particularly magnetic relationship with the mind in adolescence. Bodily based disturbances can be seen as "an exaggeration and a shift of the balance in the personality, rather than simply a set of aberrant developmental processes" (Anderson, 2005, p. 2).

Individuals enter adolescence with various internal capacities and environmental provisions. Stage theories (see for example, Levy Warren, 1996 for a discussion of the sub-phases of adolescence) describe developmental similarities within a particular phase. Stage theories capture certain elements; clearly, there are significant observable differences between an early adolescent and a late adolescent. The Kleinian conceptualization of "positions" and the Bionian conceptualizations of the ascendance of psychotic or non-psychotic elements of the personality capture the fluctuating mental states of adolescence. There is a necessary tension between developmental and diagnostic generalities on the one hand, and considerations of internal variability, fluctuation, and process on the other (see Corbett, 2001, for a discussion of the tension between views which emphasize similarity and coherence versus views which emphasize subjectivity and variability).

The adolescent personality is under considerable duress to absorb the meanings of new sexual and procreative capacities. Both early adolescence, in general (Erikson, 1956; Blos, 1967), and menstruation, in particular (Ritvo, 1976), have been discussed as normative crises. Ritvo describes menarche as having all the characteristics of a normal developmental crisis that can provide a stimulus or be an obstacle to development—in other words, leading to breakthrough or breakdown.

In my clinical experience, the sense of psychic isolation is greatest at early adolescence, but some element can re-emerge throughout adolescence. Early adolescence has been written about as the most difficult time to initiate therapy (Fraiberg, 1955) and as the time when there is the heaviest "burden of the unexpressed" (Harley, 1970).

Gardner (2001) sees the physiological changes of adolescence along with related fantasies as contributing to a sense of bodily estrangement: "the sense of the body as different, as being an object, something apart and separate from the self" (p. 61).

She sees this bodily estrangement as a crucial element in self-cutting:

> For the person who harms themselves the body is being treated as something other and apart from the self. In this way it provides both the target and receptacle for unmanageable feelings and uncontrollable instinctual impulses. This new relationship to the body is fundamentally one of disconnection, not integration, although the paradox is that only through disconnection can the body become the containing object for the fragile and fragmenting self.
>
> (p. 61)

Separation from internal and external parental objects leads to a loss of auxiliary ego and superego functions. This results in the notable instability in functioning of adolescents—seen in their dizzying shifts from acute sensitivity to insensitivity at rapid intervals. The estrangement from objects and from prior experiences of the self is well-captured in Carson McCullers's (1946) phrase "an unjoined person" (p. 3).

It can be difficult for the analyst of an adolescent to know whether a psychotic state will be a transient upheaval or something far more ominous. Eating disorders later in life have a feel different from they do in adolescence. In adolescence, an eating disorder conveys an immediate developmental problem threatening to shut down the growth of the personality. Later in life, eating disorders often acquire the sense of an established way of holding the self together.

Analysts of adolescents are well aware the transitions into high school and college are periods of risk. The onset of puberty (sometimes coinciding with the transition into high school) is a classic time for the onset of eating disorders. One patient related that the onset of her eating disorder occurred as she binged on what was left of her Bat Mitzvah cake. She was unready for the social, sexual, and academic developments ahead and broke down into an eating disorder. The familiarity of day-to-day life, family, and community at least eases the experience of psychic isolation. One anorectic late adolescent told me of her first dream when she went to college—her body was thrown by a bomb blast which her parents and I might see from far away on television. Her containing objects seemed too far away to be of much use in the catastrophe of separation.

In the next section, I use Carson McCullers's great 1946 novel, *The Member of the Wedding,* to evoke adolescent developmental unrest and psychic isolation. I then give a brief clinical example of psychic isolation in adolescence. Next, I will link psychic isolation with vulnerability to the propensity for the breakdown into bodily symptoms in adolescence. Then, I will give a clinical example in which a physical symptom (cutting) was transient.

A Literary Version of Adolescent Psychic Isolation

Carson McCullers's *The Member of the Wedding* is set in small-town Alabama. Centering on twelve-year-old Frankie and the unnamable forces in motion within her, the story takes place over a handful of long, hot summer days, primarily in the kitchen, Frankie shares with her family's African-American cook, Berenice Sadie Brown, and her six-year-old cousin, John Henry. Frankie's mother died giving birth to her. Her father remains a shadowy figure around the edges of the story. Frankie looks at him "slant-eyed" after he tells her she is now too big to come and sleep in his bed every night.

The novel palpably conveys the sense of a girl having outgrown who she has known herself to be and not yet comprehending any way forward for herself. Too old now to play with the younger children, she is not yet accepted by the older girls whom she senses have crossed some bridge into sexual understanding that she has not. She adopts a new name, "F. Jasmine," in order to leave behind the childish Frankie. The kitchen setting captures the inwardness of the changes taking place, while perverse racial inequalities and the catastrophes of World War II lurk in the background. In a central scene Frankie/F. Jasmine tries to name her uneasy, no-longer-child thoughts to Berenice:

> What I've been trying to say is this. Doesn't it strike you as strange that I am I, and you are you? I am F. Jasmine Addams. And you are Berenice Sadie Brown. And we can look at each other, and touch each other, and stay together year in and year out in the same room. Yet always I am I, and you are you. And I can't ever be anything else but me, and you can't ever be anything else but you. Have you ever thought of that? And does it seem to you strange?
>
> (pp. 114–15)

Berenice responds:

> We all of us somehow caught. We born this way or that way and we don't know why. But we caught anyhow. I born Berenice. You born Frankie. John Henry born John Henry. And maybe we wants to widen and bust free. But no matter what we do we still caught. Me is me and you is you and he is he ... Is that what you was trying to say?"
>
> (p. 119)

F. Jasmine says yes, and goes on:

> Sometimes I feel like I want to break something, too. I feel like I wish I could just tear down the whole town ... . Yet at the same time you almost might use the

word loose instead of caught. Although they are two opposite words. I mean you walk around and you see all the people. And to me they look loose.

(p. 120)

In this exchange, the tone between Berenice and Frankie has shifted from previous conversations. Berenice is now talking to Frankie as an equal who understands something of the complexities of life, instead of as a child to be protected from them. Berenice adds the word "caught" to Frankie's thoughts—like a good analyst, she understands what Frankie is saying and adds a new shape to it. Berenice's understanding of her thoughts seems to allow Frankie to elaborate them. Frankie's wish to "break something" to "tear down the whole town" implies an urge to physically break through her feeling of strangeness and isolation (consonant with the physical breakthroughs going on in her). Able to express her feelings to a containing other (someone who can apprehend, share, and tolerate her experience), she finds another way than being isolated and trapped in physical expressions.

This sort of exchange captures what is compelling about treating adolescents. There is an urgency to figure things out, to grapple with who we are, what our place and meaning in the universe is. The urgency and sense of estrangement are sometimes captured in poignant words (as in the above passage) and sometimes can only find expression by some other drastic means.

The adolescent is caught in psychic isolation in many ways—caught in an awareness of things one is not ready for yet. Caught in sexuality and gender being more defined and intense, gone is the "uneasy truce" of latency. Caught in a body transforming seemingly with a will of its own, caught in inexorable changes with parents, or parental figures such as Berenice Sadie Brown is to Frankie, and caught in the impending challenge to define a role in the larger world. The isolation is also experienced as being loose. One's own experiences seem strange and impossible to convey. One is both caught and loose at the same time. While it is true that people of any age may be caught between the effort to find words or to resort to drastic action, it is particularly true for adolescents.[3]

A Clinical Example of Psychic Isolation in Adolescence

Eleanor

"Eleanor," a thirteen-year-old whom I had seen in analysis for a year, did not tell me when she started to menstruate. When she finally did, she said: "I felt like I was glued on a fence between kid and teenager and that telling you that I started my period would be going over the fence." She said that then she would be caught in adolescence and not as free to feel she might be on either side of the fence. She said "I'm used to love in my family, not outside of it. In the family I can be myself—that love is like I can tie my shoes or leave them untied. Love outside my family, that's a different kind of love, like a tight love, right there." The flowing sense of being part of a family as a child felt threatened by her immanent sense of a relationship outside her family.

Indeed, Eleanor's presenting symptom was that she had developed a phobia that she would be kidnapped. When I first met her she told me: "In my house I think there are people who watch me when I walk down the hall. I think someone's watching me who wants to kidnap me." Eleanor's fantasy of a "kid"-napper conveyed a beginning conception of a new object who at this point felt more dangerous than exciting. Eleanor's fears caused her waking world to be infiltrated by a nightmare state. Her analysis provided an opportunity for a transitional space where she could be kidnapped and not kidnapped by me, in a way that could be named and elaborated and was in some ways under her control. These issues particularly emerged around increasing the frequency of our meetings. Her psychic space for development had broken down into concrete fears of being kidnapped—an excellent metaphor for being caught and isolated from her younger self and her childhood objects. Her prior psychic structures could not contain the mental developments concomitant with the changes in her body and in her wishes. Her fear was heard by her concerned parents and eventually allowed a breakthrough of developmental experiences that could be contained in her family and in her analysis.

I use the term "changes in internal and external object relations" in this chapter, but I do not mean to equate them. For instance, there can be a change (such as withdrawal) from actual parents, while internal object relations may be quite intense, such as fears of incestuous contact and fears of murder.

Bodily Expressions of Psychic Pain

Some adolescents can only convey the breakthrough of something they cannot psychically handle through a bodily expression of crisis. McCullers (1946) describes Frankie in a state of tension and the attempt to manage it physically:

> Just at that moment a horn began to play. ... The tune was grieving and low. It was the sad horn of some colored boy, but who he was she did not know. Frankie stood stiff, her head bent and her eyes closed, listening. There was something about the tune that brought back to her all of the spring: flowers, the eyes of strangers, rain.

> The tune was low and dark and sad. Then all at once, as Frankie listened, the horn danced into a wild jazz spangle that zigzagged upward. At the end of the jazz spangle the music rattled thin and far away. Then the tune returned to the first blues song, and it was like the telling of that long season of trouble. She stood there on the dark sidewalk and the drawn tightness of her heart made her knees lock and her throat feel stiffened. Then without warning, the thing happened that at first Frankie could not believe. Just at the time when the tune should be laid, the music finished, the horn broke off ... . For a moment Frankie could not take it in, she felt so lost.

> ... And the drawn tightness she could no longer stand. She felt she must do something wild and sudden that never had been done before. She hit herself on the head with her fist, but that did not help any at all.
>
> (p. 44)

The music expressed Frankie's saddest, wildest emotions and gave her a sense of something or someone she could be connected to. When she loses this consolation, she is trapped in her own separateness again. Maybe she hit herself on the head to try to capture what she is feeling, and to express rage at her head for what it cannot yet understand. As I imagine what Frankie might be feeling in this moment, I realize that this instance is like many moments with adolescents. They present themselves to us with some physical symptom—having banged their head against the wall, or cut themselves. As analysts we begin to try to imagine with them what compelled them to hurt themselves. Sometimes this sort of thinking can be the beginning of becoming freed from self-destructive acts. At the same time, I cannot help but think of teens who feel horrified to have these acts thought about. Seemingly, they would rather leave these acts private and not have them intruded into.

One could ask if it is useful to group the bodily symptoms of adolescence together in this way. Undoubtedly, there are differences between why one cuts and why one starves oneself. There are also meaningful differences among patients with comparatively similar symptomatic presentations. Nevertheless, I have found it useful to conceptualize bodily symptoms as expressing related developmental issues during adolescence. When an adolescent arrives in an analyst's office saying he cuts himself, he immediately draws attention to his body. Of course, confusion about the body is not the only source of the desire to hurt oneself in adolescence. The urge to stop overwhelming psychic pain and shift it into a visible bodily pain, or to hurt a parent by hurting oneself, are examples of other motivations. However, I consider the bodily symptoms of adolescence to be like radioactive markers signaling the body as a source of confusion and distress.[4]

While the extremes of bodily symptoms may appear to us as bizarre,[5] it is useful to conceive of them as still on a continuum with the bodily preoccupations of more healthy adolescents (Anderson, 2005). Girls and boys enter adolescence with an enormous range of internal capacities or vulnerabilities, as well as with enormous variations in familial or societal containing structures. The bodily self-consciousness endemic to adolescents may seem far from the extreme bodily preoccupation of anorexia, but both are conveying a developmental problem.

Many factors contribute to breakdown and the possible propensity for concrete expression through bodily symptoms. Aggression, narcissism, and familial or societal chaos or dissolution are all possible factors in adolescent breakdown, as well as many others. However, I think of psychic isolation as particularly relevant to breakdown because it leaves the psyche without internal or external resources to metabolize the whole range of affects and confusions at hand. When an adolescent feels isolated from a containing mind, not only can bodily changes seem bizarre, but the now alien-seeming body can be treated as separate and not in need of protection.[6]

The somatic changes of adolescence spur the mind to metabolize changes, but inevitably, there is a lag before the mind can catch up to the body. The bodily symptoms that tend to emerge in adolescence are often surrounded in secrecy—picture the ruminative preoccupation of anorexics—and so express isolation and alienation in powerful ways. An adolescent's unconscious sense of helplessness at his or her body changing, seemingly with a will of its own, can lead him or her to try to subordinate the body, such as in restricting in eating disorders.

On the other hand, somatic symptoms are also a potential communication by adolescents—their unconscious effort to convey what is wrong, albeit in a difficult to decipher manner. And of course, as Winnicott tells us, someone hearing the communication is required—the adolescent process can't take place without a facilitating environment. The discovery of self-destructive bodily symptoms in their child can often mobilize parents to seek treatment for their child when they might not have faced troubles presented in a less frightening manner. There is an opportunity to hear the distress in a physical symptom at adolescence that may prevent the symptom from becoming an established and addictive pattern.

Lena

Some adolescents report desperate acts they have undertaken when what they feel is too big and too fraught. "Lena," age sixteen, told me of her first incident of self-cutting. She had seen her best friend making out with a boy Lena found "gross." Lena was filled with overwhelming feelings and cut herself. Later, she showed her friend her cuts and her friend got her to seek help. Associating to "gross" in her first session with me, Lena described her father as "gross, the way he eats, these movements he makes with his mouth." Soon after, Lena reported her first dream: "I was yelling at people and then they leave, but in the second part of the dream I was able to write music and people were interested." The extreme pain and rage[7] expressed in her cutting, which might have become ritualized into entrenched self-destructiveness, could here be transformed into meaningful emotional speech and connection. A conglomeration of longings and emotions led to the cutting—jealousy, rage, and helplessness. She loved the girl and experienced her kissing this particular boy as a horror. The link between this boy and her father conveyed that this scene also evoked unwanted parental sexuality.

Lena's cutting could be thought of here as proto-symbolic—intense feelings were cutting Lena up. When she first cut, she was incapable of translating these feelings into words. The intensity of her feelings and her withdrawal from her parents precluded thinking and non-bodily representations. As she began analysis, she became intrigued with her dreams, helping to translate her feelings to a listening other, although at this early stage in her analysis she would bring me a dream and seem to leave me to think about it. This transition is an example of a beginning use of an other's mind to contain and represent new experiences and meanings—just as she had not yet been able to represent her emotional experience to her friend in a way other than showing her cuts. One might think of this as resistance—for instance, as an inhibition of self-observation arising from conflicts over aggression (Levenson, 2004). It seems to me a problem with the development of internal containment. She needed to see someone think about her internal states and dreams to begin to see this as possible.

Lena was able to begin to dream her experiences and feel they were understood in her analysis. Her self-destructiveness fell away rather rapidly. Two years later, as she was preparing to leave analysis to go to college, she brought me a poem about mourning. Lena had found a way of symbolically communicating pain to me and was no longer trapped in her body. In her final analytic session before leaving for college, she told me she'd had a dream that "a woman named Mary gave me Joseph's amazing coat of dreams."

Eleanor, the girl in the first vignette, did not have to resort to bodily harm to express her upheaval, while Lena did. However, Lena's cutting brought the response of a facilitating and containing environment to bear.

Weathering Development

I'll return to Frankie to consider some ideas about how development is sometimes weathered. Frankie initially identifies with freaks and calls herself "an unjoined person," who fits neither with the older or the younger kids. Her brother has been off in the military and is returning to marry his sweetheart. Frankie sees this couple as a mirage of beauty, adventure and perfection. Suddenly a thought comes to her: "they are the we of me" (McCullers, 1946, p. 42):

> For when the old question came to her—the who she was and what she would be in the world, and why she was standing there that minute—when the old question came to her, she did not feel hurt and unanswered. At last she knew just who she was and understood where she was going. She loved her brother and the bride and she was a member of the wedding. The three of them would go into the world and they would always be together. And finally, after the scared spring and the crazy summer, she was no more afraid. (p. 46)

The plan to be a member of the wedding inevitably leads to bitter disappointment, but it creates a temporary transitional space where Frankie can imagine a couple that she is somehow a part of. She can imagine entering a wider world without feeling too alone. A Kleinian might view this fantasy as a psychotic aspect of the personality (which can co-exist with non-psychotic parts of the personality, including reality testing). Bion might see the "member of the wedding" fantasy as a dream element—the mind's effort to dream a solution to an unconscious problem. Winnicott might see Frankie as inhabiting a transitional space, where no one should ask whether the fantasy is really possible or not. Perhaps, the question of whether such a fantasy is psychotic, dreamlike, or transitional can only be fully ascertained by the breakthrough or breakdown of further growth—or a complicated mixture of both. When Frankie's fantasy inevitably breaks down when she is not invited on the honeymoon, another transition is in store for her. Her fantasy allows Frankie to imagine her way into a next world.

Dalsimer (1986) uses *The Member of the Wedding* to describe a crucial element in the movement from pre-adolescence to early adolescence in the girl—the finding of a best friend. The best friend allows an experience of a couple, and the trying on of different possibilities through identifications and idealizations of the friend. Me/not me doesn't have to be clearly defined in this transitional space.

This "best friend" development can also be an aspect of treatment. "Catherine," an early adolescent girl in psychotherapy, relates to me as if I am a knowing older sister. She feels that watching me might help her to negotiate things she has not yet figured out. Her disinterest in talking about herself in favor of talking about me has at times been unsettling to me. However, like Frankie, I think she needs to feel a part of something with me—to be a "member of the wedding" with me. Catherine structures each session around the repetitive playing of the same game with me—similar to the intimate and repetitive kitchen rituals Frankie shares with Berenice. Rituals of sameness and stability are crucial to adolescents as their bodily and psychic ground shifts beneath them.

Within this structure of sameness, some psychic contact with sexuality can be made. Before a scheduled time away, Catherine imagined I was going to Paris to buy dresses. She regularly asks me if I am married and, if so, what my husband is like. At times, we struggle with this, as I try to draw her attention to the internal meanings of these questions. Catherine feels shut out by my not telling her about my husband. I struggle with how to let her in in a way that will benefit her, but not yield on my own process regarding what she needs from me.

Catherine is very interested in my shoes and has literally tried them on. These ways of relating challenge our ideas about how we treat adolescents. Being a child analyst is useful in this regard. In play treatments, we try to let the child's internal world take the lead, but we are inevitably active in the play. My patient and I seem to have different ideas regarding the treatment—this is an interesting and useful challenge. Some patients' ways of being in analysis or therapy fit our preconceptions more easily. My patient is requiring the growth of the container. I must adapt to her and be her kind of analyst. At the same time, I cannot abdicate the responsibility of having my own mind in relation to her. Her treatment seems to serve as a transitional space where I am and am not her older sister, and we are and are not a couple—helping her to feel less alone in facing adolescence. Her presenting symptom of bulimia has ceased.

Catherine's sort of identification with me could hold up development—preventing her from exploring her own individuality. However, it began to be clear that her mother, while quite kind, was also quite inhibited. Catherine seemed to be using her identification with me (trying on my shoes) as a progressive step in exploring pleasure and possibilities.

Conclusion

Psychic isolation is an important aspect of adolescence that can contribute to the propensity for breakdown into somatic symptomatology. Heightened sexual and rageful impulses in concert with shifting unconscious object relations and the use of primitive defense mechanisms leave the adolescent feeling isolated in new and unnamable experiences. Psychotic aspects of the personality can come to the fore. The adolescent's sense of strangeness from herself and from her internal objects creates an affective sense of isolation. The sense of strangeness can leave adolescents cut off from useful internal or external objects. Sometimes a period of psychic isolation can allow internal struggle that breaks through to new ways of experiencing self and others. At times, the transitional space of an analysis, where these new experiences can be dreamed together, allows adolescents to feel they are no longer "unjoined persons" but "members of the wedding."

Notes

1   For example, Bion describes that the "contact barrier" separating conscious from unconscious gradually develops as alpha elements cohere. The "structure" of the contact barrier is also a dynamic process that depends on the quality of alpha function or other issues such as whether alpha function is disrupted or has not been well developed in regard to particular contents.

2   As is well known, physiological adolescence involves cognitive changes, hormonal changes, and subsequent growth of pubic and other bodily hair as well as overall growth. For girls, these changes include breast development and the onset of menstruation. For boys, testosterone levels increase twenty-fold from ages nine to fifteen and result in growth of the testes and penis, the onset of wet dreams and voice changes.

3   Self-harm is considerably more prevalent in adolescents than adults. A statewide survey of self-harm in Massachusetts (2011 Health and Risk Behaviors of Massachusetts Youth) found that 18% reported self-injury ("cutting or burning without wanting to die" [p. 23]) in the prior year. One source of comparison with adults is Briere and Gil's (1998) research, which used a random sample of U.S. adults. 4% reported "having self-injured at least occasionally" (Walsh, 2006, p.41). Walsh also notes that there are "no large nationwide epidemiological studies" of self-harm (2006, p. 32). The Massachusetts Study (2011) finds an even higher number of high school students—22%—reported binge drinking and 7% reported attempting suicide in the past year (2011, p. 24). Offer's work (1971) is sometimes cited to indicate that adolescence is not as tumultuous as early analysts (e.g., Freud, 1958) described. However, Offer's work shows that, while many adolescents indicate agreement with their parents on larger societal issues, myriad rebellions occur on an every-day basis. Further, self-report research data is very different from the material of analytic sessions that allow a deeper view into unconscious processes. However, clinical data is not necessarily representative of the larger population. Healthier adolescents don't generally arrive in analysts' offices—nor may the most disturbed who may be more represented in juvenile justice systems or may have little access to treatment.

4   Campanile (2012) distinguishes actions "on the body" (my focus here) versus "actions in the body"—hysterical conversion symptoms. His description of these hysterical symptoms is fascinating, but actions "on the body" are far more prevalent in adolescence.

5   In work with bulimic adolescents, I was at first shocked to hear of bizarre rituals such as storing their vomit in jars in their closets. Many meanings could be considered in relation to this symptom. Most simply, it may convey that the act of purging—by definition, "an evacuation"—cannot really capture or make meaning since it evacuates the potential for meaning. Therefore, the evidence of the symptom must be kept. Surely, a vivid example of contents seeking a container.

6   Gardner (2001) describes "self-harm" as typically beginning in adolescence and as characterized by an adolescent "state of mind" (p. 59). She cites five states of mind typical in adolescence and also characteristic of self-harming behavior: the intensification of aggressive impulses and processes; narcissism; hypersensitivity and heightened feeling; the tendency to action and the preoccupation with death.

7   Other motivations for cutting have been discussed, such as self-soothing or the effort to disrupt feelings of emptiness or numbness, or sado-masochism (Shaw, 2012), as well as addictive cutting (Gardner, 2001). Bodily symptoms are often multiply determined (Waelder,1936) with various motivations served in the same act.

References

Anderson, R. (2005). Adolescence and the body ego: The reencountering of primitive mental functioning in adolescent development. Unpublished paper presented at the Sixteenth Annual Melanie Klein Memorial Lectureship, January 8, 2005, Los Angeles.

Anderson, R. (1998). Suicidal behavior and its meaning in adolescence. In R. Anderson & A. Dartington (Eds.), *Facing it out* (pp. 65–78). New York: Routledge.

Anderson, R. and Dartington, A. (1998). Introduction. In R. Anderson and A. Dartington (Eds.), *Facing it out* (pp. 1–6). New York: Routledge.

Barrett, T. (2008). Manic defenses against loneliness in adolescence. *Psychoanalytic Study of the Child*, 63: 111–136.

Bion, W. (1962). *Learning from experience*. London: Karnac.

Bion, W. (1967). *Second thoughts*. London: Karnac.

Blos, P. Sr. (1967). The second individuation process of adolescence. *Psychoanalytic Study of the Child*, 22: 162–186.

Brady, M. (2011). Invisibility and insubstantiality in an anorexic adolescent: Phenomenology and dynamics. *Journal of Child Psychotherapy*, 37: 3–15.

Brady, M., Tyminski, R. and Carey, K. (2012). To know or not to know: An application of Bion's K and –K to child treatment. *Journal of Child Psychotherapy*, 38: 302–317.

Briere, J. and Gil, E. (1998). Self-mutilation in clinical and general population samples: Prevalence, correlates, and functions. *American Journal of Orthopsychiatry*, 68: 609–620

Burloux, G. (2005). *The body and its pain*. United Kingdom: Free Association Books.

Campanile, P. (2012). "I had twenty-five piercings and pink hair when … ": Adolescence, transitional hysteria, and the process of subjectivization. *The Psychoanalytic Quarterly*, 81: 401– 418.

Corbett, K. (2001). More Life: Centrality and Marginality in Human Development. *Psychoanalytic Dialogues*, 11: 313–335.

Dalsimer, K. (1986). Pre-adolescence: *The member of the wedding*. In *Female adolescence: Psychoanalytic reflections on literature* (pp. 13–26). New Haven: Yale University Press.

DuPrau, J. (2003). *The City of Ember*. New York: Random House.

Erikson, E. (1956). The concept of ego identity. *Journal of the American Psychoanalytic Association*, 4: 56–121.

Fraiberg, S. (1955). Some considerations in the introduction to therapy in puberty. *Psychoanalytic Study of the Child*, 10: 264–286.

Freud, A. (1958). Adolescence. *Psychoanalytic Study of the Child*, 13: 255–278.

Gardner, F. (2001). *Self-Harm: A psychotherapeutic approach*. East Sussex: Brunner-Routledge.

Green, V. (2013). Grief in two guises: 'Mourning and melancholia' revisited. *Journal of Child Psychology and Psychiatry*, 39: 76–89.

Harley, M., (1970). On some problems of technique in the analysis of early adolescents. *Psychoanalytic Study of the Child*, 25: 99–121

Katan, A. (1951). The role of displacement in agoraphobia. *The International Journal of Psychoanalysis*, 32: 41–50.

Klein, M. (1922). Inhibitions and difficulties at puberty. In *Love, guilt and reparation and other works* (pp. 54–58). New York: Free Press.

Levenson, L. (2004). Inhibition of self-observing activity in psychoanalytic treatment. *Psychoanalytic Study of the Child*, 59: 167–188.

Levy-Warren, M. (1996). *The adolescent journey*. Lanham, MD: Jason Aronson.

Massachusetts Department of Education. (2011). Health and Risk Behaviors of Massachusetts Youth. Retrieved from: www.doe.mass.edu/hsss/program/youthrisk

McCullers, C. (1946). *The member of the wedding.* Boston, MA/New York: Houghton Mifflin, 2004.

Offer, D. (1971). Rebellion and anti-social behavior. *The American Journal of Psychoanalysis,* 31: 13–19.

Ritvo, S. (1976). Adolescent to woman. *Journal of the American Psychoanalytic Association,* 24: 127–137.

Salinger, J. D. (1951). *Catcher in the rye.* United States: Little, Brown & Co.

Shaw, J. (2012). Addiction to near death in adolescence. *J. Child Psychoth.,* 38: 111–129.

Waelder, R. (1936). The principle of multiple functions: Observations on over-determination. *Psychoanal. Q.,* 5: 45–62.

Walsh, B. (2006). *Treating self injury: A practical guide.* New York: Guilford.

Wolfenstein, M. (1966). How is mourning possible? *Psychoanalytic Study of the Child,* 11: 450–470.

Chapter 15

Death, Life, Birth and Sublimation in the Pandemic

Rosemary Balsam

"The eagle suffers little birds to sing, And is not careful what they mean thereby, Knowing that with the shadow of his wings He can at pleasure stint their melody."
Tamora to Saturninus. Titus Andronicus, act 4, sc.4, l.83–6. Shakespeare

COVID-19 has been like Shakespeare's eagle. It hovers over the globe, master of the universe, with a power for destruction that is far, far greater than puny humans – little twittering songbirds struck down in a moment, in the midst of some high sweet trill of life. We have fought back against the helplessness of this fate – as we always try to – and as we are equipped, with our smart brains and with fight and flight mechanisms alert beyond our consciousness. We have helped position ourselves – nearly two years later – better out of sight over the months. But the giant eagle prevails, hovering in the rhythms of its own whims and largely not ours. We confront with sorrow that after all we've lived through and after all our excited existence in countless eras, we are just little mortal animals on this shared small planet Earth. Imminence of possible death puts life in perspective.

The pandemic has razor sharpened many contrasts in groups into a warring fractiousness[1] within class, race, politics, nature and science. We easily detect anxiety, dread, anger and murderous rage among groups and individuals in the news and in our experiences – but what about pleasures? While this eagle swoops over continents sweeping its malignant power over us, what signs of pleasure in our daily lives spring up or exist in the here-and-now?

Effects of Environmental Constraint

Freud, in his rationale for the use of the couch and in the creation of "the frame" for analytic treatment, suggests that the diminished physical mobility (which I am analogizing to the control of households in quarantine), in the energic libidinal theory, forces the energies of individuals away from action and toward intra-psychic channels that often culminate and demand some sort of expression – verbal, in the case of communication, cultural in the case of creativeness. Yes, we grew to feel that this is too hydraulic, and a closed system of theory, but as a starting fantasy about some aspect of the mind's functioning it might be indulged

DOI: 10.4324/9781003384618-21

to play with in considerations of the mysteries of "sublimation." In analysis, the emphasis on "free association" under the conditions of physical limitation, allows us, for treatment purposes, to reap the yield of pressure on the minds of both analyst and analysand to notice more details about the contents of the person's style of mind that are communicated in the room. The choice of words and rhythms of speech can reveal unconscious leakage (after Freud (1900), for example) secondary process invaded by primary process, and gain access to more regressive levels of primary process functioning. Most schools of psychoanalysis still use "free association" as an ideal of an aspect of their treatment methods. There is revived contemporary interest in Freud's energy theories, and notions of primary and secondary process, at the interface of psychoanalysis and neuroscience – also involving research on psychedelic drugs to promote fragmentation (Rabeyron and Massicotte, 2020). They say,

> ... from Freud's distinction between primary and secondary processes, we proceed to compare the psychoanalytic model with research originating from cognitive psychology and neuroscience. The notions of entropy and free energy appear particularly relevant at the intersection of these different domains ... Thus, primary consciousness is more 'entropic' and flexible than secondary consciousness.
>
> (p. 1)

Interactive communication between analyst and analysand highlights ego defenses, marks superego modifiers and attacks and shows affects or their lack. With Freudian instinct theory, libido and aggression together and in clash will also power the imagoes of inner objects for communication and expression into the transference relationship within the room.

Jumping to group dynamics from the individual – and acknowledging their only loose approximation, the emotional outpourings of citizens about the election in the United States happened all during the pandemic, when the same group was physically stalled in their motions of everyday life. Rage seethed and flooded the community, for example, in the Capitol Riots in January 2021, breaking social and traditional geographic bounds – as if this mass of people had been freshly let out of prisons, led on by one near-naked, and other equally rageful, ecstatic and fresh-out-of restraints leaders. The rowdy, raucous, in-your-face adolescent-appearing antics and sexualized horseplay, moved out of control, and blended with terrorizing others and serious violence. Nightly riots also occurred in conjunction with angry but more restrained daytime marches from the Black Lives Matter Movement and supporters in protesting the victimhood of black young people at the hands of the police, and especially the death of George Floyd in May 2020. Much demonizing of "others" flowed forth. This turmoil stretched from the summer of 2020 until early 2021. The major newspapers reported that 2020 was the deadliest in gun violence in decades, with statistics to prove it. Mass shootings abounded. Evidence of more rage in action than business-as-usual was and is observable in this pandemic timeframe. This massive discontent and violence admixed with the dynamite of erotically violent sources is a study in itself. But these are surely judged by chronology, a counter-reaction to the massive social constraints necessary for a prolonged unprecedented time, and the annihilating fear of and vicious fantasies about others as contaminated poisoners, and killers by germs. No one was vaccinated then.

However, in this timeframe, domestic life also happened behind closed doors and in relative physical isolation, in contrast to the swirling world of cyberspace that is a godsend for imaginative and verbal communication, even without body proximity. The rest of this paper will focus on this novel and physically restrictive narrowly domestic but digitally enhanced world. The emphasis is less here on aggression than what happened to libido, to erotic or sensual or cultural pleasures in this time.

Pleasures

Since the global plague forced itself in March 2020, there was (and post-vaccination still is), a search to fill the time created by cancelled events, unsafe travel or planned meetings or work that had to be put on hold while families retired indoors for shelter, and away from the threat of being breathed upon or touched by potentially infected neighbors. Businesses ceased. Universities almost closed. Children had to tolerate being schooled via screen, at home. Hesitant of social life outside home, some timid, obsessional or teased children actually welcomed the confinement. Most others chomped at the bit, and struggled with missing sports, outdoor play and physical play with peers. Adults were pent up. Bad marriages and partnerships slid into increased violence. It is said that one in four women and one in ten men in the US experience domestic violence. It is suspected that caseloads went down during Covid because it becomes not safe to report (Evans et al., 2020). The domestic conditions however are known to be such that violence is expected – financially increased dependence of women, limited child-care, poorly organized services for black and brown families especially, etc. These are all pressures on many households that can explode in physical and sexual abuse, and gun violence. There are no reliable statistics on drug taking, but again, the public health sensibilities tell us that an increase is very likely. The Centers for Disease Control reported that in June 2020, 13% of American adults either started or increased their drug use. This discussion of such escapes, raptures, pleasure and sadomasochistic pleasures are beyond the scope of this paper on pleasure, but they are acknowledged here as very important in all-too-common dysfunctional domestic circumstances.

Bodily Pleasures

At lower decibels, as it were, many discovered pleasures, turned out to be hiding in plain sight. Several of my staid middle-aged and elderly patients, for example, talked for the first time about their masturbation activities. If their attention to their bodies was newly engaged, or more likely a revival from earlier life, they said it was a private and welcome outlet for their tension and anxieties, and the pursuit, for a brief moment, in the regressive pleasures of orgasm. Being in a lighter mood, subsequently, more possibilities seemed to open, and creative solutions to problems that had stalled in strangled angers, emerged. A fight between spouses about who was "stealing" the other's bedding during the night, resolved into the male spouse, post-masturbation, remembering by himself that the closet was full of extra blankets, and there was no need to seethe in bed feeling unloved by his mother/wife, thus sustaining his helpless rage at her! One divorced post-menopausal woman spoke of how masturbation re-assured her she still had her own body, and that it was alive. Earlier, she had never seemed to develop a sex life independent of her singular strong desire to become pregnant and achieve motherhood. Her ancient mother at the time was languishing on oxygen near death, in a nursing home.

In their fantasies, all became young to themselves – for a short time young, limitless and timeless, and beyond the malignant reach of Covid, or the vicissitudes of life. Another woman in her late sixties sought more sex with her male partner of many years, their children grown and long gone. After getting a prescription for Viagra, this usually steady, well-meaning but unimaginative man even told her that it was amazing the pleasures of youth that one could recover, when the pandemic had pushed them toward each other in close proximity for comfort, and they found their sexuality literally as a delightful "re-creation." Another male middle-aged patient spoke of heightened dis-appointment in his wife's chronic lack of sexual interest in him and began to find pornography for masturbation for the first time. Another brought into the sessions, again for the first time, his longstanding secret masturbatory life with gay pornography, while he had lived for many years a daytime roommate heterosexually arranged, but sexless marriage. His usually busy traveling business world had ceased due to the lock-down, and that had been the main preoccupation he had chosen to share in a weekly therapy over the previous two years. Silenced through the stasis of his outside world interactions, the pleasures of his actual sex world crept into his associative material, unbidden and slipped past the iron gates of his permission.

In sum, my educated, professional, middle-class older patients often paid much more attention to their sex lives than usual, as a potential source of pleasure. Young student patient cases whom I supervised, also talked more about sex – when their overly busy trainee therapists allowed themselves to hear it! The latter suffered often from an environmental din of their own constantly helpless concerns in the university setting, about whether they were providing "enough" to the mainly physically absent students in this unprecedented separation from their patients. They were behind screens, the students often off-campus and even across the country, even in other countries, and unpredictable. The young therapists' desires to manage them, above all attend to all safety factors for suicide or harming others, or wanting to be aware of intolerable symptomatology, made it hard for them to take their young patient's sex lives seriously. I believe, sexual concerns seemed too leisurely to them. One even said, "I never thought of *that* – it must be because you're an analyst!" The tensions of necessary hypervigilance were grounded in fears of death and doom, and political uncertainties all around. The much older supervisor, for example say, found stalking behavior on the internet ignored. If such a student pair were separated by continents, that did not seem a real and present bodily danger. However, psychodynamically of course stalking is a highly aggressive sexually driven issue of deep insecurity, which involves the subject's sex life and shaky identity. Such a behavior might be viewed during Covid, only as a signal of a pathetic patient's loneliness and fear of abandonment. The word "sex" might never be mentioned. This trainee said, after supervisory discussions, "I believe I had stopped thinking – thinking about dynamics. I was so beleaguered at the time trying to be a good caretaker, and by the responsibility of trying to treat so many people so far away."

Another young patient, in the relative stability and regularity of analysis by Zoom, described his adventurous and passionate first love, which was full of sexting, sex acts on Zoom together all night long, each partner yearning visually and sensually for the other, but through the camera and glass barriers. The more mature candidate was not so harassed as the previous trainee therapists and did not brush away the sexual import. Certainly, loneliness here too played a role. However, this young analysand had never had a girlfriend before, and Facetime on the phone was a safer and highly experimental and creative way under these rare environmental conditions that were not conducive to physical lovemaking, for this single late adolescent to allow his ongoing development into adult life. Freud's theoretical focus on the erotic aspects of life were (and still are) bared during these months, to a background accompaniment of the daily dirge of fantasies about illness, panic in the news, life appearing foreshortened and deprivation of the throb of the usual environmental everyday life. I observed a human focus on the body's own sources of libidinal pleasures coming much more spontaneously to the fore among the living, in this heightened situation of environmental death. Cyberspace is full of responsiveness to individuals who also crave visual or interactive satisfaction for sexually transgressive fantasies. Some individuals resorted to illicit actions in trying to seduce underage partners, and some to communicating consensually or by anonymous avatar, in cyberspace with transgressive and regressive fantasy.

Play and Videogames

Many individuals sought out ways to "play," and to entertain themselves. Many children seemed to take easily to their tablets, readily inventively to zoom together and create games with each other. Parents and grandparents, even at a distance, might be brought in to judge craft and painting competitions online. Complicated games developed from inside their own houses, or even the interior of cars (as one or other might be en route with a parent to leave something off somewhere) and could be played in tandem or groups across cyberspace. Each tablet watched and recorded. Ciri responded to their requests for help on occasion, the kids passing by their tablets and talking to each other in transit. One therapist said she newly was doing therapy with a child under his bed, having been invited into his secret precious play space! Many child therapists said they had now visited their child patients' entire houses, as opposed to the confines of therapy in the office. The computer or tablet or Facetime on phone became and is likely now a permanent fixture, an essential "third" in sustaining many social and interactive playful communications.

Typical enough of how our patients talk to analysts and therapists in our new online office venues (without risking confidentiality here) – I found online, everyday accounts about activities of regular people, that sounded very familiar from my own practice or supervision. These lives told of some other pleasures in the pandemic that were open either to children or adults.

Animal Crossing: New Horizons

Commercially, the most popular video game that has emerged in this time of stress, remarkably is not one of the many violent video games, but *Animal Crossing*. There is no other game on the market like it at this time (Spring 2021). There seems no "goal" to it. Yet, *"Animal Crossing: New Horizons* [is] the hottest entertainment property during the pandemic, with five million copies sold in March 2020 alone," at the beginning of the pandemic lockdowns (https://www.cnn.com/videos/business/2020/05/07/animal-crossing-new-horizons-nintendo-stewart-pkg-vpx.cnn). *The Washington Post* reported that, "For some, the familiar jingle that plays when starting up "Animal Crossing" is a callback to early pandemic days." (Liao, 2021). In Polygon, a website reviewing video games and their culture, Park (2021) goes on:

> The game has a wide appeal. *New Horizons* and the pandemic essentially caused a Nintendo Switch shortage worldwide as 'non-gamers' rushed to join the festivities … In March and April, [2020] millions of people played it feverishly, for hours on end, perfecting the idyllic fantasy where anything was possible. Players created perfect homes, honored loved ones, and used *New Horizons* as a protest spot in hopes of sparking real-world change. Celebrities, politicians, and influencers used it to get closer to their fans – everyone from President-elect Joe Biden and Rep. Alexandria Ocasio-Cortez … .
>
> (Carpenter, 2020)

Callum Booth, a games commentator, in "Plugg," February 2021 wrote, "… as of the end of last year, the game sold a staggering 31.18 million copies. That means that just under half of everyone who owns a [Nintendo]Switch has *Animal Crossing: New Horizons.*" Booth continues, "The median play time of *Animal Crossing: New Horizons* is 60 hours, which means there have been (roughly) 1,870,800,000 hours spent on the game. This is the equivalent to about 1,247,200,000 soccer games … Nintendo had a great year" (Booth, 2021).

I with each Nintendo switch, when the player decides to play this game, they are flown to a desert island, to inhabit it as they wish. The caretaker there is Tom Nook, a squirrel. All the people and tools etc. to create this environment are available to access. It is an opportunity to build a social system as one chooses. The avatar chosen by the player looks like cute little kid who trots around, and whose appearance, color and gender this controller can create from the many options. A village is created by the controller's villagers, who are humanoid animals. These animal figures have identifiable characteristics – like human characters in real life – grumpy, cheeky, etc., and they live in the community created by this human avatar. The main player can buy a house, pay off a mortgage, do chores – like chopping wood, sell and buy things in the store, decorate their home, visit neighbors; go swimming, build more onto the house, throw parties, hang out with invited animals. There seems no challenge other than one's own ambition to, say, have a fancier house or make a park, buy new clothes, fix things or save some money; or even to donate to a museum, seek entertainment and care for friends. One can even take time to eat, pee and poop. There is much sweetness, and also kindness to each other, ways to become more friendly, receive appreciation. There is apparently no stress as every motivated action in the game – if deemed unwise – can potentially be undone. It never seems like a last chance, and other channels can open if one is closed. People can play this game with great absorption. They can check into it, save when finished for that day, and check out; and then start from there when it pleases them – for hours. It is supposed to be played daily. Too long an absence is punishable by cockroaches, weeds and nasty villagers. But one can redeem oneself. No one ever dies.

How is sickness handled in this game, given Covid's prevalence in real life? Villagers can get sick, for example. The avatar locates them, hears their troubles, buys medicine from the store with the right number of "bells" – the medicines offered cure everything – watches outside while the sick one recovers and then stays home to rest. The recovered villager may give the avatar a gift for this service. There is no doctor, but all illness can be cured. The emphasis is on looking after each other.

Psychological Aspects of *Animal Crossing*

Booth (2021) notes and asks: "… it's a peaceful game where you don't do much of anything. Where, friends, is the violence?" So well may he ask, considering the reputation of video games in general, and the inconclusive ongoing debates and statistics about whether or not they model violence for the young or whether such social concerns are age-old hackneyed reactions to new technology. Wiederhold (2021) acknowledges the cautions:

> There is some evidence that engagement with violent video games may cause an increase in risk-taking behaviors, intensified aggression, and amplified physical arousal. Of even greater concern, especially during the pandemic, is the potential for overuse of these games, leading to mental health issues and negative life consequences.

The violence that is reported with *Animal Crossing* seems more like every day domestic sibling rivalry. The first player on the Switch can be joined by a second figure. But that figure has to tag along after the controller. Family feuds have happened about who starts the island, and populates it with creatures. If sharing is impossible, another Nintendo switch and island is the answer (fortunate for the business!). There is a challenge here as in real life, about inviting another person closer, sharing space and co-operating or creating power plays by sabotaging these friends in the same space. This privilege for the universal longed-for position of being "the only one" may be an important aspect of this game, especially during Covid where families are in tighter proximity and privacy and sharing fights can break out. Juliet Mitchell, the British feminist psychoanalyst, in 2003, offered a major insight in her book, "Siblings: Sex and Violence". She persuasively showed with clinical and historical evidence, how the eldest child's sibling rage and terror of identity annihilation, happening in all subsequent births may be a basic and primordial psychoanthropological factor in humans' warring behaviors. Cain famously murdered Abel. How often, for example, armies have been led by brothers against each other. Mitchell had to shift from seeing the inner world narrowly through the "vertical" paradigm of the Oedipus complex, and thus the child's relationship only to the parent. She saw an equal and perhaps even more powerful paradigm in the "lateral" dimension of sibling dynamics, given the formidable emotional impact that they have on each other's psyches. The challenges of sharing a digital island in *Animal Crossing* may be the more intense because the actual shared living space was more emotionally fraught, and cut-off from excursions into the outside world. Many individuals do talk online about the joy of having the island totally under their own control, where they can achieve what they want by working solo, and presumably without human (perceived chaotic) interference – surely an infantile wish fulfilled!

Other features about sharing the island have emerged. For example, if one were a young millennial, in real life suffering the physical restrictions of dating, this game provided an opportunity to experiment and discover something (remotely but yet intimately) about living with a would-be partner.

The freedom of choice of the gender, and color, of the avatar who is the subject's character, and who controls the village is surely a source of gender freedom and pleasure, affirming the recent analytic observations of Sien Rivera (2021).[2] A young contemporary psychoanalytic therapist, they describe the growth potential for trans and queer young people's gender and social experimentation using games with avatars that are readily gender fluid – as in *Animal Crossing*. Their ideas are still novel in a psychoanalytic literature that currently trends toward videogaming and life on computers as overstimulating, inciting aggression or fears the encouragement of too much omnipotence and disavowal of realities, like the body and social relationships in the world (Wiederhold, 2021). Some theorize fears of restricting ideal imaginative potentials, and fears of destroying the space for reflection, that promotes subjectivity. Our psychoanalytic world of the early 2020s tends to view cyberspace somewhat dimly at this time – decrying these active, visualization shortcuts to interaction that are favored over language, and decrying known ways to communicate affective, nuanced subtlety with others. A thoughtful, but heavily warning literature, it also perhaps shows the generational effect of a currently ever-graying professional psychoanalytic population!

Rivera, in working with children, while aware of over-use, also persuasively presents a point of view that "video games can go beyond being a method of escape; they can serve as a vessel allowing psychic healing to take place." While their paper addresses the experiences of gender non-conforming and queer youngsters, I believe many aspects of their comments on play and gaming as it relates to identity and

practiced forms of authenticity and trial fantasies are likely applicable to many individuals of all ages who can play and given the psychic fluidity and capabilities of
regression with recovery that Loewald subscribes to, as psychic health (Loewald,
1978, 1988). Rivera reminds us that Winnicott wrote, "it *is play that is universal*, and
that belongs to health" (Winnicott, 1971, p. 41), and they suggest that "ironically,
the virtual space may be the only space within which psychic reality can be embodied
at all." Children do love this game under scrutiny here.

> If one defines play as a satisfying, precarious, and creative action located within the
> potential space, stylized performances of gender and sexuality can easily be
> considered a type of play … . The avatar may serve as a facilitator of self-
> integration rather than a barrier. A virtual space may be the site of a patient's most
> adept efforts at play.

There are also apparently more adult identity and specific sexual dimension experi-
mentations possible with this game – as described in an article in The Guardian
(2020). A non-binary hairdresser Denali Winter was out of work in the pandemic
and discovered *Animal Crossing*. By sharing their code, other interested gamers could
contact Winter in their avatar roles, as a dominatrix. Clients can pay for this service
in "bells," and get punished, for example, by watering flowers and doing chores.

Animal Crossing, though, seems to provide a still oasis, perhaps a peace and control
over a virtual world through doing what one wants, if one works at unlocking the
right tools for its satisfaction, and a wishful entry into a place of simple choices.
There is ample and rewarded opportunity for benign productivity, interaction and
the welfare of the community. Video games as a whole are immersive. The player
becomes totally absorbed in this different world, not just passively, but very actively
co-creating the space with the game. The animalcharacters are known as "them
selves," warts and all, and, mirroring ideals of old-fashioned, old country village life,
are tolerated as just quirky.

A further emotional outlet is the pursuit of achievable perfection. One gamester
wrote, extolling the improvements in *Animal Crossing: New Horizons*: "With the
island designer, you can become God and shape the land and sea! You can build
massive structures across your island! You can make paintings stretching across the
land with the path/custom design feature! And you have knee-caps!" (Starlight
Saanen, January 25, 2021, on *Quora*).

In fact, mildly challenging this sense of omnipotence, there is an ultimate limit to
the quantity of available items, even in *Animal Crossing: New Horizon* – though new
additional features keep being added. When some have reached this point, they
report being tired of it, and retire, as if in satiety. They may come back for special
holidays, and nostalgia, as do humans to their home of origin. However, they may
find cockroaches and weeds and villagers complaining. These absences can be made
good if that is desirable. Undoing, re-doing and reparation, which as we know as
appealing psychic processes, become enacted and possible just at the click of one's
fingertips.

The "homing" aspects of this game suggest special meanings in light of how the idea of "home" shifted during the pandemic. In non-pandemic times, Linda Mayes, of the Yale Child Study Center presented some ideas (at Western New England Institute and Society, 2021) about the psychology of homecoming. She says that not only does "home" evoke attachment to one's people, but the word "summons a return, even as it implies a leave-taking, and attachment to place" (both of course are disrupted in child abuse, her interest). She notes "these two systems serve comparable functions in human development from emotion regulation to memory consolidation." Pandemic times strike me as paradoxical in relation to "home." Unlike other disasters interrupting lives and home life, volcanoes, hurricanes or war that demolish people's homes as a part of their disaster, the pestilence disaster found millions upon millions sitting safely, trapped right *in* their homes, in real time, but unable to get out to journey through life like Odysseus, afraid even to go to the grocery store in case they would be smitten by others with the deadly virus. Too much "at home," as it were! Thus, gamesters sat tranquilly and played "Animal Crossing" for hours upon hours … a game which very much involves the person's avatar *creating a home* to work for, and own, and a community of little roads and houses and animal people that he/she/they trots around in, actively coming and going and having adventures and then … returning home again. So, it seems our real-life peripatetic spirit for adventure as a metaphor for movement and growth, facing challenges and building a life, was being served – even in a teacup – and our human ability to escape and explore, grow, meet others, and achieve things, collaborate melded into return, hopefully wiser, to our home base to re-fuel … to start out, all over again, all in virtual time and space. The gamers' "attachment to place" (Mayes) was certainly being exercised in this game, as much as their attachment to persons. Regarding the neurobiology of the importance of "place" (and the game is a "Crossing," after all, like busy cross-roads), Mayes writes:

> The entorhinal cortex, which provides by far the largest input to the hippo-campus, contains a neural map of the spatial environment through specialized cell types. Thus, it appears that the human brain has developed complex, specific patterns of interaction with places, as has already been shown for social interactions, and while there may be overlap in these circuits, there is nonetheless also sensory specificity.

It strikes me that even as real life was virtually static – "life" in the virtual world really proceeded in *Animal Crossing*![3]

Artists at Work

This vanilla sounding game offers yet more original slants for some. The lack of an imposed story in the game, and the invitation to make any combinations one wants, can act like a well, into which people dip to express their own creativity. Here is an example from the world of fashion: The main avatar can dress up the villagers and themselves by going to the store and buying clothes. Random players can actually join in a player's island life, if that player has shared a code with them. One designer reported: "Sometimes I go to people's islands to take photos, sometimes we just talk about designing inspiration" (Cass, 2020). The platform, she says, helped her discover her passion for design. Shiv, another artist, was mentioned in the same article. A wedding and portrait photographer, she received a gift of a sari from one of her villagers in the game. "It sparked inspiration, and she spent a full day using *New Horizons'* pixel art customization to recreate her wedding lehenga ... 'I wanted to try my hand at creating something that truly represented the colors, textures, and patterns of Indian textiles,' and it allowed her to create a dream wardrobe" (Cass, 2020). With Shiv, a gift of a sari from a villager in the game triggered off her yearning for re-creation of the colors, designs peppered by the memories of her own wedding – far away from India, but appetitively re-creating an experience of joy or longing in recalling it to virtual life on the body of the figure on the screen.

"The *Animal Crossing* fashion community can be intense," says a designer named Riley. "There's a lot of competition – not personal, or with each other, it's just getting eyes on your stuff" (Cass, 2020). The hunger is experienced in the eye, and the desire is to dress beautifully, and nurture the pleasure of a little virtual creature, who in one sense "belongs" to one. The eyes are fed with the color and textures of the dress design on the screen, a visual exchange, as one watches the creature's response. I suggest that dressing these cartoon figures is akin to playing with dolls – with a desire to animate the mini-me figures with one's nurturing and parental caretaking, triggered by the pretend mother and child template. Figure 15.1 is an example of Shiv's work (Figure 15.1).

Other Pleasures: Reading, Music, Watching Series on Streaming Channels

Many patients and friends got much pleasure from reading and the comfort of having time to re-read old classics. One grateful reader reported that although he was not previously a poetry reader, during the pandemic he found comfort in poets' images, and solace and humor that salved his loneliness, and feelings of being cut off from others. Several of the patients I deal with either by supervision of therapies or analyses or psychotherapy have reported joining online poetry groups. "There is something so satisfying about reading Tennyson ... I was so moved by the losses and mourning in the imagery." The hunger for words to express experiences displaced from the real-life here-and-now, with the relief that comes from the social permission for an optimal emotional distance – not so close that it overwhelms with sadness, but sufficiently evocative with the present, or one's memories and past, that it ignites the emotion to be re-created in the sense of re-visited in an echoing framework. Yet it spares the reader from the sense "This is happening to me, right now."

To re-visit Proust is to feel we have been there before, "A la recherche du temps perdu," but now with a fuller sense of the painful pleasure of nostalgia.

Figure 15.1 The beautiful yellow silk wedding dress of the adult/mother figure is echoed and crested for the avatar doll/daughter figure. (Courtesy: https://www. instagram.com/crossingbollywood/)

Discussion and Conclusion

We survived with the help of our senses in other ways too – music, making music, dance, all in little glass squares and endless series and movies on all the streaming networks keeping our senses alive while exercising our bodies in place, and carrying on our work as best we could. Much seemed "new" and forced upon us in Covid. The horrors reigned, and we battled death too closely in roaring ambulances and freezer trucks packed up with corpses in parked disaster morgues. Gleaning pleasures even in this awful newness, our minds' capacities for creativity helped our spirits survive, in literal re-creation. Hans Loewald ends his 1988 book on sublimation in this vein, I believe attuned to our Covid struggles,

'[In] works of human imagination … [there is] … magic connected to an achievement of reconciliation – a return on a higher level of thought to early magic of thought … image, emotion, fantasy. as they become united again with … [lived] experience[s] they only reflect, recollect, represent … symbolize.

(p. 81)

We returned once more to our worlds of pain, but somehow refreshed.

Notes

1   I am speaking only of the West, in this essay, as I am not able to write about conditions in the East.
2   This paper won the Ralph Roughton Award of the Committee on Gender and Sexuality of the American Psychoanalytic Association, 2021.
3   Thanks to Elizabeth Lang for her invaluable help with "Animal Crosssing."

References

Booth, C. (2021) Animal Crossing: New horizons sold 31.8 million copies — here's some silly math on it plugg: Your sardonic source for consumer tech stories. https://thenextweb.com/news/nintendo-financials-animal-crossing-new-horizons-copies-sold-maths-switch, Feb 1, 2021.

Carpenter, N. (2020) Animal Crossing kept up with all the twists and turns of 2020: The year of Tom Nook. By Nicole Carpenter@sweetpotatoes Dec 14, 2020, 11:56 am EST Polygon. https://www.polygon.com/21828388/animal-crossing-new-horizons-game-of-the-year-2020

Cass, M. (2020) Animal Crossing keeps growing a vibrant fashion community: Walk, walk, fashion, baby. *Cyberpsychology, Behavior, and Social Networking* 24(1).

Evans, M., Lindauerand, M., Farrell, M. (2020) A pandemic within a pandemic — Intimate partner violence during Covid 19. *The New England Journal of Medicine* 383:2302–2304. doi:10.1056/NEJMp2024046

Freud, S. (1900) The interpretation of dreams. SE 4:1–310.

Liao, S. (2021) The people who spent the year in 'Animal Crossing'. https://www.washingtonpost.com/video-games/2021/03/19/animal-crossing-best-islands/Launcher, The *Washington Post*'s home for coverage of video games and esports, Mar 19, 2021.

Loewald, H. (1978) *Psychoanalysis and the History of the Individual.* New Hanve; London: Yale University Press.

Loewald, H. (1988) *Sublimation: Inquiries into Theoretical Psychoanalysis.* New haven, London: Yale University Press.

Mayes, L. (2021) Anchoring Self in Place: Homecomings Presentation given at Western New England psychoanalytic Institute for Psychoanalysis.

Mitchell, J. (2003) Siblings: Sex and Violence. Cambridge, England. Polity, 1st Edition.

Park, G. (2020) Alexandria Ocasio-Cortez is now playing Animal Crossing. And she's visiting her followers. *The Washington Post*: Democracy Dies in darkness Launcher: Video game news and analysis, May 7, 2020. https://www.washingtonpost.com/video-games/2020/05/07/alexandria-ocasio-cortez-is-now-playing-animal-crossing-shes-visiting-her-followers/

Paul Kari (2020) Dating, a talk show and a dominatrix: Animal Crossing gamers explore new horizons during pandemic. *The Guardian.* https://www.theguardian.com/lifeandstyle/2020/may/09/animal-crossing-nintendo-game-coronavirus-pandemic, May 9, 2020.

Rabeyron, T., Massicotte, C. (2020) Entropy, free energy, and symbolization: Free association at the intersection of psychoanalysis and neuroscience. *Frontiers in Psychology* 11:366. doi: 10.3389/fpsyg.2020.00366.

Rivera, S. (2021) From Battleground To Playground: A Winnicottian Reading of the Video Game Avatar as Transitional Phenomenon for the Queer, Transgender and/or Gender Non-Conforming Patient Presentation for the Ralph Roughton Award at the American Psychoanalytic Association meeting, February 2021.

Wiederhold, B. (2021) Violent Video Games: Harmful Trigger or Harmless Diversion? Cyberpsychology, Behavior, and Social Networking. January 1-2, 2021. doi:10.1089/cyber.2020.29203.editorial. Published in Volume: 24, Issue 1: January 11, 2021; Online Ahead of Print: December 23, 2020.

Winnicott, D. (1971) *Playing and Reality.* London: Basic Books.

Chapter 16

Death and the Use of Pleasure

David Lichtenstein

Pleasure

In his recent essay "Narcissism and the Pleasures of Extinction: For the Centenary of 'Beyond the Pleasure Principle'" (2021), Dany Nobus points out that

> ... almost all psychoanalysts and scholars who have accepted the death drive as a cornerstone of the psychoanalytic edifice have simultaneously felt the need to 'explicate', to 'clarify', to 'render intelligible' its modus operandi by overlaying it with another text, by replacing the original text with an alternative interpretative framework that would allegedly be better suited than Freud's own (meta-) biological paradigm.

Nobus himself engages in an explication that explores the interplay between the death drive and narcissism, especially in its self-annihilating aspect. He argues that the key to the enigmas of the death drive may be found in Freud's other work, and especially his work on narcissism. But of course, any critical reading, including Nobus' of Freud, entails marking aporia and proposing new links, in this instance the link in the apparent contradiction between self-love and extinction. "Narcissism is by definition adverse to creative cross-fertilisation and to the progressive re-vitalisation of the species that emanates from 'allo-sexual' investments, because the latter are fundamentally predicated upon the reduction of its 'auto-sexual' counterparts" (Nobus, 2021).

The need to work and rework Freud's notion of a psychic drive toward death that yet arises from a bodily demand, as all *Trieb* does, by definition, reflects not only the unresolved character of the essay (in Freud's own assessment) but also the (narcissistic) difficulty in thinking one's own death not only as a distant eventuality but as a constant presence. My work in this essay is addressed to that difficulty and especially to the difficulty of recognizing the presence of death in psychoanalytic work itself.

In the opening paragraphs of "Beyond the Pleasure Principle" (1920), Freud addresses the way that he has used this principle in psychoanalysis. It is according to what he refers to as an economic factor. It is tied to maintaining a stable balance in the level of excitement in the mind. Referring to G.T. Fechner's ideas about the

DOI: 10.4324/9781003384618-22

pleasurable effects of psycho-physical stability, Freud initially agrees with Fechner that the pleasure principle is a principle of constancy (1920). The pleasure principle is not directed at increasing either mental or physical excitation but at their reduction, or as Freud says, at least to maintaining their constancy, an economic balance of stimuli and excitation.

This principle rests upon a restrictive and technical meaning of pleasure itself(*lust*), a concept that would in fact have a very wide range of meanings if not restricted *a priori* in this way. In following Freud and in trying to appreciate what he is up to when he finally goes *beyond* this principle of constancy, we are obliged to first recognize this narrow and restrictive use of the term that he will ultimately go beyond.

Taking Freud at his word, the pleasure principle is the principle of an economic balance factor as such. The core notion is not pleasure as much as it is balance in the economic sense. Disturbing this balance is unpleasure and restoring it is pleasure. We could follow the trail back to the beginnings of metapsychology in Freud's "Project for a scientific psychology" (1895), where he introduces the neuronal model of psychosexuality in terms of homeostasis, to perhaps understand the reasons for this restrictive concept, but I am interested instead in the movement beyond and the new tools it has given us to think about the psychoanalytic process. Freud asserts in 1920 that while it had seemed that this tendency toward maintaining a constant balance seemed an apt principle of psychic motivation, it is evidently not so. The psyche is driven by something beyond the principle of internal balance.

It was about the question of pleasure and its role in the psychoanalytic view of motivation that Lacan began his seventh seminar entitled "The Ethics of Psychoanalysis" (1959–1960). He notes that the link between pleasure and "the good" goes back to Aristotle. Thus, in the overall view, Freud's recurrent efforts to define it and his inquiry into its limits have ancient roots. Lacan's project in that seminar was to show what new dimensions psychoanalysis brings to this ancient topic. Among those, perhaps the most important and central to Lacan's view is that a new distinctly psychoanalytic concept of the human subject only emerges in Freud's movement beyond the pleasure principle, in the redefinition of pleasure itself and in the death drive. The nineteenth-century conception of the psychological subject rested happily on the principle of economic balance, and it seems as though Freud initially thought the psychoanalytic subject might as well. However, the encounter with certain features of unconscious motivation including repetition, narcissism, traumatic return, and self-destruction led to an altogether different idea of human subjectivity. It is to the death drive that Freud is drawn when he ventures beyond the pleasure principle and thus in working out what this means, we are challenged as well to address how the meaning of the death drive (*Todestrieb*) affects the idea of the psychoanalytic drive (*Trieb*) as such.

The idea that the psychoanalytic concept of the drive is implicated in a new conception of the human subject is still a current topic of debate in our field. Lacan's explorations of 60 years ago are relevant precisely because the field at present is still engaged in trying to resolve some of the questions he raised, whether this is known or acknowledged by contemporary analysts or not.

Thus, in Morris Eagle's most recent book, *Toward a Unified Psychoanalytic Theory: Foundation in a Revised and Expanded Ego Psychology* (2022), we find Eagle confronting the problems of a psychoanalytic theory of the subject, the extent to which the concept of Ego needs to be expanded in relation to this theory, and how a theory of motivation and the idea of "affect regulation" relates to the economic model as well as to the psychoanalytic conception of the drives. Without this being explicitly noted by Eagle, it is essentially the same set of problems addressed by Lacan in his Ethics Seminar (1959–1960). However, where Lacan approaches the problem by expanding the notion of the psychoanalytic drive (and especially the death drive), Eagle and many other Anglo-American analysts argue that we should discard or at least minimize the role of the drive due to its narrow focus. As Eagle (2021) puts it, "'Liberating' ego psychology from drive theory allows recognition of the wide range of human aims, motives, desires, and feelings that many individuals defend against consciously experiencing and acknowledging" (p. 251). In other words, the functions of the repressed unconscious in Eagle's view should not be limited to a narrow concept of balancing the psychic economy. If, however, we accept the definition of the drive as beyond this balance, no "liberation" from drive theory is required. An expanded concept of the Ego might better be supported by an expanded concept of the drive. Lacan's strategy might indeed be useful to Eagle's project.

Another contemporary exploration beyond the pleasure principle is Avgi Saketopoulou's essay, "The Draw to Overwhelm: Consent, Risk and the Retranslation of Enigma" (2019). In proposing the neologism *overwhelm* (as a noun), Saketopoulou refers to "excitation … beyond the pleasure principle, into pleasure that is suffered" (p. 18). This is essentially Lacan's (1986/1997) idea of *jouissance*, including its link to the death drive. Although Saketopoulou doesn't cite that connection, she relies a great deal on the work of Jean Laplanche who was an active participant in Lacan's seminars in the late 1950s when the concept of *jouissance* was introduced. Her discussion of the function of a certain dissolution or "shattering" of the ego in psychoanalytic treatment so as to allow for new significations (translations) is in keeping with the idea that the drive *beyond* entails a wider idea of subjective possibility than that of a balanced economy.

In reconsidering the drive beyond the pleasure principle to enhance our understanding of what takes place in psychoanalytic treatment, I would also cite Nestor Braunstein's important study of the same, *Jouissance: A Lacanian Concept* (2021). That this work has now been translated into English allows the Anglo-American analytic community to benefit from the rich and complex work on Freud's step beyond the pleasure principle. Braunstein effectively charts the concept of *jouissance* in its relation to Freudian thought, the drives, *libido*, etc. and presents how Lacan developed the idea and struggled with its implications.

In what follows, I hope to draw that untranslated (untranslatable?) French term out of a certain obscurity that surrounds it, both because of the difficulty of Lacan's exposition and the difficulty in the concept itself, I will address the topic outside of the Lacanian discourse per se. I want to see if the ideas that surround this term can be rendered useful for contemporary Anglo-American psychoanalysts who might not be familiar with the Lacanian framework.

Texts such as Hannah Segal's "On the Clinical Usefulness of the Concept of the Death Instinct" (1992), and recent books such as Mitchell Wilson's *The Analyst's Desire: The Ethical Foundation of Clinical Practice* (2020) as well as Eagle's *Toward a Unified Psychoanalytic Theory* (2021, op. cit.) address, each in different ways, the concept of the subject in psychoanalysis in relation to theories of motivation, desire, and drive and thus are engaged in a related project even if in some instances neither *jouissance* nor the death drive are addressed directly.

If the pleasure principle involves an overly restricted and narrow idea of pleasure, the idea of the death drive, as well as the other ideas outlined by Freud beyond the pleasure principle such as the compulsion to repeat, primary masochism, the structure of melancholia can be viewed in terms of an expanded, more nuanced, notion of pleasure itself. Jacques Lacan's introduction of the term *jouissance* can then be understood as an effort to conceptualize this wider notion and in a sense recover pleasure from the pleasure principle after going beyond it. Since *jouissance* is a rough synonym for pleasure, that is, the two words fall within the same rather complex semantic field, the difference between them may illustrate an important dimension of the psychoanalytic theory of motive.

In the indispensable *Dictionary of Untranslatables* (2004/2014), "a philosophical lexicon", the word pleasure requires over 10 pages of attention to unpack its history of diverse meanings. The differences among these and the choices made to privilege one or another aspect of the overall concept reflect complex ethical and philosophical decisions. There are no neutral positions about the meaning of pleasure. It is a notion deeply implicated in ideas of the human subject, the nature of virtue, and truth.

This is so because the human experience of pleasure cannot be separated from the meaning of that pleasure for the subject who experiences it. And, like all meaning, the meaning of human pleasure cannot be taken out of time, the time of the experience. The pleasure I experience is never detached from the event and context in which I am experiencing the pleasure. The fact that I am experiencing a certain pleasure at a certain time in a certain context is an act that situates me as a subject. I am interpellated, called into being as a subject, by my pleasure/*jouissance* insofar as it provokes a question in the other, experienced as an implicit demand, "What is your pleasure?" It situates me by posing the question of its meaning. Even the idea of a "simple pleasure" involves a claim, a claim that has meaning that is already or could certainly be put in doubt, which would of course affect the nature of my experience. In calling it a "simple pleasure" I already imply that it could be more than that, else why declare it to be simple. I am already answering for it.

If in this way, the meaning and implication of the experience of pleasure are an essential part of the pleasure itself, Freud's earlier reliance on the principle of an economic balance was bound to fall short. In generating meaning there will always be surplus and indeterminacy, factors that will not be balanced. In the course of psychoanalytic work and in the refinement of its concepts, the complexities of satisfaction, enjoyment, consumption, and use were bound to go beyond a pleasure principle too simply conceived. This has implications for the structure of the subject in psychoanalysis because it implies that derivatives of the drives are already in some way caught up with questions of sense and meaning, with signification and trans-lation. This is how Lacan, Laplanche, and others in the French tradition come to situate the subject and the drive as an effect of language and the symbolic function rather than as an entity, a biological given, independent of these functions. While Laplanche (1992) rejects Lacan's use of the category Symbolic, he nevertheless relies upon the idea of the "message" to convey this link between the drives and signifi-cation. What is beyond the pleasure principle in the death drive, the compulsion to repeat, etc., is inherent in the ever-partial satisfaction consequent upon ever-incomplete meaning. Pleasure is an event in the history of the subject and partakes of its complexities and limitations.

Along the way in Cassin's (ibid.) philological history of the meanings of pleasure, one of the many meanings we encounter is that of Augustine's *fruitio,* about which the editors say, "... the French term jouissance is an exact translation" (p. 795). *Fruitio* is a notion, in Augustine's Latin, that combines the ideas of enjoyment and use. It is the pleasure that comes in taking pleasure. Taking pleasure in pain would thus be less alien than we usually think of regarding pleasure in the simpler sense since the element of use is present. Certain apparently masochistic practices, like cutting for instance, can then be seen in this sense as the use of the body, and indeed as marking that use upon the surface itself. Many of the debates among psycho-analytic schools, debates about libidinization, about the relative primacy of relational and libidinal motives, about gratification and adaptation are in fact debates about how to conceptualize enjoyment, use, and pleasure in this wider, more nuanced sense.

Pleasure evokes a range of meanings that indeed expands even as one considers it.

> The great diversity of pleasure's semantic field seems so universal that Jeremy Bentham, the philosopher of pleasure and happiness, seeking to determine the range of meanings in English, ended up forging the concept of "fruitfulness" to designate pleasure's ability to produce further pleasures ... .
>
> (ibid., p. 798)

In other words, the concept itself is generative of multiple instances of itself and thus seems limitless in its possible meanings. Pleasure begets the satisfaction of enjoyment. Bentham enumerates 54 synonyms many of which, such as happiness and play, are clearly founts of additional meanings as well.

The interplay of experience and self-reflection under the broad umbrella of "pleasure" is indeed a challenge and as Eagle (2021) as recently argued leads us to examine the very notion of the subject of that reflective experience, the "I" or Ego who enjoys that pleasure while reflecting on its meaning. It is noteworthy that in his effort to revise Ego Psychology as a framework for unifying contemporary psycho-analytic thought, Eagle arrives at the problem of the psychoanalytic theory of the subject, a problem very much associated with Lacan's study and seemingly at odds with what had seemed a more settled notion in Ego Psychology. It is the subject continually subverted by the meaning of its desire even as it is articulated that interests Lacan (2007), and this seems to be where Eagle's thought is also taking him.

Repetition

I recently wrote about the treatment of a young child (Lichtenstein, 2019) to frame a discussion about the death drive as a clinical concept. In that treatment, the subject in question was dealing with the actual death of a parent. Her treatment was meant to help her to deal with this loss. She established from the first moment of the treatment a manner of working where the compulsion to repeat and to set up repeated encounters with the dilemma of ending and beginning was particularly apparent. Apart from what was said, and the gradual elaboration of a verbal history in the treatment, there was a meaning conveyed by the urgency of her focus on certain games that repeatedly enacted themes of disappearance, shock, and deception. It was the form of her play that spoke to the dilemma she found herself in trying to make sense of the disappearance of a parent.

The enjoyment of the games was in their repetitive use, but also in their play on horror, loss, and surprise and the engendering of pleasure/pain. In short, there was a *jouissance* encountered and repeated in the work that simultaneously conveyed meaning, the limits of meaning, and that which is beyond the limits of meaning. The intensity of the play, using both the child's and the analyst's physical presence as a marker for absence in the playful assumption that hiding and discovering can effect. In one sense, the games were nothing unusual, the kind of games children play, but in another, as with Freud's grandson in the crib, they offered the basis to see a momentous encounter—in the case of Freud's grandson a representation of separation from his mother, in the case of my patient the effort to represent the enigmatic and intolerable permanent loss of a parent.

We can go beyond the singularity of the treatment described and instead consider how the subject as encountered in psychoanalysis always presents as driven by something other than balancing the economy of pleasure. The subject in question in my case was dealing with an actual death which allowed certain connections to be made to the functions of impossible loss and repetition; however, those functions operate as well when other questions face the subject in analysis. There is no reason to think that the death drive was more influential in her case than in others, and indeed because the child was dealing with a proximal experience of death there is a risk of misunderstanding, as though the form of the death drive is a result only of an encounter with an actual death rather than what is in fact the case, that it is a result of the inescapable encounter with loss as such.

The subject as such, which is the discursive being who is speaking, is always driven by an encounter with the function of absence, a fading or disappearance, aphanisis[1] and a repetitive and uncanny return to point zero that suggests death. Discursive being, observing the laws of discourse rather than those of physics, is rooted in the interplay of presence/absence inherent in the symbolizing function. It is in this sense that we can consider the death drive to be an essential element in our view of subjectivity as encountered in the practice of psychoanalysis. There is an inherent repetition in this encounter with absence that underlies the place of the speaking subject. We are repeatedly losing ourselves in what we say.

While this might seem to be an unwarranted and unfair shift from the meaning of death as organic ending to that of a symbolic death, and thus to be a preservation of the idea of the death drive only by emptying it of its real meaning (*pace* Nobus), I think the truth of the matter is more complicated. In biology, the distinction between life and death is in fact not easily made as is evident in the case of the virus a biological entity that occupies a zone between life and death. Indeed, the question in this ambiguous zone is about the replication of genetic codes, and thus indeed a metaphor ("code") from the cultural to the organic, reversing the direction of Freud's metaphors from the organic to the psychic. Insofar as an essential element in the definition of life is the organism's ability to reproduce, the question of viral repetition and how it figures in and differs from cellular reproduction is at the heart of the biological considerations of life and death just as repetition and the possibility of the new operates in the psychic realm.

Replication, the uncanny return of the same, the double, and the various forms that the trope of repetition can assume, has long had notable literary and philosophical resonances. It is found in the work of Poe, Nietzsche, and others (Levine, 2020, pp. 11–25). Kierkegaard's (1843/1964) essay on Repetition is especially noteworthy especially in its appreciation of the psychic interplay between stasis and innovation. Of course, we should also include Freud's discussion of the Sandman and the subsequent literary and philosophical discussions of that work (Levine, ibid.). It is clear that Freud was quite familiar with cultural context of this problem and indeed made explicit as well as implicit reference to the idea of the eternal return of the same in the essay on uncanny as well as in BPP. Repetition as a compulsion but also as an element in treatment was of course addressed in "Remembering, repeating, and working through" (1914). The link between repetition and the death drive is one that renders the idea of the latter meaningful in a clinical context. It is in repetition that the idea of stasis and the zero is meaningful and also the idea of the new or invention can be marked. That we find genetic replication to be at the core of the distinction between life and death brings new meaning to Freud's metabiological speculations. I want now to return with this idea to the psychoanalytic process.

Speaking to the analyst in the context of transference that for our purposes can be defined as the repetition of the original loss entails the possibility of a kind of saying that will have proven to be a zero point, a point of departure for the arrival of something new. This possibility arises out of the illocutionary aspects of speech (Austin, 1962). The act of saying something not only conveys the conceptual content of what is said but implicates the subject in the very act of saying. Like the "I do" in the wedding ceremony, it is not just an affirmation that I am an agreement with the marriage, that is, I am not just taking myself as an object and reporting that this person (who I am) is in agreement, but rather that I, as a speaking subject in the moment of the utterance, avow my commitment qua subject. Likewise, if in the transferential context of an analysis, I say, "I love/hate you" to the analyst I might depending on its illocutionary function be describing in an apparently objective manner, a feeling of love/hatred, as if to say, "sometimes I have a feeling of love/ hatred towards you". I am attenuating and distancing myself from the passion involved and informing the analyst of my emotions. Whereas if I say the "I love/hate you" as a subject in the moment of utterance, what we can call following the French usage, "an enunciation", I am *avowing* my love/hatred not just describing it. In that, I am using/enjoying my place as a subject of passion. When this occurs in the context of transference so that the other to whom I am enunciating this passion is experienced as more than he or she is as an ordinary person, the effect is meaningful in the particular way that makes psychoanalysis possible. It is the *jouissance* encountered through the utterance, the exciting pleasure/pain use of speech, that both ruptures the subject of polite discourse and allows a new subjective position to emerge.

In order for that to become a starting point, a new position for the speaking subject, it will have also proven to be an end point. This traversal of the zero, of the end that is a beginning, is an essential principle of psychoanalytic treatment. Indeed, without it, psychoanalysis is just another form of psychoeducation. This coming of the new in the place of a dead end is not about pleasure in the way we would understand it. A pleasure may be sought in the form of repetition—"the finding of an object is always a re-finding"—however, that does not convey the dynamics of an ending and a coming into being of the new. Indeed, one can approach the analyst as a potential source of some already known pleasure/unpleasure, for instance, approval, acceptance, friendly interest, or their negations. What ultimately matters in the course of an analysis, however, is something else something beyond those known objects, some new encounter with an object which as Loewald (2000) argues will also be a new form of object created in the work of psychoanalysis. This is closer to what I have in mind.

Use

The place of invention or creation in psychoanalytic work is not easily addressed. The archeological metaphor remains influential and privileges the idea of uncovering something already there. The limitations in this model are addressed by Laplanche (1992) in his linking of the drive and the signifier. How in putting the "already there" into words, something new may come into being, indeed something new that profoundly alters the "already there" is the sort of reverse causality addressed by Freud's *nachtraglichkeit* (*après-coup*) that has been translated in various ways into English, i.e., deferred action or "afterwardness", which generally fail to capture the idea of the reversal of normal causality, that is, the extent to which the later event causes a change in the earlier event. This reverse causality is a necessary element in the idea of invention in psychoanalysis because it is only in that way that something new can affect the already there. Another way to consider this paradoxical process is in terms of re-inscription with the idea that a re-inscribed memory trace is both the earlier thing (as memory trace) and a new thing (as re-inscription). This brings us back to the idea of repetition, because in repetition there is a re-inscription of the same that is by virtue of the "re-" (re-petition, re-inscription, and re-turn) is both the same and not the same.

As Kierkegaard (1964) put it, "The dialectic of repetition is easy, because that which is repeated has been, otherwise it could not be repeated; but precisely this, that it has been, makes repetition something new" (p. 18).

Thus, something new comes into being through repetition insofar as it is articulated or inscribed anew, but we are again brought to the question of what this has to do with death as well as with that which is "beyond the pleasure principle". In what sense is death encountered here in the death drive?

At moments Freud takes us to the matter of organic mortality, death in the common sense of the end of organic life, but in other, it is clear that this is only meant to be taken as an analogy, that the drive as a demand made on the psyche is demanding something beyond a single organism's death in this drive to return. Thus, Freud introduces the Nirvana principle and the universal zero or void. What is this universal void that is other than the organism's death and what does it have to do either with the pleasure/unpleasure balance or rather with something else that becomes the aim of the drive when it moves beyond that principle?

A concept that is useful in addressing this question is the archaic and awkward notion of usufruct. Its most general meaning is the right to use or enjoy something. It doesn't mean that one is enjoying in the sense of pleasure but rather enjoying in the sense simply of deriving the benefits of use. For example, if one enjoys the rights to a property, one is not necessarily always deriving pleasure from that use. Indeed, at moments one might be frustrated and disappointed but that wouldn't change the juridical fact that one is enjoying the rights to the property. It is this meaning of enjoyment, namely that which comes from the benefit of use, whether pleasurable or unpleasurable, that is needed in order to make sense out of the aim of the death drive. We might then say that the human subject has the rights, the usufruct, to the drive itself as a unified concept in its expression of both life and death and it is this use, a use that ultimately defines the subject, that is beyond the pleasure principle.

As usufruct, right of enjoyment, *jouissance* is juridical in nature. That is to say that it is in some way governed by or implicated in the function of law. In other words, the right to enjoyment usufruct/*jouissance* is always essentially and in principle limited insofar as law is the establishment of limit. The drive can be enjoyed but always as limited, for instance, limited to the lifetime of the user, which is to say, by death. My goal now is to show how this logical and general framework of a juridical limit and enjoyment of the drives regarding life and death is clinically relevant.

Donald Winnicott (1969) touched on this problem in his essay, "The use of an object". In his conclusion, he states, "The object is always being destroyed. This destruction becomes the unconscious backcloth for love of a real object; that is, an object outside the area of the subject's omnipotent control" (1969, p. 714).

That the object is "outside the area of the subject's omnipotent control" is another way of asserting that the use (enjoyment) of the object is limited in some way.

For Winnicott the limit arises from the reality of the object being used, a reality that he calls shared (p. 711). This "shared reality" (p. 711) of the object is an essential feature (for Winnicott) of the transitional object as such. It is both real and imagined in Winnicott's self-described paradoxical logic. That it might be purely imagined and thus not a transitional object as such is referred to by Winnicott in asserting that the object in question is not merely "a bundle of projection" (p. 711). However, it is not merely a real object in the world either, precisely because it is an object that can be destroyed by the subject, that is to say, it is an object subject to destruction, disappearance, and absence. To exist in the form that Winnicott is asserting it must exist in order to be used in this manner, it must be an object defined paradoxically by the necessity of being both present and absent. To say that it must fulfill this logic is to say, again, that it is governed by law in the general sense I have been using it. The law that governs the use of an object qua transitional object is that it must destroyed, i.e., absent, and also must return (survive) as present. There may be things that don't observe this principle (projections, as such) but they won't be considered transitional objects and will not be subject to the use (enjoyment, *jouissance*) in question. The links between Winnicott and Lacan on the nature and the use of the object are addressed well by Alain Vanier (2012).

The idea that links the conceptualization of clinical work in such apparently disparate theorists as Loewald (2000), Winnicott (1969), and Lacan (1973/ 1998) is that the use of the object, and the analysand indeed the analysis itself coming to occupy the place of the object that is being so used by an emerging subject, is a use that involved the interplay of destruction, absence as an absolute void on the one hand and return and/or reappearance on the other. Whether or not it is conceptualized as an expression of the drive (as it is by Lacan) or is conceived more phenomenologically, as by Loewald and Winnicott, each in their way, it remains an idea that links a certain idea of use, (enjoyment, *jouissance*) with destruction, separation, death, as well as with return and the idea of the "new".

The contemporary theorists such as Wilson (2020) and Eagle (2022) in their respective efforts to develop a new synthesis across psychoanalytic schools should also implicitly address the problem of the subject who comes to be in the process of psychoanalysis, and indeed who comes to be precisely insofar as there is a new use of the object and the object relation, is another indication of the importance of the notion of use and enjoyment I am considering here. It is precisely the idea of the subject as such conceived in a new way through psychoanalytic work that is at stake. Eagle (personal communication) has recognized this through his work on "a revised and expanded ego psychology".

The one who enjoys (the subject of jouissance) comes into being also as the one who accepts the limits to enjoyment. This duality is the way to conceive of this new subject of psychoanalysis once the notion of enjoyment is appreciated in its fully paradoxical and/or contradictory character of life/death. In Lacanian language this is the fading of the subject in the jouissance of signification. It is insofar as the subject is speaking in the face of the gap or absence that this coming to be as a (new) subject emerges. Braunstein (2021) describes this formative absence as a debt. In order to use the symbol (and exactly as in the use of the transitional object it is impossible to resolve the question is it yours or is it not yours) there must a loss of omnipotent use (of jouissance) since the symbol is real (in Winnicott's sense). It is found in and "borrowed" from the other and governed by the basic law of representation—this is primal repression.

In taking up a place as a speaking subject, the limits on enjoyment must be recognized and a certain symbolic debt incurred. The symbolic act is predicated on the loss of omnipotence in relation to enjoyment (jouissance). The subject who speaks and in so doing enjoys the possibilities (the use and benefits) of symbolic being emerges in the very place of its own fading. It is this pulsation as the repetition of absence and presence that reflects the interplay of the death drive and its affirmative erotic potential, the interplay of the life and death drives as described by Freud (1920). However, as this underlies the very possibility of a speaking subject, it links the making of meaning to the dualities of the drives as such.

The problem faced by the patient I discussed in the 2019 essay was how to make sense of the loss of a parent. It is not a problem that can be solved by an explanation or the imparting of a meaning that is already known. There can be no satisfactory answer to the challenge of making sense of a senseless loss. There can be no psychic balancing of the account. Any analysis here is the creation of meaning in the face of its impossibility. Indeed, does one ever know once and for all the meaning of a profound loss? In a certain sense, this is the problem faced in every psychoanalysis, even if the conditions of the loss are singular for that analysis, the abiding question is can meaning be made in the face of that impossibility. Where it was, there I will have come to be. Even if coming to be there, I can only fade again in the face of the impossible and unknowable meaning. The games of hide and seek, of here and gone and here again, that the child (patient) introduced in the very first session in our treatment established in a formal way the pattern that would gradually be filled out by speech and by our partial understanding (since an understanding of life and death can only be partial at best). These games as structures of symbolic possibility were the framework that allowed a subject to come into being in the place of loss. And that likewise allowed loss to come into play in the place of the subject, thereby allowing and indeed deploying the death drive in signification. Playing with the disappearance, indeed, annihilation of the subject was a crucial element in the creation of meaning.

The question is not simply whether something can be said but whether the I, as the subject who is speaking, can come to say something that has a new recursive effect for the subject. This is the heart of psychoanalytic work. It is a kind of knowing that only has value as a moment of saying. However, in order to be a mutative event as the psychoanalytic act may be, it cannot be just any saying repeating, as it were, the already known. It must be a saying in the moment of loss, in the encounter with traumatic absence, that the transference brings into being. In this sense, there must be the presence of death in the use (enjoyment) of symbolic being that psychoanalysis makes possible.

Note

1 A term from the Greek word for disappearance, first introduced by Jones (1927) and developed by Lacan (1973/1998).

References

Austin, J. L. (1962) *How to do things with words.* Oxford: Clarendon Press.

Braunstein, N. (2021) *Jouissance: a Lacanian concept.* SUNY Press.

Eagle, M. (2021) *Toward a unified psychoanalytic theory: foundation in a revised and expanded ego psychology.* Routledge.

Freud, S. (1895) Project for a scientific psychology. *SE*:1:283–392.

Freud, S. (1914) Remembering, repeating, and working through. *SE* 12:145–156.

Freud, S. (1920) Beyond the pleasure principle. *SE* 18:7–66.

Jones, E. (1927). The early development of female sexuality. *International Journal of Psychoanalysis* 8:459–472.

Kierkegaard (1964). *Repetition.* Harper.

Lacan, J. (1997) *Seminar VII: the ethics of psychoanalysis.* Norton.

Lacan, J. (1973/1998). *Seminar of Jacques Lacan: on feminine sexuality, the limits of love and knowledge.* Norton.

Lacan, J. (2007). *Ecrits.* Norton.

Laplanche, J. (1992) Interpretation between determinism and hermeneutics: a restatement of the problem. *The International Journal of Psychoanalysis* 73:429–445.

Levine, M. (2020) *RISS, Materialien 6 Hamburg*, pp. 11–25.

Lichtenstein, D. (2019) A clinical instance of the death drive in a child analysis. *Research in Psychoanalysis* 28(2):78–82.

Loewald, H. (2000) *The essential Loewald: collected papers and monographs.* University Publishing Group.

Nobus, D. (2021) Narcissism and the pleasures of extinction: for the centenary of 'beyond the pleasure principle'. https://www.journal-psychoanalysis.eu/narcissism-and-the-pleasures-of-extinction-for-the-centenary-of-beyond-the-pleasure-principle/

Saketopoulou, A. (2019) The draw to overwhelm: consent, risk, and the retranslation of enigma. *Journal of the American Psychoanalytic Association* 67:133–167.

Vanier, A. (2012). Winnicott and Lacan: a missed encounter? *The Psychoanalytic Quarterly* 81:279–303.

Winnicott, D. W. (1969) The use of an object. *International Journal of Psychoanalysis* 50:711–716.

Wilson, M. (2020). *The analyst's desire: the ethical foundation of clinical practice.* Bloomsbury Academic.

Chapter 17

Destructive Envy and the Narcissistic Grip*

Dominique Cupa

Translated by Michael Civin

When Paul Denis offered me a reflection on envy, I first thought about primary envy in the manner theorized by Melanie Klein in Envy and Gratitude: "Defense against envy often takes the form of devaluation of the object. I have suggested that spoiling and devaluing are inherent in envy. The object which has been devalued need not be envied any more. This soon applies to the idealized object, which has been devalued and therefore no longer idealized" (1993/1957, p. 217). My mind drifted to a patient with whom I do analytical work face to face, once a week, in an institution … Perhaps reformulating my understanding of her might help me understand better some aspect of Lola's daughter-mother relationship. She began her therapy by saying that she had "no envy of anything", which seemed explained much better by applying this notion of primary envy in its relationship to destructiveness. I also had in mind the way in which my patient told me repeatedly about the layout of her studio, her staged productions in my office space and the frequent use of projective identification that I observed in the negative transference and countertransference. Without being "Kleinian", I think, like Michel Neyraut, that a certain number of Freudian and Kleinian conceptions "are more complementary than they are contradictory; they are situated at different epistemological levels" (Neyraut, 1974, p. 225).

Michel Fain adds an enlightening clarification, because I present a work on daughter-mother relationships: "M. Klein constantly builds upon a foundation of the breast that Freud, himself, constructed around the oedipal. This is why, along with D. Braunschweig, we thought that the manifest contradictions between Freud's conceptions and those of M. Klein were along the lines of a contradiction inherent in the structure of the human being, a contradiction attached human bisexuality: all that is feminine in us is closer to the Kleinian phantasmagoria than Freudian intelligibility" (Fain, 1971, p. 306).

The unconscious phantasmagoria evoked by Klein and the interpretations she proposes, aiming to enter the deep layers of the psyche have always aroused my interest, but also my disagreement. I don't use her interpretative style, which among other things ignores the repercussions as shown by Michel de M'Uzan (1994, p. 105) by opposing Kleinian tactics and Freudian strategy. If, in Freud, envy is above all

---

* From Cupa, D. (2021). Envie destructrice, emprise et narcissisme. *Revue française de psychanalyse*, (3), 573-585. Paris, France. Reprinted with permission.

DOI: 10.4324/9781003384618-23

"envy of the penis" in women, a female correlate of the castration complex, for Klein the oral envy of the breast dominates the psyche and infiltrates the envy of the penis in women, the genital in natural continuity with primary orality.

"Every child", she writes, "feels envy at some point, and desires to possess the attributes and abilities that belong to parents: those of the mother first, followed those of the father. Originally, envy is directed against the breast of the mother and the milk she produces, but in reality the envy is directed at the creativity of the mother. One of the effects of envy is expressed by the desire to turn the tables, to reduce parents to infantile helplessness and draw sadistic pleasure from this reversal" (1957/1983, p. 196).

This excessive "fundamental primitive feeling" collides with "deprivation" and "frustration", provoking hatred and destructiveness as well as a "primary moral anguish". Beyond the reference to drive duality, this quote implies the question of narcissism, which Klein does not link in so many words to envy even though Karl Abraham, who influenced her, makes this link.

This is the question of envy in its link to narcissism, its attacks and responses they elicit that I question in resonance with my clinical work. I also have in mind that Freud, noting that it is difficult to capture the primary narcissism of the child, seeks it out from the position of the parents towards their children". We are obliged, "he writes", to recognize in it the revival and reproduction of their own long abandoned narcissism. He specifies that there "is a tendency to attribute every perfection to the child", "*His Majesty the Baby* ... will fulfill wishful dreams that parents did not fulfill" (Freud, 1914/2005, p. 234).

The child is the projective container of parental narcissism, parental envy, mirrored by that of the child who wishes to possess all the perfections of the parents, being fully satisfied.

What then happens when a parent does not feel narcissistically satisfied? Either by disappointment: the child does not have all the perfections, or by fear that the child overshadow her, as is the case with Snow White's stepmother. Doesn't that parent develop a certain hateful, even destructive, envy of the child, a mirror of the latter's hateful envy towards him?

Lola and Her Mother or the "Envious Fragmentation" of the Child

She said: "I have a weight, an inertia, I don't envy anything". She was totally invested in her headaches, which were present 24 hours a day. She neither complains nor speaks of pain; she does not seek to find a meaning, a cause. She fixates on these internal persecuting companions. The future consists of the next meeting with herself or with her mother who lives in Provence. She vegetates in the studio her parents set up. She has no friends. She stopped her biology studies. She does not work. She could be very pretty but can't seem to be able to invest her femininity; even her narcissism is abandoned.

For a long time I have the feeling that facing me I have me a little girl in distress. However, Lola is over 50 years old. Paradoxically, she seems to be cathected to the meaninglessness of clothing, aspiring to an evacuated state, inducing a state of emptiness that she tries to countercathect by hanging onto her pain.

Part of Me Envies the Analyst

Lola has already had a lengthy therapy. Her headaches have been around since adolescence. Back then she had an anorexic episode and depression with suicidal ideation. The headaches start. Her mother imposes a draconian vegetarian diet on her, to put on a device to clamp the nose, requires her to wear woolen panties, forbids her to go out: she must remain locked in her room, " like today". This being the case, at the start of our work, Lola praises the qualities of her generous, kind, solid mother who always took good care of her.

Her father is presented initially as an invalid under careful care that mother and daughter share. It was only late in our work that he appears as a hero having a mistress accepted by his wife, because she finds no satisfaction in sexual relations and, for that matter, in very little else.

Evocations of her mother bear witness to the imago of an almighty object that is in front of a tenuous ego which exists only as a maternal extension. This phallic narcissistic woman ran a small business. The representation of maternal figures is twofold, one archetypally intrusive, the other tender. Paternal representations at the start of treatment attest to the projection of the maternal imago onto the paternal imago, which evokes an undifferentiated maternal and paternal configuration (characteristic, according to M. Bouvet, of a non-neurotic state). The beginning of a differentiation of these imagoes with its parallel in the shift from psychic functioning in imagoes to functioning in actuality appeared recently.

Lola quite quickly brings up a nerve-wracking dream in which she lost her purse:

I'm going to a party. I can't find my handbag anymore. I ask the receptionist where it might be. She shows me a cupboard. As there is not a lot of light, I think it's my cellphone.

Lola has no associations.

I just tell her that, "like the person in her dream, I receive her". She is surprised.

I think to myself of the handbag as a lost feminine attribute, of a closet that might contain inaccessible genitalia. Would the bag be a corpse in that closet? I think this fits well with her asexual presentation. The cellphone allows you to talk to each other, but at a distance. I understand her surprise as a defense against my introduction of the transference. Might I be the embodiment of the intrusive imago? Could it be a request for a "maternal" homosexual initiation into sexuality? In this dynamic of intrusion/abandonment anxiety, paradoxically, it seems to me that intrusion is both feared and sought.

The most difficult thing for me is to endure Lola's countless repetitions session after session. She talks and she talks. My patience, my masochism are put on trial. We are in the repetition of the same as de M'Uzan theorizes. In this non-neurotic patient, the economic dimension is invasive, it discharges "unbound" excitations in the face if which meaning falters. Her speech has no expressive value; it is not related to fantasies.

I have the feeling that a fundamentally negative transference is unfolding, because for a long time she rejects my interventions, which at times provokes my hostility, because it undermines my work, makes me helpless. How to understand her rejections?

I agree with Klein in thinking that "doubts about the value of analysis arise from the fact that the patient has split the envious, hostile part and that he presents constantly to the analyst certain aspects which he believes more acceptable. These partial cleavages exert a considerable influence on the analysis" (1927/1983, p. 22). *But then so what does she envy in me that would provoke her hostility? My ability to listen to, to make connections?*

Aren't her flood of words and the rejection of my interventions also defenses against the threat of the intrusive maternal imago projected on me in the transference? Don't they possibly risk mobilizing traumatic traces through associativity, even to bring into resonance and correspondence the very themes whose revival threatens to unleash violence against herself, a decompensation of the ego?

Traumatic Control and Destructive Rage

After a few months, Lola devotes her sessions to telling me about cockroaches who invaded her studio. She shows me the little bites made by the insects, scratches herself in front of me, which leads me to wonder about her autoerotism. She insistently repeats how her bed, each of her walls, her carpet, etc., and she herself are attacked by these insects. She lets herself be bitten, sometimes cursing them, but does nothing to get rid of them.

I ended up telling her that: "If I were in his place, I would call the services of the mair (i) e [mayor/city hall], because it is a painful situation to allow yourself to be attacked in this way".

In the moment, I think that there is an external projection of the internal attacks of the maternal objects which persecute her with re-projection of bad objects which attack her ego from without. I try to promote an identificatory closeness without being injunctive, which would risk reproducing maternal intrusiveness, this guided by the conception of the "maternal function of the therapist" according to Pierre Marty (1990, p. 95).

In the apres-coup, however, I question my intervention from the perspective of reality. Countertransferentially, I realized that I saw the invasion of insects by my patient as *a sort of traumatic stranglehold:* I can't hear it any more, a phallic narcissistic defense against her destructiveness. Then I wonder if the envy that Lola shows for me is not linked to the intrusive control of her mother.

Lola ends up asking for help and making use of the intervention of sanitary services; the cockroaches being wiped out, she empties her studio, ransacking what remains, destructive rage of envy against the maternal imago that I represent. Because of me, her "claustrum" would be penetrated and she felt helpless. I then associate to the beginning of Colette and Ravel's lyric fantasy, *The Child and the Sortilèges,* that

Klein commented on (1929/1974, p. 254). The child lacerates the curtain, destroys the pendulum of the clock, tears books to pieces, injures a squirrel, etc.

The passivity of my patient in the face of the invasion of insects and its reversal in destructive rage will also make me think of a work by Gérard Szwec (2018), which links this to the absence of negation and to psychosomatic imbalances. Lola shows herself incapable of refusing my invitation, of saying "no" to me, which provokes a destructive rage in her.

The Damaged Narcissism of the Envied Subject

To differentiate a me with an empty inside from an outside full of objects to find takes time, as the distinction between subject and object progresses, as Winnicott suggests. Lola shares her painstaking efforts with me, her great difficulties in choosing each of these objects. I play the game. She finds a tiny capacity for libidinal investment, seeking an echo in my supportive and libidinalizing listening. So, for example, she searches for and extensively tests out the color of the paint on the walls of her room. She would prefer a soft gray, distant from the dark color of the paper chosen by her mother, which I support by a short "indeed". I then think of a positive transference to the frame; my enveloping listening would allow her to patch up the tears in her skin-ego (Anzieu, 1985).

Lola talks, once again repeats a lot and now gets up to demonstrate for me, in my office space, the organization of her interior. She finds my calm satisfying and talking to me relieves her. A beginning of introjection of a soothing object, but like the soft color of the paper, if the tenderness is present, it lacks liveliness, humanity.

Another scenario then unfolds that Lola calls "her mother's crises" that she also stages in my office by imitating her mother in a rage through projective identification and acting out the rage. I am thinking here of "Imitative current" Denis (1997, p. 92) linked to assuming control which can go as far as reproducing the behavior of others. This could be a necessary condition for being.

Lola's mother can't stand her daughter opposing her and screaming, threatening her physically and insulting her, which amazes my patient who cannot respond to her, who cannot say "no". She tells me that her mother often treated her and still treats her like a parasite.

The sadistic "bad mother" has been placed center stage so I will try a link between cockroaches and mother.

Lola partially accepts what I propose and replies that she never had the right to protest. The only time she complained, her mother told her that if she had known about her, she wouldn't have given birth. Lola feels annihilated; it's a wound worse than an insect bite. Her mother also always says hurtful things about her body, about what she does or thinks.

"Why does she blame everything I am?" Lola wonders.

This is what constitutes her narcissism that Lola feels damaged, destroyed by her mother. I think then of the furious envy of a mother deprived of the imaginary child fulfilling her narcissism, of a woman who cannot be satisfied. When Lola mistreats her internal objects/internal maternal chaos, is it not a question of tentative eagerness to regain maternal omnipotence in a destructive act against oneself and the other? Florence Guignard (1997, p. 127) notes that narcissism of the envied subject is put to the test, particularly when she has close relations with the envious subject.

Envious Maternal Control

A repetitive dream appears that she has had for a long time in which she is walled up alive. There is no way out. No one comes to help her. She can't seem to associate; she does not tolerate the connection between me and her mother who forbade her to go out. *I think of an envious maternal control.*

Around that time, she requested an administrative document from the institution. (The document was left on my desk, her sessions taking place late at night when there was no secretary.) When I give her the document, she is depressed: it isn't what she wants. I point out to her that she is depressed, which she accepts. In returning the document to a secretary the next day, I get angry. In my anger, I notice that I have demeaning thoughts for the institution. Handing over the new document to her the next session, I tell her that I have started to be angry for her. My projective identification touches her. I perceive internally, in my representations linked to the affect of anger, the devaluing aspect with respect to the mother.

Forced to submit, Lola cannot express her anger for fear of retaliation. She is also caught between disillusionment and love for her mother, having to choose between grief for the lost object and infantile omnipotence.

Lola was then able to enter into a more reflective stance, recognizing her mother's violence and increasingly admitting her own aggressive actions. She could express her exasperation with regard to her mother and inability to oppose her. I note that no guilt appears in Lola.

Klein argues that the early form of guilt associated with envy in its primary appearance cannot be experienced as genuine guilt; it regresses into persecutory anxiety because of the immaturity of the infant, resulting, according to Winnicott, in merciless ruthlessness.

It was around this time that Lola told me the story of her only lover. She was in her thirties, he found her beautiful, but too complicated and mistreated her dangerously. She was pregnant and had an abortion. I then said to her: "We never talked about it".

She replies: "I am not telling you everything". She could tell me that she does not tell me not everything, which signified progress for Lola.

Envy That Is Destructive to Creativity

After several months, Lola begins her session by telling me in a very confused manner how angry she is with a town hall employee. Her aggressive story is very complex; for me it seems Kafkaesque. So I said to her: "What you are telling me is Kafkaesque, a kind of imprisonment, as in your recurring dream".

Lola remembers as a child she slept in a small alcove. "When I turned at night against the wall, I thought I was walled up."

It is the first memory of childhood that she relates.

She associates to a movie that she saw on television. This is the story of an architect who built a tomb for a king. She emphasizes that the servants had been buried alive and that there were scratches all over the tomb. The architect fell in love with the king's wife and vice versa. The king has them buried in the tomb with lepers, but they escape with the help of a servant.

She associates to the idea that she never shared anything with her parents, no emotion, no listening, she couldn't talk to them. She then thinks back to the response from her mother about her abortion. Without affect, she said: "She eliminated me, killed my desires, what does she have against me?"

She reconsiders her difficulties in speaking. "We take it upon ourselves" (she gestures towards herself).

D: "We keep it for ourselves?"
L: "Yes, because we run into a wall. We're locked up."
D: "So how do you get yourself out of there?"
L: "Me, I'm getting out of there right now ... When I wanted to talk to her again about abortion, she replied that it was nothing. She didn't understand my desire for a child. She has always told me "you must not get married; you must not have children".

She frowns.

We are at the end of the session. I simply tell her: "We will pick up about all of this".

Lola's agonizing dream can be interpreted as a kind of imprisonment in the mother's womb. She would be the object that the mother does not want to give birth to/everything about giving birth, its "extension", its non-detachable child-penis. But even though the fantasy of returning to the mother's breast refers to a fantasy of coitus with the mother, *this fantasy of being immured in the mother's womb can be the image of submission to the envy of the mother who leaves her no way out.*

Her associations reveal fantasies of attack by sadistic scratches of the maternal body experienced as a tomb from which our work releases her. She comes out of the uterine tomb with the help of a servant-analyst and an architect- analyst who helps her build her interior. The cleavage between "good" and "bad" object is striking and I wonder then if one day we will reach the depressive position. The murderous king does not figure as a third object; he is only a simple duplication of the maternal imago. Lola's inadequate Oedipal resolution leaves her in a violent dual relationship.

It seems to me that we are at a transitional moment and that a real transfer appeared. Certainly, it is imprisoned in the controlling maternal uterus, in the alcove-screen-memory where her bed was, far from the parents' room with whom she "has no engagement". In doing so, a primal scene fantasy arises, structured in a "two-way" manner: a good and a bad parent, a fantasy into which she inscribed herself, the third object here is only the double of the object.

Linked to this is the painful memory of her abortion associated with the hateful envy of the mother who negates her, advises her not to have either a man or a child. I think then also to the lost bag of the first dream. As Klein points out (1957/1983, p. 46),

> *destructive envy attacks creativity which is as its core and its primordial instantiation the creation of children.*

Lola's mother is sterilizing, in enormous solitude; Lola has an abortion. For this mother Lola is not the child fulfilling her desire: she would neither be beautiful nor brilliant, not a boy, an unsatisfactory child of an unsatisfied woman.

> *Lola is the envied object of a hateful envy, because of her having disappointed her mother's expectation of both narcissistic and object-oriented satisfaction.*

Lola – "imprisoned" in the envious maternal destructiveness to which she submits, violated by maternal care, prohibited from masturbation by woolen breeches, forbidden to think, imprisoned in her defensive system – took the path of hateful disinvestment to the point of evacuating herself, depriving herself of her own substance; "negative narcissism" according to André Green where the ego is itself, even if you are not involved. The pain of headache remains the only form of possible world of deadly masochism according to Benno Rosenberg. In the analytical work with Lola, we identify the encystment of the mirroring relationship and its deleterious effects.

Lola who didn't want anything, not even from herself; she was locked in *the tomb dug by destructive envy, exacerbated with respect to her mother and vice versa.* To try to escape the implosion caused by the object, both in its presence and in its absence, her ego was paradoxically cornered, having to resort to her destructiveness, disinvesting herself of any serious struggle for a solution against the invasion by the envious object who is at the same time desired and dreaded.

A beginning of openness seems to be happening today: Lola was moved by laudatory words from a neighbor and she began to recall the difficult history of her mother's relationship with her own mother. The latter, belonging to a line of nobility, would have wanted to give birth to a boy; however, her only child had been Lola's mother. In addition, Lola's mother did not marry the man the grandmother wanted her to marry and was disinherited. Lola's mother does not appear to have responded to her mother's narcissistic wishes and this pattern was repeated with Lola and her mother.

But isn't Lola caught in the type of cross-currents of control that Denis describes? According to him the ego struggles for its preservation and its reinforcement, which involves the bringing into play ways of controlling the behavior of objects in the outside world to obtain the satisfaction that serves to limit their control. The external object becomes "bad" when it does not promote satisfaction for the subject. Can't we think of the installation of control as constituting the iron fist of envy in the seeking satisfaction, including narcissistic satisfaction? When installing control is not limited by the experience of satisfaction, the urge to control is heightened. She is seeking a narcissistic feast, rendering herself more powerful than the object.

Envy, Narcissism and Destructiveness

The envy between Lola and her mother dominates in a dual relationship in which the Oedipus is absent and does not mediate the envious mother-daughter relationship. It is a question of envy and not jealousy. Klein makes clear the difference between one and the other. Envy implies a dual relationship and goes back to the relationship of dependence on the mother; jealousy, which is based on envy, is situated in a relationship that is at least triangular. Lola is disappointing for her mother because she does not fulfill her desire to have a child with "all the perfections" of *His Majesty the Baby* and hurts her narcissism, which in turn undermines the narcissism of her daughter. The daughter, on the other hand, has a mother who does not have "all the perfections"; violence mirroring what is seen in the mirror. The reproaches that the mother makes to her daughter could be understood as the effects of destructive primary envy becoming destructive maternal primary envy towards her daughter. Doesn't Lola's mother re-enact the disappointment caused by her own mother, Lola's maternal grandmother? Gulgnard (2005, p. 32) points to the transgenerational transmission of envy. This was probably the case between Libussa and her daughter Melanie Klein, and between Melanie and her daughter Melitta. Freud specifies in his text on narcissism that "the thorny point" is that the child must also be the bearer of "the immortality of the (parental) self that reality beats up" (Freud, 1914/2005, pp. 234–235). *Doesn't the child have to bring itself to life to survive the parents' envy of its ideal ego? Doesn't he have to be the envied object of satisfactions which the parent had to abandon?*

I return, now, to my questioning concerning envy in its link to primary narcissism. Klein makes little use of the concept of narcissism. For her, it derives from the introjective and projective processes of the infant. She always emphasized that the first object relation is intertwined with the first identification, that love and identification are indistinguishable in the introjection of the "good object" that will become the core of the self. Envy concerns the negative aspect of projective identification.

A footnote in *Envy and Gratitude* (p. 18) seems particularly interesting to me, where she points out a remark that Elliott Jacques made to her on the etymological root of the word envy. This word comes from the Latin *invidia*, which derives from the verb *invideo*, to look at someone in a negative way, to consider him or her with distrust, resentment, to cast an evil eye on him or her. This confirms, she writes, the distinction she makes between envy and greed, and underscores the projective aspect of envy.

For his part, Jacques Lacan (1948/1966, p. 98) in his report on "Aggression in psychoanalysis" takes up this etymology of envy. Envy, according to him, appears in the infant at the moment when it apprehends his object as something it is "deprived" of, causing "frustration". He situates this experience in the mirror that "brings into view" the loss of the mother. For Lacan, praising Klein, and his conception of "the function of the primordial imaginary enclosure formed by the imago of the maternal body", aggressiveness with its envious state is in "tension" with the narcissistic structure.

Destructive envy, according to Klein, and aggression, according to Lacan, is linked to the dual mother/child relationship. In my own opinion, this affect belongs to the projection of the primitive constitutive hatred of the external object with regard to the introjective movement of the hallucinatory satisfaction of the libidinal component of desire.

Klein (1957/1975, p. 25) argues that when frustration is followed by gratification the infant integrates his destructive anxieties better, because the mother has contained them; she becomes an object that supports the formation of the ego. The enjoyment and the gratitude that her "presence" allows serve as a counterpoint to the destructive impulses, the envy and the greed.

Destructive Envy, Control and Narcissism

For Lacan, it is the maternal turning away from the baby in the Name of the Father that brings the child into the Symbolic, into Oedipal triangulation attenuating aggression in the Imaginary. With the Oedipus complex, the identificatory re-organizations lead, according to him, to the "pacifying" function of the ideal-ego.

Thus, I think that envy is a primary, hostile affect specific to the primary narcissistic relationship in infants, which can be all the more violent, "passionate", if the Imaginary reflects an envious negative image, as is probably the case between Lola and her mother. In this case, wouldn't the child become envious by necessity because the envy of the child is enhanced by the reflected maternal envy?

The toxic activity of envy undermines the narcissistic foundations, leads to profound disturbances in the installation of the primary identification and the oedipal organization. It distorts feelings such as jealousy and greed. It can be propagated from generation to generation.

I agree with Fain who points out that a characteristic of Klein's and Winnicott's work is marked by the disappearance of the woman who, at certain moments, leaves her child to enjoy her mate's penis. If the mother dominates, she excludes the female lover. When the mother becomes the woman lover and is absent (this is not the case of the mother according to Lola), she then uses her narcissism to make herself appealing to the penis of her man and no longer in connection with her infant. On his side the male responds with auto-erotism (auto-erotism quite absent for Lola). The censorship that the lover imposes does not prevent the realization of the hallucinatory desire "underpinned without yet knowing it by a primary desire for the penis" (Fain, 1971, p. 320).

It seems to me to be worth recalling the role of the transferring of maternal narcissism in relation to the child towards the link to the father. The maternal narcissism is not only absorbed by her child, but the child offers itself to the mother's man in order to enjoy it. The father, as lover of the mother, serves to loosen the vice grip of the envious narcissistic control.

Last Remarks

I did not devote much attention to the question of Lola's headaches. In summarizing his work on headaches, Marty argues that in this type of patient they can be understood as "a last bulwark" against psychosis (1990, p. 21). This is in line with Claude Smadja's reflection (2017, p. 68) that makes a connection between somatization and delirium. Somatization would be "like a somatic neo-reality whose significance seems to be associated with a preservation of the external world". It seems to me that her headaches can also be understood, following the work of Rosenberg (1991, p. 87), as attached to a dysfunction of primary erotogenic masochistic nucleus of the ego, an "incompletion of primary masochism" as Marilia Aisenstein (2023, p. 16) maintains. This "incompletion of primary masochism" must have been overwhelming given the envious affects libidinally linking little Lola and her mother. *Lola's infantile somatic reality inhabited by envy, rage, or even despair during experiences of excessive frustration were not transformed into pleasure due to the lack of "mother's capacity for reverie" in Bion's sense. The pains of the headaches would then be of the order of a secondary erogenous masochism trying to heal the primary masochism and the core of the ego.*

My journey with Lola may make it clear, as Christian Delourmel (2014, p. 98) argues, why these patients have difficulty using analysis. Indeed, he notes that this seems to have the value of a permanent trauma that they must ward off by resorting to forms of resistance that immobilize their psychic life. They maintain a type of paradoxical defenses so intensely that they have the conviction that only a state of "non-life" can prevent the danger of a psychic collapse in the sense of Winnicott. Listening deeply to their distress allows us better to understand why we need tenacity and patience to respect these vital defensive supports as long as necessary. It allows us to tolerate them better in ourselves and thus to "survive analytically" these analytic journeys.

References

Aisenstein M. (2023). *Desire, pain, thought. primary masochism and psychoanalytic theory*. Paris, Ithaca, Routledge.

Anzieu D. (1985). *The Skin Ego*. Paris, Dunod.

Delourmel C. (2014). Le narcissisme dans son articulation avec les états limites et le négatif. In B. Chervet (Ed.), *Hommage à André Green*: 85–100. Paris, SPP Editions.

Denis P. (1997). *Emprise et satisfaction, Les deux formants de la pulsion*. Paris, Puf.

Fain M. (1971). Prelude to the phantasmatic life. *Rev Fr Psychanal* 35(2): 291–364.

Freud, S. (1914). On narcissism. In J. Strachey (Ed. and Trans.), *The Standard Edition of the Complete Psychological Works of Sigmund Freud*, 24: 67–102. London, Hogarth Press.

Guignard F. (1997). L'envie, terre de désolation. *Rev Fr Psychanal* 61(1): 123–134.

Guignard F. (2005). L'envie, terre de désolation II. In F. Wilhelm (Ed.), *L'envie et Ses Figurations Littéraires*: 21–32. Dijon, Éditions Universitaires de Dijon.

Klein M. (1974). La situation anxiogène de l'enfant au miroir des représentations artistiques. *Essais de psychanalyse*. Paris, Payot. (Originally published 1929.)

Klein M. (1975). *Envy and gratitude*. Paris, Gallimard. (Originally published 1957.)

Lacan J. (1966). *L'agressivité en psychanalyse, Écrits*. Paris, Seuil.

Marty P. (1990). *Psychosomatics of the adult*. Paris, Puf, "Que sais-je?"

M'Uzan M. de (1994). *La Bouche de l'Inconscient*. Paris, Gallimard.

Neyraut M. (1974). *Le transfert, Étude psychanalytique*. Paris, Puf.

Rosenberg B. (1991). *Masochisme mortifère et Masochisme gardien de vie*. Paris, Puf.

Smadja C. (2017). Le travail de somatisation, *La psychosomatique*. Paris, Puf.

Szwec G. (2018). Absence de négation, rage destructrice et déséquilibre psychosomatique. *Rev Fr Psychosom* 54(2): 67–84.

Chapter 18

"... whatever ..."

Michael Civin

Listen doc, I'm here because my dad says he's gunna cut off the credit card if I don't come. He's probably full of shit. He's always full of shit. A year can go by and I don't hear a fucking word from him until something like this smacks him in the face and he thinks it's gunna make him look bad. That's all he cares about, his reputation and his fucking money. You know how many therapists he's sent me to so it looks like he gives a shit about me? Throw some money at it and pretend it'll go away. So I'm here until he forgets about it. I'd like to shove his fucking credit card up his ass ... whatever.

(Tony, 2020)

If *la belle indifférence* represents one form of the 19th-century hysteric's relationship to the body of the drives, then "whatever" represents, perhaps, one form of the contemporary subject's relationship to desire. At the intersection of desire and the perception of impossibility occasioned by countless repetitions of disappointment, the utterance "whatever," whispered into the ether half-mutely and without object, quells anxiety with an evocation of the Nirvana Principle (Freud, 1920, pp. 55–56). "Whatever" subverts the destructive hatred of frustration and its annihilatory consequences with a headlong plunge toward the inorganic, toward the absolute zero of Thanatos. But this defensive plunge toward nothingness also subverts imagination, fantasy, and even Eros itself. Where we used to delve into the patient's masturbatory fantasies, now we learn only what kinds of porn they watch.

> This role of fantasy hinges on the fact that 'there is no sexual relationship', no universal formula or matrix guaranteeing a harmonious sexual relationship with one's partner: because of the lack of this universal formula, every subject has to invent a *fantasy* of his or her own, a 'private' formula for the sexual relationship – for a man, the relationship with a woman is possible only inasmuch as she fits his formula.
>
> (Žižek, 1997, p. 7, italics mine)

But whatever happens when there is no fantasy, no private formula, but only the part drive/part object discharge of insular, virtual sexuality even when the part object happens to be the body part of some insignificant other.

DOI: 10.4324/9781003384618-24

One does not give ground on desire without guilt because doing so implies putting it to sleep and nullifying its pro(*pulsion*) … Freud surely experienced sadness standing between the columns of the Acropolis, but his guilt would have been so much greater had he not reached the observation tower and remained at the foot of the hill, not wanting to surpass his father.

(Braunstein, p. 262, referring to Freud *SE XXII*)

And when that father, that "O," has vanished in the faceless company of the dead mother (Green, 1986, pp. 142–173), then perhaps … "whatever."

Building upon Freud (1924), Benno Rosenberg (1991) framed masochism as the "guardian of life," observing the important role of primary erotogenic masochism in the human subject's capacity gradually to erotize increasing amounts of tension, hence unpleasure. Seen from this perspective, primary erotogenic masochism represents the infant's capacity to endure the unpleasure of absence through hallucination, essentially establishing a precursor to the development of a capacity to postpone immediate gratification. However, since hallucination in and of itself does not actually nourish, if the length of time between the onset of drive frustration, unpleasure, is too great, a failure of primary erotogenic masochism ensues with a resultant imperative in a reduction (or eventually a virtual elimination) of the pulsation of the libidinal drive.

In quite a different formulation of a somewhat similar construct, we might locate Winnicott's notion of the development of a transitional space. In the presence of a good enough facilitating environment, the infant is endowed with a capacity for play that gives forth to the proximal stage of psychic development through creation of an indecipherability of the me/not-me (read hallucination). The establishment of this intermediate zone of potentiality (potential space) thus, similarly, forms the precursor of a capacity to tolerate and grow from an absence of immediate gratification if the good enough environment exists (i.e., the delay is neither too short nor too long). But what if this "good enough" environment appears and vanishes like an apparition? This endless repetition of something that I term *impotential space* leads to "… whatever … ."

Tony

When Tony entered treatment in the winter of 2018–2019, he was a first semester freshman at a major New York City university, dangling from failing out only by the string of his father's donation-generated influence and a "mandate" to attend psychotherapy. The eldest of four boys, reared on a Sands Point waterfront estate, prepared at among the finest of New England's academies and summered on his mother's compound on Santorini, he had, grossly to understate, bathed in luxury. Having parlayed his wife's generational wealth into a vast fortune by playing early and hard on tech stocks and pooling his gains into Berkshire Hathaway, Tony's father sanctified the boys' life with a penumbral, but nonetheless forcefully punitive, presence while their mother perfected her golf, tennis, and bridge and, perhaps, sexuality at one or another of the prestigious clubs of which they were members. Diagnosed by multiple psychiatrists and psychologists with ADHD, he coasted with studied diligence through prestigious private schools and then through prep school on native intelligence, a cloud of cannabis, a snow drift of cocaine, and molly mixed with endless hours of porn and compulsive masturbation. And through it all he prided himself on perfecting the art of factitious attentiveness and interpersonal indifference. Friendless and isolative at school and scorning his classmates, at least twice a week Tony escaped his subjectively perceived prison, stealing his way through backroads to the nearby town where he mingled with townies, gambling, drugging, and hooking up with any mouth that would give him a blow job until dawn's enforced recidivism wrenched him reluctantly back to his spurious world. Indifferent to the multiple times, he had been confronted with his blatant disregard for the academy's "strict" standards, Tony mockingly feigned contrition and, naturally, continued to flaunt his contempt, unmoved by his parent's foisting him off on a revolving door of highly regarded mental health professionals.

When Tony swore that he would drop out of college before he even started if he had to live in student housing again, his ever-compliant father bought a co-op just a short walk from campus. For the first weeks, Tony kept his nose to the grindstone, but as midterms rolled around he tossed his studies aside and stole his way through the brightly lit streets the city into almost endless partying. Weeks of clubbing followed by faceless hookups "afterhours" brought him to the brink of collapse. Ultimately, a nearly fatal overdose of MDMA and a five-day hospital stay caught his family's attention.

For three weeks, twice per week and always on time, the pencil thin boy with an incongruently cherubic face and dyed silver hair faced me with a gaze that somehow managed to be simultaneously vacant and truculent, parrying all my prodding with empty syllables. Finally, given the likelihood that my ever-escalating resentment contained a thinly veiled message I asked Tony why he bothered coming for his sessions. I began this chapter with his answer.

Therapy continued with the same apathetic torpor through the holidays and into January when Tony's failing marks earned him a leave of absence. In an abbreviated final session, he told me that he would be confined to his parents' home. Then, turning with a barely visible shrug and his back to me, whispered "whatever" as he vanished without bothering to close the door.

It is what it is ...

Where "whatever" is, as noted earlier, whispered objectless into the ether, this alternative contemporary currency, "it is what it is," is more often aimed in the direction of, if not exactly to, an object. On the surface, this trope appears quite similarly suggestive of deep dives toward Thanatos; however, oftentimes the clinical presentation appears with a distinct qualitative difference.

It seems reasonable to assume that the primary erotogenic masochism described by Rosenberg (1991) unfolds in a more or less continuous gradient rather than discontinuous quantum leaps or dichotomous states. The economics of the capacity of the libidinal drive to endure unpleasure through fantasy (erotogenic or, from a more Kleinian perspective, destructive, as in the scooping out of the beast) certainly couldn't be expected to adhere to straightforward formulae. Perhaps then, following Rosenberg, life (Eros) is guarded by masochism to varying degrees as a function of almost infinite sets (Matte Blanco, xxx) of parameters surrounding the economics of the drives. Similarly, if the sexuality of a "sexual relationship" rests on the elaboration of a private fantasy that is perforce the negation of a relationship might there not arguably exist a gradient among the relative strengths of such an elaboration? Can't we imagine that differing amounts of ground on desire without guilt are given and that as a result the depths of sleep and the nullification of its pro(*pulsion*) vary commensurately? And isn't it only fair to imagine that we might a vast range of "facilitating environments," hence a continuum of spaces among those that have potentiality?

Lynne

Lynne first came to treatment when she was 17, in her final semester of high school. Having already been accepted into the same college that Tony attended, she had begun for the first time in her life to cut classes, drink, smoke, and have sex with numerous partners. Frantic with concern, Lynne's mother brought her to therapy upon learning that her daughter was pregnant. The youngest of four children with the same mother and three different fathers, only she and her brother shared and, in her memory, only fleetingly, Lynne said that she knew it was her duty to feel shame and remorse. Her mother, she told me with a flat, unmodulated tone that seemed intended to convey urgency had sacrificed her life to make sure that Lynne had everything she needed to succeed. Even though her tone remained as unmodulated as before, Lynne seemed barely able to breathe, telling me that even with the great insurance her mother had from a job that forced her to work almost endless hours, the copays drained the woman of anything she might even think of having for herself. The therapy lasted less than two months. After the abortion, Lynne's mechanical contrition channeled her into even greater striving, doing everything she could never do to keep even with the interest compounding on her debt.

If it weren't for her name, I would never have recognized Lynne almost five years later. Her unevenly cropped, darkly tie-dyed hair, her black makeup on one eye and lip and red on their opposing pair and her deep, apparently braless, cleavage temporarily distracted me for a minute from noticing that she had gained at least 50, perhaps even 80, pounds. She immediately launched into the same type of nearly breathless, unmodulated recap of the time since I had last seen her. She had continued to excel at school, graduating with a nearly perfect GPA, a double major in Communications and Psychology and a solid, if boring and repetitive, six-figure social media position at a cutting-edge tech startup in the fashion industry. Her social life had taken quite a different turn, sounding like a drunkard's-walk through gender identities and object choices, each even less satisfying than the previous one. She let me know that her current pronoun set was it/it, but that she didn't care about mis-gendering. For the past year or so she had called herself a digisexual, shunning direct human interactions and experimenting with technologies aimed at syncing mechanized masturbation to pornography. On the surface, she had returned to therapy because of her misgivings about having assembled an online following of subscribers to her jerry-rigged techno-porn website that had suddenly, startlingly ballooned. Almost as an afterthought Lynne mentioned that she barely spoke with her siblings – "They envy me. That's how out of it they are. They envy me." Her mother brought Lynne close to affect – "She's proud of me. I can't." She paused for a few seconds, looked around the room as if she were studying the paintings, and turned her gaze back to me.

"It is what it is," she intoned. I had no idea if it grasped the double entendre.

Discussion

While both Tony and Lynne certainly stand out as singularly striking individuals, nonetheless neither differs generically from a type, or perhaps two types, of character who drifts somewhat peripatetically into our offices with increasing frequency in recent years. These two vignettes emerge, of course, from younger patients, from the "hook-up" culture of late millennials and Gen-Zers. Still, these trends have leeched into their elders; or, perhaps, causality becomes far less clear when we pause to consider the multi-generational layers of drug use (both recreational and prescription), digital immersion, divorce, and extra-marital affairs leading to split families, absentee parenting, alcoholism, and so on. However, the multi-generational nature of this phenomenon notwithstanding, from my anecdotal experience and that of a number of my colleagues,[1] we share little doubt that these "whatever" phenomena have accelerated rapidly, if not even asymptotically over the past 20 or so years. And so, to the extent that what we witness represents at least somewhat of a more general phenomenon we are presented with the opportunity to explore from a psychoanalytic perspective at least three intertwining trajectories each of which unfolds and diffracts in humanly typical complexity: (1) What pulse[2] of the Group/Society might lend itself to such a massive surrender to apparent indifference? (2) What is the pulse of the person within the group, in particular the person who comes to our office? (3) Is the person who comes to our office a patient and, if not, is there a way, perhaps, to facilitate some psychical movement in that direction?

Let me try to use the vignettes to give roundabout illustrations of some of the issues that may come into play when we think about the larger social phenomena of "whatever." Lacan (1957) introduced the notion of the paternal metaphor to enable the child understand/remain curious about the mother's absence as an Oedipal phenomenon. Aha! So that's where mommy's been hanging out. This paternal metaphor, this name-of-the-father, however challenging and daunting, institutes a law that organizes the psycho-sexual world of the subject. But what about Tony? Certainly, he would have never had any sense that his mother would have been likely to have been with his father. With a credit card for a father, there was no organization and with no organization if he had ever found a reason to go hunting for his mother, well … of course, "whatever." Of course, for Lynne the failure of the paternal metaphor takes a different twist. For her, for all but something that might have been a rumor, there was no father. For Lynne, whose mother was never missing there had been no perception of the need of an instantiation of a law to organize. It appeared that organization by default was all that there ever was, with the everlasting solidarity among the siblings according to one law: that there was only brotherly love and above all love for the mother. Hence, "it is what it is."

I am using these two vignettes to suggest aspects of a more general collapse of the paternal metaphor in our contemporary world at a quite rudimentary level. Of course, the argument can be taken in many different, perhaps even more philosophically compelling, directions: the collapse of the geo-political/socio-economic paternal order and with it the concomitant collapse of psycho-sexual paradigms. I am pointing out that, based on anecdotal clinical observation among collaborating colleagues, a quite massive surrender to voluntary indifference is typified by the cases of Tony and Lynne.

In our work when we invoke the mantric case by case, we add extra top spin to each individual case. Why exactly did Tony continue to irritate me so much? In the much-endorsed clinical model of "essential depression" elaborated by Pierre Marty, Michel Fain, and their successors in the French School of Psychosomatics (Birksted-Breen, 2010, pp. 449–462), the suggestion would be that for the type of patient of which Tony would be an excellent example the therapist would have little or no countertransference. This line of thought (and their clinical experience) evolves from the idea that in the patient's earliest life there was a relatively consistent failure of primary erotogenic masochism such that the capacity for communication through projective identification (the essence of countertransferential experience) was inadequately developed. In so many ways, Tony was the very picture of a modern "operational thinker." He left no evidence of any form of phantasmatic life of any sort, everything within his reach was concrete and intentionally effluent. In the model of essential, or blank, depression, the push toward Nirvana, toward the inorganic, is a push in the direction of absolute homeostasis, toward uninterruptibly permanent peace. The part of Long Island in which Tony was raised is known colloquially as the Gold Coast, harkening back to Gatsby's days and before. Perhaps, then, here is part of the key to Tony's "whatever" at the intersection of desire and impossibility and the reason that it left me with such unabated irritation. Tony was touched at birth by Midas, turned in effect to another little bit of gold that could be neither eaten nor nourished. Although they amount to the same thing in the long run, there are two differing metaphoric pathways toward the endless "whatever" of Nirvana; in one, you bring your own pulsion to zero while in the other you decimate the pulsion of the entire universe. When Tony left my office, he didn't even bother to close the door. Tony's "whatever" was one, I think now, of total decimation. By no means am I claiming that every time we hear this flat two syllable over and out, we are hearing the thinly veiled signature of aggressive drive come unhinged. I imagine that many instances correspond more closely to the blank depression of disaffection, but I suspect that Tony's case may be closer to the rule than the exception.

Earlier I drew a distinction between the "whatever" without identifiable object and the "it is what it is" directed at least toward, if not exactly to, an object. I suspect that Lynne's case reveals something more consistent with Marty's operational thought or the blankly depressive disaffection (MacDougal, 1984).[3] Lynne also revealed no traces of preconscious functioning, no dreams, no detectable phantasmatic life at all; if anything, the mechanized automata of her cyborg-sexual world typified her affectless presentation. Throughout both courses of Lynne's therapy – she continues her treatment currently – she offers such little insight into the inner workings of her being through her own associative material, her own dreams, parapraxes, tropes, or induced countertransference.[4] I will write a bit about what I consider the therapeutic process to be for patients like Lynne (and Tony, with a weighty asterisk), but for the moment I want to forward a few, perhaps plausible, speculations about Lynne's early life to see how well they match up with aspects of the theoretical models. Of course, we always need to keep in mind that excavating the stochastic scraps of Lynne's childhood and piecing them into a structure runs the risk of mimicking Sir Arthur Evans's magnificent Knossos. The principal set of notions that I am proffering involve failures of primary erotogenic masochism, impotential space, and the dead mother.[5] Each of these notions revolves around the capacity of the neonate/infant to sustain adequate pulsion, binding or fusing of the drives, to move in the direction of proximal states of psychosexual maturation. With a failure of primary erotogenic masochism, as noted above, the neonate who, challenged to suffer well the lack of the breast for too long, succumbs to the failures of hallucinatory figurability to nourish and grants the death drive an upper hand. In impotential space, the primary caretaking environment fails adequately to facilitate the substrata of resources necessary for pulsational potentiation to combust with that singular form of spontaneity that links source, drive, aim and object in one frame of reference, or mother and baby in another, in such a manner that the inertial energy can be traced back neither to the internal nor the external. The dead mother was not always dead. This is not a story about intense postpartum depression. She was a presence for the neonate at birth and for some time thereafter; certainly for long enough to launch the child into a meaningful form of psychical life; certainly for the oral drives to coalesce at the breast, at least for long enough to traverse the theoretical moment of primary narcissism and launch psychosexuality into the realms of primary erotogenic masochism. But then, or perhaps sometime shortly thereafter – probably before the nascent muscular autonomy of the middle anal stage – something happens. Perhaps a host of things happen more or less simultaneously, things that the serve to yank the mother clear of the child's psychosexual orbit. The child is probably still nourished and changed, though perhaps not with the same frequency and certainly not with anything approaching the same care. But the child is not seen, not felt and no longer known. There is no such thing as a baby (Winnicott, 1971) – dead mother, dead child (Bollas, 1999).

Lynne is the youngest of four. Her father who was also the father of her elder brother stayed around, it seems, until she was, perhaps, a toddler. The two older siblings have two other fathers. We don't know if there were any marriages, for how long the relationships lasted, if there were other relationships/marriages before or after, etc. We know that Lynne communicates a sense that her education was of extreme importance to the mother. Lynne also lets us know that she feels her mother worked herself to the bone for Lynne's benefit – something we might think to be in the true spirit of moral masochism. Also, Lynne started doing drugs and got pregnant as a teenager. Might the mother have been present enough in Lynne's earliest days, perhaps while the father was still in the picture, to provide some of the deep emotional support, early fostering even of an ideal ego even, that later on turned into a harshly driven superego, handing off the holding, feeding, pampering and soothing to the two older siblings? If so, isn't it easy enough to imagine the ground slab for the sorts of failures depicted above, selectively or serially? Lynne's teenage turn to drugs and promiscuity might also suggest an identification with some aspect of the mother's own psychosexuality, one that serves simultaneously as a rebellion against and an identification with internalized aspects of the mother's own infantile sexuality in a manner that might well constitute a replay into the kind of impotential space described above. What about the *it*? What can we speculate about the absolutism of Lynne's commitment to the operational, to transform the psychosexual into the digisexual? What is there in Lynne's early background as we know it that might lead to this wholesale eradication of difference? Of course, we can't know. But nonetheless it does seem that there is something about the interpersonal, about the human even, not just the sexual, that Lynne experiences as transgressive. Could it be something about the hatred that the Dead Mother felt for the imperative to die on the cross that she carried for the sin of sexuality that had given way to children? Might it be that "it is what it is" is so much more preferable to *I* am what *I* am, because *it* needs no anaclitic nourishment from the breast that had, perhaps perforce, its own macabre mise en scène to avoid annihilating its most beloved new offspring for the torture she brought with her birth? If you have the chance to visit Crete, I recommend Knossos; it's just a couple of miles outside of Heraklion.

Finally, what can we say about treatment. With the little vignette about Tony I have highlighted a sort of hyper-aggressivity that attends, in my clinical experience, to much of the "Nirvana" intentionality of the "whatever" presentation. It might be fair to call this negative, or death, narcissism d'après Green (1999), who considers it, in general, a worthless pursuit to attempt to treat. Tony, at least, didn't allow me the opportunity to waste my time. As a general rule, from my perspective, I don't feel that I agree wholeheartedly with this conclusion. Perhaps very few people can actually ride a real rodeo bucking bull, but if you look hard you can still find mechanical bull rides in cheesy Dive Bars scattered hither and yon; and, with a bit of practice, a few bruises, and a down-shift of pride a psychotherapist might eventually wave his ten-gallon hat to the thinned-out crowd.

The sort of operational patient that *it* was, presents quite a different challenge. I think that the central notion here is a bit different. When Lynne says, "it is what it is" we know that "it isn't what it is." The problem is that we can't tell her that. Our task revolves around facilitating her discovery that there may be countless versions dispersed over time, space, and person of what it/she is and might be, or might have been, or might still be, or might still have been. Arguably, for Lynne you let the sessions drift along week in and out patiently, tossing back an occasional tidbit that seems as though it might have a scansion like quality, waiting for something meaningful, startling, or with the potential for graspable transference to emerge.

Conclusion

These two utterances, "whatever" and "it is what it is," which in recent times we hear so often both inside the consulting room and out-and-about, signify the disaffected retreat toward Thanatos at the intersection of drive (life or death, love, or destruction) and impossibility. The blank depression that accompanies these words is not the depression of a vicious superego usurping the energy of the id to attack the ego; rather, it is a bottomless pit, a depression devoid of both thought and affect, a cryogenic plunge toward the negative narcissistic safe-haven of inorganicity. In less extreme cases, perhaps, the words reflect an ongoing struggle against the repetitive frustrations of failed object cathexes; to be sure, still a narcissistic retreat, but nonetheless a struggle that may leave some opening for a connection.

As others in this volume suggest, the phenomena, in this case echoing through these words, reflect a turning of the contemporary search for pleasure in the faintly lit dusk of a world in which both striving and prohibition risk vanishing into the dark void of a total eclipse. In the place of desire, one vector in this turn, the one taken by Tony and countless others, substitutes a jouissance of pervasive substance abuse, relentless auto-erotism and anti-social isolation interrupted only by part-object encounters at best vaguely discernable from thoughtless instinct. A different vector, the one taken by Lynne, strives for a totalitarian mechanizing of the human, reduced to completely operational "thinking," to the robotic in which both desire and judgment dissolve in a society bereft of any meaningful organizing/containing function.

From the perspective of a psychoanalytically oriented therapist, the overarching question remains: what, if anything, can we do to make use of our training and skill with these contemporary individuals whom we can't genuinely describe as patients? The quest for a "technique," barely begun, already reveals that no *deus ex machina* will descend from the heavens to bring the drama to a quick and efficient conclusion. One tack is clear: first, we have find a way to facilitate the individual's transformation into a patient. Could that happen with any of the Tonys who cross our thresholds? Could I have found a way that eluded me to help him stay the course? For now, we struggle with these as unanswered questions fraught with repetitive destructively negative therapeutic outcomes. For the Lynnes, who continue to appear in our offices quasi-mechanically and equipped with neither thought nor affect, we know that we must, at the very least, remain patient.

Notes

1 Many such examples have been presented over the past few years by participants and guest lecturers in the seminar on the "Disaffected Patient" – hosted by Rose Hill Psychological Services.

2 The word *pulse* is used here as a somewhat crudely fashioned transformation of the French word *pulsion*, which is the generally accepted translation of the German *treibe*. The reasons for favoring this term over *drive*, which is favored in turn over Strachey's *instinct* are significant and, even though in a certain way perhaps relevant to the themes of this chapter, beyond its scope.
3 The contemporary disaffected patient has been the topic of study for the past several years in the seminars referenced earlier.
4 In truth, I believe that the remarks that I make next are, in fact, a version of induced countertransference inasmuch as the speculations that I make emerge from the times that I have spent in her presence and the material that I have gleaned from her. That much said, not surprisingly, these speculations remain quite largely intellectual with precious few hints of the stuff of the somatic/figurational that truly enriches the capacity for concordant identification (Racker, 1968).
5 We might easily also include the abject of Kristeva (1982), the double of Botella and Botella (2005), the pictogram of Piera Aulagnier (2015), the penetrable and impenetrable (Miller, 2020), and so on.

References

Aulagnier, P. (2015) Birth of a body. Origin of a history. *IJPA* 96: 1371–1401.
Birksted-Breen, D. (2010) Is translation possible? *IJPA* 91: 687–694
Bollas, C. (1999) *The Mystery of Things*. New York: Routledge.
Botella and Botella (2005) *The Work of Psychic Figurability*. New York: Routledge.
Braunstiein, N. (2020) *Jouissance. A Lacanian Concept*. New York: SUNY Press.
Freud, S. (1920) Beyond the pleasure principle. *SE XVIII*: 55–56.
Freud (1924) The economic problem of masochism. *SE XIX*: 159–170.
Green, A. (1986) *Negation and contradiction in on Private Madness*. London: Hogarth Press.
Green (1999) *The Work of the Negative*. London: Free Association Books.
Kristeva (1982) *Powers of Horror: An Essay on Abjection*. New York: Columbia University Press.
Lacan (1957) *Seminar V: The Formations of the Unconscious*. Cambridge, England: Polity Press.
MacDougal, J. (1984) The "dis-affected" patient: reflections on affect pathology. *Psychoanalytic Quarterly*, 53: 386–409.
Matte Blanco, I. (1975) *The Unconscious as Infinite Sets: An Essay in Bi-logic*. London: Gerald Duckworth & Company (H. Karnac Books, 1998).
Miller, P. (2020) *The Early Shapes of Psychic Life as Forerunners of (Bi)sexuality*. Presentation at the Association of Psychoanalytic Medicine, New York City, 11 February.
Racker, H. (1968) *Transference and Countertransference*. New York: International Universities Press.
Rosenberg, B. (1991) *Masochisme Mortifère et Masochisme Guardien de la Vie*. Paris: PUF.
Virgil (2013) *The Aeneid*. Vintage Collection, translated by Robert Fitzgerald.
Winnicott, D. W. (1971) *Playing and Reality*. London: Tavistock Publications.
Žižek, S. (1997) *The Plague of Fantasies*. London: Verso.

Afterword

Anand Desai

The editors of this volume have brought together eminent psychoanalysts and social scientists to revivify Freud's economic model of the drives at a time when the relevance and value of this theory are difficult to overstate. Drawing on expertise in fields adjacent to psychoanalysis—anthropology, sociology, history, political science, gender studies—this collection provides a prism through which what is changing about the human experience today can be refracted and considered.

My goal in this brief afterword is to add a few details to the picture of the world evoked here—one in which the contemporary subject lives "in a state of constant emergency," bombarded, addicted, desperate, delibidinized (Tsolas). In the context of ongoing natural and viral and political crises, we surpass one million deaths from COVID-19 and witness multiple mass shootings of innocent civilians, including yet another slaughter of children at school. Over the past year, we have seen a stark increase in mass shootings, homicide, and violent assault.

In May 2022, the CDC released data that showed an alarming rise in the number of drug overdose deaths in the United States and confirmed that 2021 marked the nation's highest ever recorded annual death toll from drug overdoses. Asked whether she thought this was a uniquely American problem, Nora Volkow—Director of the NIH's National Institute on Drug Abuse—confirmed that some aspects are indeed uniquely American (the nationwide scope of the problem, for example). Speculating about what has made Americans vulnerable to drugtaking, she pointed in part to "diseases of despair that are causing people to escape their realities."

In 2022, an intriguing study (Herbenick et al., 2022) was published showing marked changes over the past decade in the frequency and repertoire of sex in the United States. In the large study sample, limited to individuals ages 14–49, the investigators used detailed measures of sexual behaviors beyond oral, vaginal, and anal intercourse in an attempt to address whether the decline in coital (penile-vaginal) frequency might be explained by increases in non-coital behaviors. But it was not. Rather, they report "significant decreases across all partnered sexual behaviors assessed and, for adolescents, decreases in the proportion of adolescents reporting solo masturbation in the prior year." This latter finding was non-trivial and noted to deserve close further study. The proportion of adolescents reporting neither solo nor partnered sexual experiences had risen, by 2018, to roughly 45% of men and 75% of women. Overall, these findings are consistent with studies from multiple countries similarly documenting declines in sexual frequency (for example, Britain, Sweden, Germany and Japan, among others). And finally, this study also found, particularly in those aged 18–29, a growing prevalence in the United States of aggressive sexual behavior—"rough" sex including choking or strangling. While the details are not yet clear, particularly with regard to whether or not the rough sex is wanted and pleasurable, what is now seen in studies of thousands of randomly sampled college students is that choking or strangling has become a majority behavior during sex. Researchers were surprised at the form of the aggression in sex—not the hair-pulling or light-spanking they had anticipated—and have begun to pursue actively this emerging trend. At the same time, over the past 20 years, there has been a substantial rise in the number of people identifying as "asexual."

These are perplexing, multifactorial developments germane to the focus of this volume—namely, the contemporary search for pleasure and an examination of the nature, cause, impact, and prognosis of the changing forms of enjoyment. A journalist (Julian, 2018) who surveyed the landscape and literature of what she called "the sex recession" mused that

> Over the course of many conversations with sex researchers, psychologists, economists, sociologists, therapists, sex educators, and young adults, I heard many other theories ... . I was told it might be a consequence of the hookup culture, of crushing economic pressures, of surging anxiety rates, of psychological frailty, of widespread antidepressant use, of streaming television, of environmental estrogens leaked by plastics, of dropping testosterone levels, of digital porn, of the vibrator's golden age, of dating apps, of option paralysis, of helicopter parents, of careerism, of smartphones, of the news cycle, of information overload generally, of sleep deprivation, of obesity. Name a modern blight, and someone, somewhere, is ready to blame it for messing with the modern libido.
>
> (Julian, 2018, p. 81)

While there is no clear explanation for the decline in partnered and solo human sexual behaviors, a few themes recur in Julian's reporting—now almost four years old. For one, a seemingly radical collapse of the space in adolescence for sexual and romantic exploration. In this crucial developmental time, there has been a great reduction of idle, non-scheduled time; and this is concurrent with an accepted notion that sex, romance, love be subordinated to and delayed until the achievement of academic and professional pursuits. One of many things that might warrant interrogation is the generally, culturally accepted efforts "to 'protect' teenagers from most everything, including romance, leaving them ill-equipped for both the miseries and the joys of adulthood."

Another recurring theme is the seemingly sudden shift in the acceptability of in-person flirtation: "romantic pursuit is now being cordoned off into a predictable, prearranged online venue, the very existence of which makes it harder for anyone, even those not using the apps, to extend an overture in person without seeming inappropriate." There are also rising rates of body dissatisfaction, clearly correlated with social media use, an observation touched off by a Dutch study and confirmed internationally. There is less comfort in one's own skin and nakedness. Of final note here, everyday experiences such as sleep deprivation and background distraction have been shown to severely dampen sexual arousal.

In the wide-ranging conversations Julian engaged in and reported, two apparent and apparently related contradictions seem relevant here. First,

We live in unprecedented physical safety, and yet something about modern life, very recent modern life, has triggered in many of us autonomic responses associated with danger—anxiety, constant scanning of our surroundings, fitful sleep. Under these circumstances, survival trumps desire.

And second,

How can such little things—a bad night's sleep, low-grade distraction—defeat something as fundamental as sex? One answer, which I heard from a few quarters, is that our sexual appetites are meant to be easily extinguished. The human race needs sex, but individual humans don't.

The editors and scholars of this volume have spoken to these developments, and future editions of this work might take up more specifically this seeming desiccation of bodily sexuality in the individual and the population. An economic perspective on the drives, the emphasis here on "libido as psychic energy, accounting for variations, transformations, extensions, coverings-up, fixations, regressions, time-lags, enmeshings and unravelings" (Tsolas) can help to make sense of converging currents: increases in drug addiction, suicide, and violent assault; decreases in solo and partnered sexual activity with growing prevalence of violence in adolescent and young-adult sex. We know that most young male mass shooters are "asexual," be it voluntarily or involuntarily ("incels"), and yet a simple hydraulic model does not suffice. The more complex economy of the drives resurrected and offered here, and perhaps future research into drive ecology at the level of the group if not population, will certainly help us understand more deeply what is changing, and how, and what might be done about it—from the level of the psychoanalytic process and dyad up through education and policy. The trenchant work of the editors and scholars presented here, reinvigorating an aspect of Freud's genius and its arc in the history and present of psychoanalytic thought, strikes us, at least in North America in 2023, as a matter of life and death.

References

Herbenick, D., Rosenberg, M., Golzarri-Arroyo, L., Fortenberry, J. D. & Fu, T. Changes in Penile-Vaginal Intercourse Frequency and Sexual Repertoire from 2009 to 2018: Findings from the National Survey of Sexual Health and Behavior. *Archives of Sexual Behavior* 51, 1419–1433 (2022).

Julian, K. The Sex Recession. *The Atlantic* (2018).

Index

Note: *Italicized* page numbers refer to figures. Page numbers followed by "n" refer to notes.

Abraham, K. 186
absolute realism 75
addictive behavior 7, 47–48, 106; addictive contemporary subject of instinct 107–109; addictive girdle, double wall of 104–107; autoeroticism 86–88; compulsion, prevention of 94–96; fetishistic objects 91–94; infantile part of 83–85; jouissance and 101–103; in narcissist vulnerability 81–98; negativity 97–98; question of representation 88–89; resistance 97–98; toddler with hair pulling compulsion 85–86; transitional space 90–91
adolescence 95, 102, 116, 127, 132, 187, 208; bodily symptoms in 9, 144–156; physiological 156n2; psychic isolation in 8–9, 48, 144–156
Adorno, T. 67–68, 73
affect regulation 175
Aisenstein, M. 195
Anderson, R. 147
anger 67–69, 102, 159, 190
Animal Crossing: New Horizons 164–169; psychological aspects of 165–168
anorexia 94, 116, 152, 187
anti-social isolation 205
An Trá Ghearr ("The Short Strand") 33
anxiety 2, 6, 37, 41, 72, 74, 82, 83, 91, 94, 95, 97, 100, 104, 108, 135, 138, 145, 159, 161, 187, 190, 194, 197, 208, 209; castration 8, 105, 107, 112–120, 142; narcissistic loss 114–116; objectal loss 117–118; in women 7–8, 111–122

Anzieu, D. 89, 101, 102, 104, 110n1, 122
apoptosis 4, 20
Aristotle 174
artificial intelligence 24, 26, 94
artists at work 168–169, *170*
Augustine: *fruitio* 177
Aulagnier, P. 206n5
autoeroticism 11, 83, 84, 86–88, 94, 115, 117, 188, 194
autoplastic modification 7, 48

Bancel, S. 23
Beauvoir, S. de 121
binding 39, 48, 89, 107, 123, 124, 131, 203
Bion, W. R. 9, 88, 89, 96, 146, 147, 154, 156n1, 195; theory of thinking 145
"bipolarity" of the ego ideal 16
bisexuality 70, 136, 185
Black Lives Matter Movement 160
body 1–3, 7–9, 22, 26, 27, 48, 49, 57, 61, 82, 84–88, 90, 96, 101–104, 109, 112–117, 119–121, 124, 125, 127, 129–131, 134, 135, 137, 138, 156n4, 161–163, 166, 169, 177, 189, 197; biological 9; bodily estrangement 148; bodily expressions, of psychic pain 151–153; bodily pleasures 88, 161–163; bodily symptoms, in adolescence 144–156; dissatisfaction 208; law of motion of the 16, 26; maternal 112–114, 191, 194
Booth, C. 164, 165
Botella, C. 206n5
Botella, S. 206n5

Braunschweig, D. 87, 185
Braunstein, N. 101, 109, 175, 183
Briere, J. 156n3
bulimia 116, 133, 155, 156n5

Campanile, P. 156n4
castration anxiety 105, 107, 112, 114–119; feminine 8, 119–120; men 142
cathexis 64, 86, 87, 89, 123, 125
CDC *see* Centers for Disease Control (CDC)
Centers for Disease Control (CDC) 161, 207
Chasseguet-Smirgel, J. 16
civilization 3, 5, 8, 16, 25, 27, 108, 131
cognitive theories 25
compulsive destructiveness 8
compulsive self-destruction 138, 142
constancy, principle of 47, 49, 123, 125, 174
Constructivism 75
contact barrier 86, 156n1
corporeal functioning 112
countertransference 97, 105, 141, 185, 188, 202, 203, 206n4
COVID-19 15, 19, 23, 39, 100, 101, 105, 108, 128, 159, 161–163, 165, 166, 170, 207
creativity, envy and 191–193
cyberspace 161, 163, 166

Dalsimer, K. 154
Dante: great sadness 48, 122
Dartington, A. 147
Das Ding 40
Davoine, F. 37, 38, 43
dead mother complex 16, 34, 39, 42
death 5, 22, 40, 41, 43, 44n1, 48, 50, 61, 100, 120, 122, 156n6, 204, 205, 209; cell 4, 20; cultural 6; desire 21; drive 4, 8, 9, 47, 49, 88, 104, 106–109, 123–125, 131, 173–179, 181, 183, 203; fantasies 139; during pandemic 159–171, 207; psychic 15; sacred 64n5; and use of pleasure 173–184
decathexis 39, 47, 97
de Freytas-Tamura, K. 66
delibidinization 15, 207
Delourmel, C. 195
de M'Uzan, M. 47, 104, 185, 187; *Slaves of Quantity* 7, 107
Denis, P. 185, 189
dependence, situation of 112–113
depression 1, 4, 7–8, 10, 37, 38, 41–43, 48,

69, 83, 87, 100, 102, 130, 144, 187, 202, 205; maternal 34; of middle of life 120–121; pathological form of 111; postpartum 203; in women 111–122
deprivation 2, 112, 115, 117, 163, 186, 189, 192, 194, 208, 209
destruction 2, 7, 9, 22, 49, 53, 66, 77, 92, 95, 97, 106, 108, 115, 132, 137, 138, 142, 159, 181, 182, 205
destructive envy 105, 185–195
destructive rage 188–189
Dictionary of Untranslatables 176
digital capitalism 20
discontentedness 15
discrimination, gender-specific 62
double wrapping 104
drive 3–5, 83, 205; active 61–63; congestion of 59; death 4, 8, 9, 47, 49, 88, 104, 106–109, 123–125, 131, 173–179, 181, 183, 203; drive-demand 58; drive-wish 58; ego 108; libidinal 198; passive 61–63; phonic 5, 24–25, 27; psychic 131, 173; psychoanalytic 174, 175; sexual 108, 112; theory 47, 49, 50, 62, 63, 64n2, 93, 125, 175; uncanny 50–64
DuPrau, J.: *City of Ember, The* 145

Eagle, M. 177, 178, 182; *Toward a Unified Psychoanalytic Theory: Foundation in a Revised and Expanded Ego Psychology* 175, 176
Eagly, A. H. 64n6
eating disorders: anorexia 94, 116, 152, 187; bulimia 116, 133, 155, 156n5
economic balance 83; principle of 174, 176
ego 67–69, 74, 75, 84, 93, 123, 141, 175; auxiliary 148; congruence of 68; control 60; corporeal 102; development 130; drive 108; egoism 3; ego-pleasure 11; erotogenic masochistic nucleus of 195; ideal 16, 67, 68, 72, 73, 112, 116; libidinal nourishment of 102; narcissistic 108; premature 128, 131; psychology 175, 177–178, 182; skin 7, 89, 93, 101–104, 107, 110n1, 189; superego 1, 8, 30, 59, 67, 68, 70, 72, 96, 108, 112–114, 116, 118, 131, 136–138, 141, 142, 148, 160, 204, 205; vulnerability to psychosis 97

email 51, 59, 63
energy 1, 11, 16, 47, 61, 69, 81, 82, 107, 123, 125, 131, 137, 160, 203, 205, 209
enjoyment 4, 9, 11, 12, 31, 43, 47–49, 108, 113, 114, 117, 176–178, 181–183, 194, 208
envy 24, 47, 106, 201; control 194–195; and creativity 191–193; damaged narcissism of envied subject 189–190; destructive 105, 185–195; "envious fragmentation" of the child 186–188; envious maternal control 190; and narcissism, relations between 9, 47–48, 193–195
eros 8, 11, 47–49, 53, 87, 107–109, 123–125, 131, 197, 200
erotic sexuality 84
estrangement 8, 37, 48, 135, 144, 148, 150
ethical impotence 2, 47
ethics 21
excitement 16, 24, 26, 27, 86, 91, 96, 113, 173; auto-excitement 119
exclusion 39, 67
expectation, messenger of 113–114
explosion 22

Fain, M. 82, 87, 131, 185, 194, 202
fantasy 11, 27, 59, 70, 71, 74, 83, 84, 88, 93–96, 116, 117, 123, 135, 140, 146, 151, 154, 161–163, 167, 187, 188, 191, 192, 200; death 139; hallucinatory 87; homosexual 113; libidinal 81; masturbatory 197; oedipal 95; regressive 163; sexual 88, 96; transgressive 9, 163; unconscious 68, 72, 90
fascism 76, 77
Fechner, G. T. 47, 123, 125, 173–174
femininity 7, 43, 48, 61, 62, 65n8, 117, 120, 142, 186; Irish 34
fetishistic objects 91–94
"fight or flight" mode 61
Fliess, W. 139
fragmentation 1, 160; "envious fragmentation" of the child 186–188
free association 75, 82, 160
French School of Psychosomatics 83, 202
Freud, S. 1–6, 15, 47, 68, 113, 117, 122, 124, 138; "Beyond the Pleasure Principle" 124, 173; "child is beaten, A" 115–116, 140; 'Civilization and

Its Discontents' 2, 87–88; "Ego and the Id, The" 125; on envy 185, 186; "Ethics of Psychoanalysis, The" 174; Group Psychology and the Analysis of the Ego 68, 73; Instincts and their Vicissitudes 70; "Interpretation of Dreams, The" 123; metabiological speculations 179; nachtraglichkeit (après-coup) 12, 88, 133, 135, 180; on narcissism 193; New Introductory Lectures on Psychoanalysis 73–74; Outline of Psychoanalysis, An 74; phallocentric theory of psychosexual development 116; "Project for a scientific psychology" 174; on psychic space 93; "Psychoanalytic View of Psychogenic Disturbances of Vision, The" 107; Science of Thought 25–27; theory of the drives 47; on Trieb 61
friendship for thinking 30, 31
friendship of thinking 30
fruitio 177
frustration 3, 86, 95, 186, 194, 195, 197, 198, 205

Gardner, F. 148, 156n6, 156n7
Gaudillière, J.-M. 37, 38, 43
gay pornography 162
gender non-conforming 166
gender-specific discrimination 62
genital sexuality 63, 135
Gil, E. 156n3
Glover, B. 67
Grant, A.: "There's a Name for the Blah You're Feeling. It's Called Languishing" 100
Green, A. 2, 8, 16, 33, 34, 39, 42, 94, 97, 124, 125, 145, 192, 198, 204
Guignard, F. 190, 193

hallucination 83–87, 91–94, 96, 112, 198, 203; hallucinatory fantasy 87; hallucinatory satisfaction 9, 11, 93, 114, 123, 194; hallucinatory wish-fulfillment 74; hallucinosis 96; negative 92, 94, 96
hammer-blow wish 58–61, 63, 64n2, 64n5
Hammerschlag-Wunsch 58, 64n2
hedonism 5, 25, 26
heterosexuality 162
Hippolyta, myth of 103–104

Hoffer, W. 85
homosexual 187; bond 70, 71; fantasy 113; transference 70, 127
hostility to thinking 31
human beings 5, 8, 30, 31, 62, 76, 111, 112, 122, 123, 132, 185
human evolution 3
human subject 18, 174, 176, 181, 198
humiliation 67, 68, 130, 138

ideal ego 16, 67, 68, 72, 73, 112, 116
illusion-disillusionment 92
impenetrability 47, 103, 206n5
impotence 6, 116, 123, 127; ethical 2, 47; impotential space 49, 198, 203, 204; political 2, 47
indifference with respect to thinking 31
infantile insomnia 82
infantile sexuality 1, 83, 84, 86–88, 116, 204
infant–parent relations 7
inhibition of thought 25
injustice 67
instinct 5, 7, 16, 24, 50, 64, 74, 82, 90, 97, 160, 205, 206n2; addictive contemporary subject of 107–109; animal 3; of self-preservation 61, 81, 124; sexual 125
intellectualism 26
intellectual nihilists 73
intercourse 17, 84, 207
intelligibility 41, 75, 173, 185
Internet 19, 21, 88, 109, 162
invulnerability 47, 103, 104
Ireland 33–44; generational shifts in paternal metaphor 6; Irish neck 37–39; Irish personhing 39–40; Irish rebirth 42–43; Irish torso 34–37, 36; Irish zombies 41–42; nationalism 33–34; Provisional Irish Republican Army (IRA) 33, 39; Sinn Féin 33
isolation 4, 21, 90; anti-social 205; narcissistic 140; physical 161; psychic 8, 48, 144–156; sexual 15; social 1, 4, 6, 12, 15

Jacques, E. 193
James, H.: Turn of the Screw, The 1
James, W. 76
Jones, E. 184n1
jouissance 4, 7, 9, 47, 116, 119, 175, 176, 178, 180–182, 183; addictions and 47, 101–103; double wall of

addictive girdle 104–107; Hippolyta, myth of 103–104; impossible, reaching for 100–110; instinct, addictive contemporary subject of 107–109

Kahn, C. 6, 64n1; Feux rouges (Red Lights) 50
Keyes, C. 100
Kierkegaard 179, 181
Klein, M. 48, 112, 114, 115, 145, 147, 154, 189, 191, 200; on envy 185–186, 188, 192–194; Envy and Gratitude 185, 193; intelligibility 185; phantasmagoria 185
Kristeva, J. 4, 6, 15, 18–19, 33, 38, 42, 87, 206n5; "Day After, The" 18, 20; Passions of Our Time 18

Lacan, J. 4, 9, 40, 116, 119, 177, 178, 182, 184n1, 201; "Aggression in psychoanalysis" 194; Ecrit 5, 24, 107; "Ethics of Psychoanalysis, The" 174, 175; on jouissance 49, 101, 175, 176; paternal metaphor 201–202; use of the category Symbolic 177
La Défense 50, 51, 63
Lady Gregory: Cathleen Ni Houlihan 44n2
language 3, 19, 21, 24, 25, 27, 78, 82, 88, 124, 145, 166, 177, 182; acquisition 8
Laplanche, J. 4, 50, 61, 81, 98, 175, 177, 180
latency 114, 125, 131, 132, 145, 147, 150
Law of Fulfillment 5, 25
Laws of Sexual Difference 24
Le Soldat, J. 49, 50, 58, 60, 62, 63, 64, 64n2, 64n4, 64n5, 64n7
Lévy, P.-H. 20
libido 1, 2, 123; libidinal development 90; libidinal drive 198, 200; libidinal energy 11, 81, 82; libidinal fantasy 81; libidinal freedom 73; libidinal motives 177; libidinal nourishment of the ego 102; libidinal pleasures 163; libidinization 3, 177; narcissistic 107; object 107; as psychic energy 47
Limitless 127
Loewald, H. 9, 167, 170, 180, 182; Sublimation 9
loneliness 8, 19, 21, 48, 144, 163, 169
lust 4, 174

Macron, E. 66
Marty, P. 188, 195, 202, 203
masculinity 7, 43, 62; Irish 33, 34, 42
masochism 8, 11, 87, 115, 124, 131, 132,
    137, 138, 177, 187, 192, 198, 200,
    202, 203; erogenous 113, 119, 195;
    feminine erotic 117, 119; moral 8,
    142, 204; primary 89, 176, 195;
    sado-masochism 156n7, 161
masturbation 84, 88, 96, 101, 106, 108, 109,
    161, 162, 192, 197, 199, 201, 207
maternal environment 7, 93
maternal investment 113–114
maternal phallic narcissism 113
Mayes, L. 168
McCullers, C. 9, 151; *Member of the
    Wedding, The* 145, 148–149, 154
McDougall, J. 83, 91, 93
McKeown, L.: *Johanna Monahan* 34–36, 38,
    39, 43
melancholia 35, 68, 70, 89, 119, 137, 138,
    142, 143, 176
menopause 120
menstruation 147, 150, 156n2
mental confusion 68
mentalization 8, 125
metapsychology 3, 83, 141, 174; definition
    of 1; psychoanalytic 89
Mino-Mycenaean period 114
Mitchell, J.: "Siblings: Sex and Violence" 166
moral masochism 8, 142, 204
mourning 35, 38, 39, 95, 118, 120, 121,
    144, 145, 153, 169
music 108, 128, 151–153, 169, 170
mutuality of speech 15, 21

nachtraglichkeit (après-coup) 12, 88, 97, 133,
    135, 180, 188
narcissism 47, 98, 111, 120, 130, 132, 152,
    156n6, 173, 174, 204; bodily 117,
    119; damaged narcissism of envied
    subject 189–190; and envy, relations
    between 9, 47–48, 193–195; female
    117; narcissistic ego 108; narcissistic
    failures 88; narcissistic grip 185–195;
    narcissistic isolation 140; narcissistic
    libido 107; narcissistic lockdown 72;
    narcissistic loss anxieties 114–116;
    narcissistic loss, object of 116–117;
    narcissistic pathologies 89; narcissistic
    regression 137; narcissistic suffering
    8; narcissistic transference 70;

narcissist vulnerability, addictive
    behavior in 81–98; object of
    narcissistic loss 116–117; phallic 113,
    116, 121; primary 17, 107, 186, 203;
    primitive 11; secondary 107;
    solipsistic 48
National Institute on Drug Abuse 207
negativity 97–98
neo-capitalism 20
neoliberalism 18, 20, 21
neo-needs 90, 91, 94, 95
neuroscience 160
neurosis 101, 111, 125; psychoneurosis 95
Neurotica 74
neurotic disposition 68
Neyraut, M. 185
Nietzsche, F. 16, 179
Nirvana principle 15, 47, 106, 125, 181,
    197, 202, 204
Nobus, D. 179; "Narcissism and the
    Pleasures of Extinction: For the
    Centenary of 'Beyond the Pleasure
    Principle'" 173
non-neurotic configurations 111

objectal loss: anxieties 7, 117–118; object of
    118–119
objective truth 77
object of narcissistic loss 116–117
object of the objectal loss 118–119
object-relations 2
oedipal conflict 111, 114, 115, 118
Oedipus complex 50, 112, 114, 137,
    166, 194
Offer, D. 156n3
Ogden, T. H. 91, 97, 98
omnipotence 3, 15, 17, 32, 48, 49, 73, 92,
    94–97, 106, 129, 166, 167, 181,
    183, 190
ontology 2, 30
Ornstein, A. 68, 73, 75
Orwell, G.: *1984* 66, 76–78; *Looking Back on
    the Spanish War* 77
otherness 19, 22, 87, 19, 121, 131

pain 2, 4, 7–9, 11, 37, 49, 71, 82, 83, 85–87,
    92, 94, 96, 97, 104, 112–114, 118,
    126–131, 134, 135, 141, 142;
    psychic 121, 151–153, 171, 177,
    178, 180, 186, 192, 195; somatic 125
pandemic 1, 4, 7, 15, 18–21, 39, 47–49, 83,
    85, 100, 101, 109, 159–171; artists at

work 168–169, *170*; bodily pleasures 161–163; environmental constraint, effects of 159–161; music 169; play and videogames 163–165; pleasures 161; reading 169; watching series, on streaming channels 169
parent–infant relations 82
Park, G. 164
partnering 25
passibility 65n9
passive wishes 50, 62
passivity 8, 49, 63, 65n9, 97, 131, 135, 136, 142, 189
paternal metaphor 6, 201–202
Paxton, R. 76
Pearse, P. 43–44n1; "Mother" 35
personality theory 2
personthing 39–40
perverse 7, 17, 27, 89, 101, 103, 122, 125
phallocentric theory of psychosexual development 116
phantasmagoria 77, 185
phantasmatic functioning 112
phantasy 49, 58, 61
phonic drive 5, 24–25, 27
phylogeny 2
physiological adolescence 156n2
play 34–39, 42, 43, 44n1, 49, 50, 59, 67, 68, 72, 83, 85, 88, 90, 92, 96, 97, 102, 134, 136, 137, 140, 149, 151, 155, 160, 161, 163–167, 177, 178, 183, 189, 193, 198, 201
pleasure 3–5, 8, 9, 15, 48, 49, 74, 86, 89, 109, 123, 161, 181; bodily 88, 161–163; contemporary 47; early barriers to 11–12; ego-pleasure 11; libidinal 163; loss of 7; pleasure–displeasure principle 11; pleasure–unpleasure principle 2, 11, 180, 181; use of 173–184
political despotism 48
political impotence 2, 47
politico-economic virality 22–23
Polygon 164
Pontalis, J. B. 4, 50, 61, 81
Protocols of the Elders of Zion, The 66
Proud Boys 66
Proust 169
pseudo-representation 96
psyche 1–4, 6–8, 11, 25, 48, 49, 68, 82, 86, 87, 90, 92, 96, 98, 101, 102, 104, 109, 131, 137, 152, 166, 174, 181,

185, 186; psychic blankness 33, 34; psychic drive 131, 173; psychic economy of addiction 83; psychic space 93
psychic isolation, in adolescence 8–9, 48, 144–156; clinical example 150–151; literary version of 149–150
psychic pain 83, 121, 142; bodily expressions of 151–153
psychoanalysis 2, 4, 5, 7, 24, 25, 27, 31, 74, 75, 84, 85, 88, 92, 93, 101, 109, 111, 160, 173, 174, 176, 178–180, 182, 183, 207; historical 43; psychoanalytic drive 174, 175; psychoanalytic metapsychology 89; resistance to 8, 133–143
psychological subject 174
psychoneurosis 95
psychopathology 25, 27, 111
psycho-physical stability, pleasurable effects of 174
psychosexuality 2, 11, 48, 50, 58, 81, 174, 204; psychosexual maturation 203
psychosis 72, 97, 101, 125, 195
Psychosomatic School of Paris 8
psychotic disposition 68
puberty 116, 121, 134, 147, 148

quiescence 123

radical receptivity 65n9
rapprochement 81, 85
Ravel, M.: *Child and the Sortilèges, The* 188–189
reading 169
Realität 74
Realitätsgerecht 68
reality 66–78, 123; ad knowledge, truth-correspondence between 75; collapse of judgement of 67; shared 182
re-creation 162, 168, 170
Red Lights 50; interpretation 58–63, *60*; plot 51–58, *51–58*
reductio ad absurdum 15
regression to dependency 97
regressive fantasy 163
re-inscription 180–181
repetition 7, 11, 40, 88, 96, 174, 180–181, 187, 197, 198; addictive 81, 83; compulsion 39, 93, 97, 138, 141, 142, 179; and death drive, link between 179

replication 179
repression 8, 30, 36, 42, 43, 50, 68, 89, 98, 113, 116, 123, 124, 136, 139, 175, 183
resistance 12, 43, 76, 97–98, 153, 195; to psychoanalysis 8, 133–143
re-turn 181
Rivera, S. 166–167
Roman Saturnalia 68
Rorty, R. 75–78; *Pragmatism as Anti-Authoritarianism* 16
Rose Hill Psychological Services 205n1
Rosenberg, B. 192, 195, 198–200
Roussillon, R. 89, 98

sacred death 64n5
sado-masochism 156n7, 161
Saketopoulou, A. 49, 64n2, 64n3, 65n9; "Draw to Overwhelm: Consent, Risk and the Retranslation of Enigma, The" 175
Salinger, J. D.: *Catcher in the Rye* 144
satisfaction 3–7, 16, 26–27, 47, 48, 83, 85, 86, 91, 94; erotic 84; hallucinatory 9, 11, 123, 194
Science of Thought 5, 25–27
seduction 22, 117, 139–141; narcissistic 106
Segal, H.: "On the Clinical Usefulness of the Concept of the Death Instinct" 176
self-accusation 74
self-calming 95, 96, 131
self-harm 87, 156n3, 156n6
self-healing 95
self-preservation 70, 74, 85, 123, 140; instinct of 60–61, 81, 107, 124
self-sabotage 137
self-soothing 7, 48, 82, 84, 156n7; compulsive 82, 86–88, 93
sexting 163
sexuality/sexualization 1–2, 10, 69, 71, 96, 113, 123, 200; bisexuality 70, 136, 185; erotic 84; genital 63, 135; heterosexuality 162; homosexuality 70, 71, 113, 127, 187; infantile 1, 83, 84, 86–88, 116, 204; psychosexuality 2, 11, 48, 50, 58, 81, 174, 203, 204; sex recession 208; sexual difference 5, 7, 24, 25, 48, 103, 106, 111; sexual drive 108, 112; sexual identity 112–113; sexual isolation 15; sexual penetration 116, 147; virtual 197
Shakespeare, W. 159

Simenon, G. 6, 50
singularity 18, 19, 22, 90, 141, 178
Sinn Féin 33, 36, 37; *1916: Our History, Our Future* 34
skin ego 7, 89, 93, 101–104, 107, 110n1, 189
Slaves of Quantity 7, 47, 104, 107
Smadja, C. 195
Smith, W. 76, 77
social isolation 1, 4, 6, 12, 15
Society of Friends of Thinking/Friends of Thinking Society 31
soma 101–104
somatization 47, 119, 121, 131, 195
stability 123, 137, 148, 155, 163, 174
stigmatization 42
Stones, R. 11
Strachey, J. 206n2
sublimation 9, 49, 58, 64n3, 84, 122, 128, 160, 170
suicide 1, 6, 41, 47, 100, 145, 156n3, 162, 209
Sulkowicz, K. 67
superego 1, 8, 30, 59, 67, 68, 70, 72, 96, 108, 112–114, 116, 118, 131, 136–138, 141, 142, 148, 160, 204, 205; melancholic 137
superficiality 25, 117
sur-vivants 5, 23
symbolization 9, 38, 87–89, 97, 98, 106, 112, 113, 115, 119, 124, 171, 178

Tausk, V. 84
Tavington, W. 40
Thanatos 10, 47, 49, 107, 124, 197, 199, 205
Thatcher, M. 34
theory of infantile sexuality 116
theory of thinking 145
thought 3, 8, 10, 24, 49, 132, 205; freedom of 77; inhibition of 25; of satisfaction 5, 25–27
toddler with hair pulling compulsion 85–86
totalitarianism 73, 77, 205
transference 109, 130, 135, 140, 160, 179; countertransference 97, 105, 141, 185, 188, 202, 203, 206n4; homosexual 70, 127; narcissistic 70; negative 97, 98, 138, 185, 188
transgenerational order 24
transgression 4, 75, 105, 114, 204; transgressive eroticism 64n5; transgressive fantasy 9, 163

transitional space 7, 9, 48, 82, 85, 89–92, 94, 151, 154, 155, 198
trauma theory 61
traumatic control 188–189
trichotillomania 85–86
Trieb 50, 61, 173, 174
Turkle, S. 94

United States 208; drug overdose deaths 207; emotional outpourings of citizens about election in 160; social unrest in 7
unpleasure 4, 58, 174, 198, 200; clinical vignette 125–130; enemies of 8, 123–132; pleasure–unpleasure principle 2, 11, 180, 181
usufruct 49, 181

Vanier, A. 182
victimization 67, 142
videogames 163–165
violence 1, 47, 53, 58, 71, 72, 137, 141, 165, 188, 190, 193; domestic 161; gun 160, 161; historical 42; prevalence of 209; structural 42; of unpleasure 124
virtuality 6, 15, 19, 47–49
Völkische Beobachter 66
Volkow, N. 207

watching series, on streaming channels 169

weathering development 154–155
Wiederhold, B. 165, 166
Wilson, D. 40
Wilson, M. 182; *Analyst's Desire: The Ethical Foundation of Clinical Practice, The* 176
Winnicott, D. W. 84, 85, 89, 90, 98, 114, 116, 120, 153, 154, 167, 183, 189, 190, 194, 203; on envy 194; on maternal environment 93; 'Metapsychological and Clinical Aspects of the Regression within the Psychoanalytic Situation, The' 97; *Playing and Reality* 92; psychoanalysis 93; on regression to dependency 97; on transitional objects 94; on transitional space development 198; "use of an object, The" 181–182
Winter, D. 167
Wirklichkeit 74
Wirkung 74

Xenos 2, 107

Yeats, W. B.: *Cathleen Ni Houlihan* 44n2

zombiehood 41–42